Strategies in Learning an
Second Language

APPLIED LINGUISTICS AND LANGUAGE STUDY

General Editor
Professor Christopher N. Candlin, Macquarie University, Sydney

For a complete list of books in this series see pages v–vi

Strategies in Learning and Using a Second Language

ANDREW D. COHEN

LONGMAN
LONDON AND NEW YORK

Addison Wesley Longman Limited
Edinburgh Gate
Harlow, Essex CM20 2JE
England

and Associated Companies throughout the world

*Published in the United States of America
by Addison Wesley Longman Inc., New York*

© Addison Wesley Longman Limited 1998

The right of Andrew Cohen to be identified as the author of this Work has been
asserted by him in accordance with the Copyright, Designs and Patents Act 1988.

First published 1998

ISBN 0 582 305888 Paper

British Library Cataloguing-in-Publication Data
A catalogue record for this book is available from the British Library

Library of Congress Cataloging-in-Publication Data
Cohen, Andrew D.
　　Strategies in learning and using a second language / Andrew D.
Cohen.
　　　　p.　cm. — (Applied linguistics and language study)
　　Includes bibliographical references (p.) and index.
　　ISBN 0–582–30588–8
　　1. Second language acquisition.　2. Language and languages—Study
and teaching.　I. Title.　II. Series.
P118.2.C64　1998
418′.007—dc21　　　　　　　　　　　　　　　　　97–33360
　　　　　　　　　　　　　　　　　　　　　　　　　　CIP

Set by 35 in 10/12pt Ehrhardt
Produced through Longman Malaysia, LSP

APPLIED LINGUISTICS AND LANGUAGE STUDY

GENERAL EDITOR

PROFESSOR CHRISTOPHER N. CANDLIN

Macquarie University, Sydney

Strategies in Learning and Using a
Second Language
ANDREW D. COHEN

Teaching and Language Corpora
ANNE WICHMANN, STEVEN ⁶IGELSTONE,
GERRY KNOWLES *and*
TONY MCENERY (EDS)

Language and Development: Teachers
in a Changing World
BRIAN KENNY *and*
WILLIAM SAVAGE (EDS)

Autonomy and Independence in
Language Learning
PHIL BENSON *and* PETER VOLLER (EDS)

Literacy in Society
RUQAIYA HASAN *and*
GEOFFREY WILLIAMS (EDS)

Phonology in English Language
Teaching: An International Approach
MARTHA C. PENNINGTON

From Testing to Assessment: English
as an International Language
CLIFFORD HILL *and* KATE PARRY (EDS)

Language as Discourse: Perspectives
for Language Teaching
MICHAEL MACCARTHY *and*
RONALD CARTER

Language and Discrimination
A Study of Communication in
Multi-Ethnic Workplaces
CELIA ROBERTS, EVELYN DAVIS *and*
TOM JUPP

Translation and Translating: Theory
and Practice
ROBERT T. BELL

Exploring Error Analysis
CARL JAMES

Communication Strategies:
Psycholinguistic and Sociolinguistic
Perspectives
GABRIELE KASPER *and* ERIC KELLERMAN
(EDS)

Language, Literature and the Learner
Creative Classroom Practice
RONALD CARTER *and* JOHN MCRAE (EDS)

Theory and Practice of Writing: An
Applied Linguistic Perspective
WILLIAM GRABE *and* ROBERT B. KAPLAN

Measuring Second Language
Performance
TIM MCNAMARA

Interaction in the Language
Curriculum: Awareness, Autonomy
and Authenticity
LEO VAN LIER

Second Language Learning:
Theoretical Foundations
MICHAEL SHARWOOD SMITH

Analysing Genre – Language Use in
Professional Settings
V.K. BHATIA

Rediscovering Interlanguage
LARRY SELINKER

Language Awareness in the Classroom
CARL JAMES *and* PETER GARRETT (EDS)

Process and Experience in the
Language Classroom
MICHAEL LEGUTKE *and*
HOWARD THOMAS

Contents

Author's acknowledgements

I would like to acknowledge Chris Candlin for encouraging me to consider putting this volume together. The original intention was simply to gather up a series of recent writings related to language learner strategies. It became clear that all of them would need significant updating and revision.

Since the project constituted an integration of different writings, I must acknowledge those who helped me shape the various chapters. I wish to thank Rebecca Oxford for her many contributions to Chapter 2, dealing with definition of terms, as well as for her insights on strategies-based instruction and in the design of the research project on strategies-based instruction reported in Chapter 5, for which she was a consultant. I would also like to thank Anna Chamot for her helpful input during the design of the strategies-based instruction study. I would like to thank Kimberly Scott for her assistance in putting together a portion of Chapter 3 on assessing learner strategies. Many thanks go to Susan Weaver for her innovative contributions in the field of strategy training, her co-authorship of the material on strategy training in Chapter 4, and her role in the planning and writing up of the research study in Chapter 5 as well. In addition, I would like to thank Joel Levin, Micheline Chalhoub-Deville, Dick Schmidt, and Robert Bley-Vroman for comments which contributed to revisions in the write up of Chapter 5. Thanks go to Stephen Hawras for his research contribution to the mental translation in reading portion of Chapter 6, and to Jim Lantolf, Elaine Tarone, Peter Gu, Maria Brisk, Dick Tucker, and Merrill Swain for their feedback on various portions of this chapter. Thanks also to Lyle Bachman and Elaine Tarone for feedback on portions of Chapter 7 on test-taking strategies.

I would also like to acknowledge the University of Minnesota for granting me a sabbatical leave (1996–97) during which time I had the relative calm necessary for writing up this manuscript. In addition, I want to thank the two universities and their respective departments that granted me visiting scholar status during this period – the Department of English as a Second Language at the University of Hawai'i and the School of Education at the Tel-Aviv University. It was through the use of their facilities and interactions with a host of fine colleagues that this book came to fruition.

Finally, I would like to thank my wife, Sabina, for her endless support for my professional endeavors in general and for her support on this book writing project in particular. In addition, I would like to thank my parents, Rena and Harold Cohen for ensuring that I receive the best education possible, with many language learning experiences.

Andrew Cohen

Publisher's acknowledgements

We are indebted to the following for permission to reproduce copyright material:

Applied Language Learning for a revised version of the paper 'Verbal reports as a source of insights into second language learner strategies' by A D Cohen in *Applied Language Learning*, 7 (1–2): 5–24 (1996); Edward Arnold for a revised version of the paper 'The language used to perform cognitive operations during full-immersion maths tasks' by A D Cohen in *Language Testing* 11 (2): 171–195 (1994); Cambridge University Press for a revised version of the paper 'Strategies and processes in test taking' by A D Cohen in *Interfaces Between Second Language Acquisition and Language Testing Research* (eds) L F Bachman and A D Cohen; Centre for Advanced Research on Language Acquisition for extracts from the papers 'Second Language and Use Strategies: Clarifying the Issues' by A D Cohen and 'The impact of strategies-based instruction on speaking a foreign language' by A D Cohen, S J Weaver and Tao-Yuan Li (originally published in their working paper series); Chulalongkorn University Language Institute for a revised version of the paper 'The role of learner strategy training in ELT methodology' by A D Cohen in *Explorations and Innovations in ELT Methodology* (ed) A Wongsothorn et al (Selected papers of CULI and International Conference) (Bangkok, Chulalongkorn University Press); Heinle & Heinle Publishers for a revision of the paper 'Making learning strategy instruction a reality in the foreign language curriculum' by S J Weaver and A D Cohen in *Faces in Crowd: the individual learner in multisection courses* (ed) C Klee (1994); Dr. Teresa Pica for a revised version of the paper 'The role of language of thought in foreign language learning' by A D Cohen in *Working Papers in Educational*, 11 (2): 1–23 (1995); the University of Hawaii at Manoa, Second Language Teaching and Curriculum Centre and Rebecca Oxford for a revised version of 'A synthesis of approaches to assessing language learning strategies' by A D Cohen and K Scott in R L Oxford (ed), *Language Learning Strategies Around the World: Crosscultural Perspectives*, Technical Report 13: 89–106 (1996); TESOL Quarterly for a revised version of 'The production of speech acts by EFL learners' by A D Cohen &

E Olshtain in *TESOL Quarterly* 27 (1): 33–56 (1993); Academic Press Inc for our Figure 7.1 'Three pictured response alternatives for an L1 reading item' from 'Standardized tests: objectives/objectified measures of "competence"' in A W Cicourel et al *Language use and school performance* 1974.

This book is dedicated to my father, Harold J. Cohen, whose keen mind, steadfastness of purpose, organizational skills, and intellectual curiosity were a continual source of inspiration to me. Although he passed away several months before this volume was to appear, it gave him great joy to know that I had written it.

1 Introduction

This book is written primarily for teachers, administrators, and researchers of second and foreign language programs. There are practical suggestions for teacher trainers and teachers as to how to be of greater support to their students in their learning effort. Both teachers and researchers may find the discussions of multilingual behavior and test-taking strategies helpful to them in their endeavor to understand better the language learning experience of students. Researchers and prospective researchers may find the discussions of terminology and research methods of benefit to them as they determine the topics that they wish to investigate and choose their means of investigation.

The book is intended to bring together in one volume a series of different themes which nonetheless are tied together by their focus on second language learners and their strategies. Portions of Chapter 2 and Chapter 4, and all of Chapter 5 (a research report on strategies-based instruction) are appearing in print for the first time. The rest of the material has appeared in one or another article, but in all cases has been substantially revised and updated for this volume. In fact, the major challenge in this project was in creating a framework which would enable the various themes to come together into a meaningful whole. While this volume is fortunately not the first to deal with research methods for investigating language learning and language use strategies, there is still very little literature available. The book deals primarily with a particular set of second language (L2) issues, namely those concerning language learning and language use strategies. The main focus is on the adult learner, with one major exception, Chapter 6, which includes a study dealing with immersion pupils in the elementary grades ages 8 through 11. This work was included because it relates well to the theme of multilingual thinking.

The first issue of concern in the book is that of sorting out terms. Chapter 2 revisits the distinction between language learning and language use strategies and further distinguishes them. While experts in the field may not agree on the nomenclature, it is at least helpful to be clear as to the phenomena that are being described, regardless of whether they are referred to by means of the same labels. Hence, the chapter provides a discussion of terminology. The purpose of these definitions and the ensuing discussion is to facilitate empirical investigation, rather than to fine-tune the distinctions between different theoretical models for analyzing types of strategies.

The second issue of concern is that of research methods since the accuracy of strategy descriptions depends on the rigor of the data collection instruments and of the methods for data collection and data analysis. Chapter 3 presents a review of instruments available for assessing L2 strategies, followed by a detailed discussion of how verbal report can be utilized so as to maximize its benefits.

Chapter 4 then takes up the theme of strategy training, focusing primarily on strategies-based instruction as perhaps the best means of increasing learners' awareness as to the benefits of systematically using strategies. To the extent that teacher trainers and teachers make use of the suggestions in the chapter, it may constitute an important source of support for the learners. Chapter 5 reports on a research project conducted in order to determine the effects of strategies-based instruction on learners engaged in university-level foreign language instruction. The motivation for this study was to provide evidence regarding the impact of specific language learning or language use strategies on achievement in the foreign language. It was gratifying to see that if the study is planned carefully enough, such evidence can be obtained.

The next issue that the volume considers is a relatively neglected one, namely, the differential use by bilinguals and multilinguals of the various languages available to them for the purposes of cognitive processing – whether it be the sorting out of the logic behind some grammar rule, the search for a solution to a word problem in math, or the development of an argument in an expository essay. After examining the language of thought issue in general, we will focus on two specific themes – mental translation into the first language by adult learners during foreign language reading and the language used by elementary-school pupils for performing cognitive operations during full-immersion content courses.

The final theme addressed is that of the strategies used by respondents in language assessment situations. Chapter 7 starts by defining test-taking strategies, and then exemplifies strategies for taking tests of reading and writing, using indirect formats (multiple-choice and cloze) and more direct formats (summarization tasks, open-ended questions and compositions). Next, an empirical study dealing with strategies for producing oral speech acts in simulated task situations is presented. The last portion of the chapter underscores the point that the construction of valid tests can benefit greatly from feedback by test takers as to the strategies that they use in responding to assessment instruments.

2 Second language learning and language use strategies: defining terms[1]

2.1 Introduction

It is promising to see that more recent textbooks dealing with linguistics, applied linguistics, and more specifically second language acquisition, have begun to include reviews of the language learning and communication strategies literature. A chapter or more on strategies can be found, for example, in the following three textbooks: Ellis (1994), Cook (1993), and Towel and Hawkins (1994). Rather than reviewing one or another of these treatments of strategies here, suffice it to say that there are in circulation a number of terms for describing second language learning and second language use strategies. In fact, the literature contains conflicting views as to the meaning of sometimes rather basic terms, such that the reader is not certain what the terms actually refer to and how to make use of them in understanding second or foreign language instruction. This chapter will not attempt to unravel the meanings of all such terms, but will discuss some of the prominent ones and endeavor to arrive at a set of working terms for practitioners. This effort was greatly assisted by a paper written jointly with Rebecca Oxford five years ago (Oxford and Cohen, 1992).

The current chapter will begin by providing working definitions for language learning and language use strategy terminology. Next, five problematic issues that have arisen in the language learning strategy field will be considered: the distinction between the term *strategy* and other terms, the role of *consciousness* when referring to those processes which are strategies, the criteria for classifying language learning and language use strategies, a broadening of the concept of *strategic competence*, and the linking of *learning strategies* to *learning styles* and other personality-related variables. Finally, an example will be given of how an action-oriented program of strategies-based instruction at the university level has integrated these themes into a single program for teacher training.

2.2 Defining 'second language learning and second language use strategies'

Before presenting the strategy definitions, there is as always a need to call attention to the issue of whether to refer to the language being learned as the *second language*, the *foreign language*, or the *target language*. Technically, learning a second language means that the language being learned is that which is spoken in the community in which it is being learned, while a foreign language is not spoken in the local community. The term *target language* simply refers to that language being learned, whether as a second or foreign language. The reality is that sometimes a language which is widely spoken in a given community is still learned as a foreign language because the learners may have little or no direct contact with it (e.g. the case of Arabic in Israel for many learners). Likewise, there are foreign language learning situations where the learners find or create for themselves a large enough community of speakers of the language so that the learning experience for them is more that of second language learning (e.g. learning Hebrew while living in a section of Los Angeles where there is a concentration of native Hebrew speakers). In this volume, while *foreign language learning* will be used to refer exclusively to a situation where the language is not considered to be spoken in the local community, *second language learning* will refer to the language spoken in the community and will also at times serve as the generic term used to refer to both second and foreign language learning.

In an earlier volume on language learning, I defined *learning strategies* as 'learning processes which are consciously selected by the learner. The element of **choice** is important here because this is what gives a strategy its special character. These are also moves which the learner is at least partially aware of, even if full attention is not being given to them' (Cohen, 1990: 5). It still seems appropriate to me to link the notion of consciousness to the definition of strategies, though as we will see below, this is a controversial issue. In my view, the element of consciousness is what distinguishes *strategies* from those processes that are not strategic. Additions to this definition could include the split between language learning and language use strategies, and mention of the specific stage in processing – that is, strategies before, during, or after the performance of some language behavior. Thus, *language learning* and *language use strategies* can be defined as those processes which are consciously selected by learners and which may result in action taken to enhance the learning or use of a second or foreign language, through the storage, retention, recall, and application of information about that language.

The following represents a broad definition of second language learning and second language use strategies. *Second language learner strategies* encompass both *second language learning* and *second language use strategies.* Taken together, they constitute the steps or actions consciously selected by learners either to improve the *learning* of a second language, the *use* of it, or both. *Language learning strategies* include strategies for identifying the material that needs to be learned, distinguishing it from other material if need be, grouping it for easier learning (e.g. grouping vocabulary by category into nouns, verbs, adjectives, adverbs, and so forth), having repeated contact with the material (e.g. through classroom tasks or the completion of homework assignments), and formally committing the material to memory when it does not seem to be acquired naturally (whether through rote memory techniques such as repetition, the use of mnemonics, or some other memory technique). Note that repeated contact with material could be seen as a form of rehearsal, although rehearsal usually implies that the material is at least partially learned already and can therefore be rehearsed. Adult learners may have a keen sense of just what it is they may need to commit to memory (e.g. certain complex vocabulary or grammatical forms) and what they can leave to more automatized language learning, often referred to as *acquisition*. For the purpose of this discussion then, a distinction is being made between that language material which is learned at least to some extent consciously and that material which is learned or acquired with little or no conscious control.

The strategies for learning the subjunctive in Spanish as a foreign language, for example, could include grouping together and then memorizing the list of verbs that take a subjunctive in constructions such as *quiero que vengas* 'I want you to come,' or noticing the difference in imperfect subjunctive inflections between the form in the *-ar* conjugation, *cantara* 'sing,' as opposed to that used with the *-er* and *-ir* conjugations, *comiera* 'eat' and *existiera* 'exist' respectively. The specific strategies for memorizing this group might involve putting these verbs inside a box in the notebook and reviewing the contents of the box regularly, as well as noting what these verbs have in common semantically. If the concern is to learn the verbs themselves, then strategies for learning new vocabulary would be helpful, such as through flash cards and possibly including on the flash card a keyword mnemonic to jog the memory. A *keyword mnemonic* involves both an *acoustic link* – i.e. a native language word or phrase (the keyword) that is similar in sound to part or all of the target language word, and an *imagery link* – i.e. an image of the keyword 'interacting' with the native language word or phrase.[2]

Strategies for *using* the material (whatever the current level of mastery) include four subsets of strategies: *retrieval strategies, rehearsal strategies, cover strategies*, and *communication strategies*. *Retrieval strategies* would be those strategies used to call up language material from storage, through whatever memory searching strategies the learner can muster. In the above example with the subjunctive, retrieval strategies would constitute those strategies used to call up both the correct verb (if necessary) and the correct subjunctive forms as well when the occasion arises in or out of class.[3] For those learners who keep a list of verbs taking the subjunctive, a strategy may involve visualizing the list in their mind's eye and cross-checking to make sure that the verb that they wish to use in the subjunct-ive form actually requires the subjunctive. Likewise, a language use strategy would entail using the keyword mnemonic in order to retrieve the mean-ing of a given vocabulary word. So, say that a learner encounters the verb *ubicar* ('to locate'), which she had learned by means of the keyword mnemonic 'ubiquitous,' and she wants to retrieve the meaning of the word. The language use strategies would include any efforts by the learner to retrieve the meaning of the word *ubicar* – involving the linking of the Spanish sounds /ubik/ with the English /yubɪk/, and then perhaps seeing an image of someone who keeps turning up everywhere the language learner looks for her.

Rehearsal strategies constitute another subset of language use strategies, namely, strategies for rehearsing target language structures. An example of rehearsal would be form-focused practice, such as practicing the Spanish subjunctive forms for different verb conjugations so as to be able to use them correctly in a mid–term exam. A learner could also rehearse a subjunctive form in preparation for using it communicatively in a request in Spanish to a boss for a day off. As suggested above, some rehearsal strategies could be part of language learning as well as part of language use. Bialystok (1990: 27) gives the example of memorizing how to request a loaf of bread and two rolls at the bakery. So in this case memorizing serves as a learning strategy, but most likely followed by the language use strategy of actually employing the material in a communicative exchange.

Cover strategies are those strategies that learners use to create the impres-sion that they have control over material when they do not. They are a special type of compensatory or coping strategy which involves creating an appearance of language ability so as not to look unprepared, foolish, or even stupid. A learner's primary intention in using them is not to learn any language material, nor even necessarily to engage in genuine com-munication.[4] An example of a cover strategy would be using a memorized and partially understood phrase in an utterance in a classroom drill in order to keep the action going. Some cover strategies produce simplified utterances (e.g. learners use only that part of a phrase that they can deal with), while other strategies may actually complexify the utterances, but again in an effort to simplify the learner's efforts at generating utterances in class (e.g. saying something by means of an elaborate and complex circumlocution because the finely tuned vocabulary is lacking or in order to avoid using the subjunctive). Both simplification and complexification in the classroom may represent an attempt to compensate for gaps in target language knowledge.

Communication strategies constitute a fourth subset of language use strategies, with the focus on approaches to conveying a message that is both meaningful and informative for the listener or reader. Much focus has been given to this category of strategies in the literature (see Tarone *et al.* 1976; Tarone, 1977, 1981; Faerch and Kasper, 1983a; Paribakht, 1985; Poulisse, 1990; Bialystok, 1990; Dörnyei, 1995; Dörnyei yei and Scott, 1997). Communication strategies have been seen to include intralingual strategies such as that of overgeneralizing a grammar rule or vocabulary meaning from one context to another where it does not apply, interlingual strategies such as that of negative transfer (i.e. applying the patterns of the native or another language in the target language where those patterns do not apply), topic avoidance or abandonment, message reduction, code switching, and paraphrasing (i.e. using synonymous words or phrases, or using circumlocution). We note that communication strategies may or may not have any impact on learning. For example, learners may use a vocabulary item encountered for the first time in a given lesson to communicate a thought, without any intention of trying to learn the word. In contrast, they may insert the new vocabulary item into their communication expressly in order to promote their learning of it. (See below in this chapter for a discussion of the Bachman (1990) taxonomy with regard to communication strategies.)

Language learning and language use strategies can be further differentiated according to whether they are cognitive, metacognitive, affective, or social (Chamot, 1987; Oxford, 1990). *Cognitive strategies* encompass the language learning strategies of identification, grouping, retention, and storage of language material, as well as the language use strategies of retrieval, rehearsal, and comprehension or production of words, phrases, and other elements of the second language. *Metacognitive strategies* deal with pre-assessment and pre-planning, on-line planning and evaluation, and post-evaluation of language learning activities and of language use events.[5] Such strategies allow learners to control their own cognition by coordinating the planning, organizing, and evaluating of the learning process. There is a rather extensive literature demonstrating that the higher-proficiency students are more likely to use metacognitive strategies than the lower-proficiency ones and to use them more effectively as well (see

Vandergrift, 1992; Anderson and Vandergrift, 1996, for a description of one such study, focusing on listening strategies).

Affective strategies serve to regulate emotions, motivation, and attitudes (e.g. strategies for reduction of anxiety and for self-encouragement). *Social strategies* include the actions which learners choose to take in order to interact with other learners and with native speakers (e.g. asking questions to clarify social roles and relationships or cooperating with others in order to complete tasks).

Since strategies themselves have sometimes been referred to as 'good,' 'effective,' or 'successful' and the converse,[6] it needs to be pointed out that with some exceptions, strategies themselves are not inherently good or bad, but have the potential to be used effectively – whether by the same learner from one instance within one task to another instance within that same task (e.g. at one point in a text v. some other point), from one task to another, or by different learners dealing with the same task (see 2.3.3 below for an example). Perhaps if enough learners in a given group successfully use a given strategy in a given task, then claims could be made for the effectiveness of that strategy in that instance for that group. Otherwise, it is safest to refer to what often amounts to a panoply of potentially useful strategies for any given task.

The literature is replete with studies suggesting that higher-proficiency or lower-proficiency learners use more or fewer strategies than the other group – usually indicating that the better learners use more strategies but sometimes just the opposite. In one example of many, a study of language learning strategy use by 374 students at three course levels at the University of Puerto Rico, found greater use of learning strategies by more successful learners (Green and Oxford, 1995). However, in a small-scale study at the Guangzhou Foreign Language Institute with six higher-proficiency and six lower-proficiency English majors, it was found the higher-proficiency learners used fewer communication strategies when communicating both concrete and abstract concepts to a native speaker in an interview setting, as well as using those strategies more effectively than did the lower-proficiency learners (Chen, 1990).

Presumably, the findings from the first study are indicating that more is better. The findings from the second more qualitative study, on the other hand, would suggest that higher-proficiency learners may be able to perform well using fewer consciously selected strategies, at least on those communicative tasks in that study. In contrast, the lower-proficiency learners may keep trying different strategies without comparable success, and so they end up using more strategies altogether. Thus, the total number or variety of strategies employed and the frequency with which any given strategy is used are not necessarily indicators of how successful they will be on a language task. Whereas the successful completion of some tasks may require the use of a variety of strategies used repeatedly, the successful completion of others may depend on the use of just a few strategies, each used only once but successfully.

Another approach to strategy description is through labeling the function of each strategy that is selected. Bialystok (1990) would consider the classification of strategies according to their function as too simplistic because they can have multiple functions. The issue she has raised is an important one. Those who have done empirical research on strategies have seen that what is ostensibly the same strategy can have more than one function. However, strategies often do have one function, and even if they have more than one function, there may still be one principal function. In any case, it would seem useful to continue to identify the functions that strategies actually assume in given tasks.

2.3   Terminological and conceptual issues in need of clarification

Having considered working definitions for language learning strategy terminology, let us now consider five problematic issues that have arisen in the learning strategies field and suggest means for dealing with each one.[7]

2.3.1   The distinction among strategies, substrategies, techniques, and tactics

The first issue concerns a distinction made among *strategies, substrategies, techniques*, and *tactics*, and the lack of clarity that this distinction has generated in the research literature. The term *strategies* has, in fact, been used to refer both to general approaches and to specific actions or techniques used to learn a second language. For example, a general approach strategy could be that of forming concepts and hypotheses about how the target language works. A more specific strategy could be that of improving reading comprehension in the new language. Among the *substrategies* aimed at improving reading comprehension could be any one of the strategies for determining whether a text is coherent – e.g. checking whether the direction and ordering of elements is clear, seeing if it is consistent and complete, and so forth. An even more specific strategy would be that of attempting to summarize the text in order to see if the ordering of the points makes coherent sense. A still more specific strategy would be to fine-tune the type of summarizing – e.g. that they be short,

General strategy   Forming concepts and hypotheses about how the target language works
Specific strategy   Improving reading comprehension in the new language
More specific   The use of strategies for determining whether a text is coherent
Still more specific   Strategies for summarizing a text to determine its coherence
More specific than that   The use of ongoing summaries written in the margin in telegraphic form

FIGURE 2.1   The range of substrategies from more general to more specific

telegraphic summaries written in the margins of the text every several paragraphs (see Figure 2.1).

So the issue is one of how to refer to these various cognitive or metacognitive processes. The literature includes the terms *strategy*, *technique* (Stern, 1983), *tactic* (Seliger, 1984), and *move* (Sarig, 1987), among other terms, and also includes the split between *macro*-strategies on the one hand and *micro*-strategies and tactics on the other (Larsen-Freeman and Long, 1991). A solution to the problem would be to refer to all of these simply as *strategies*, while still acknowledging that there is a continuum from the broadest categories to the most specific or low-level. For learners and teachers as well, experience has shown that lists of suggested strategies for given tasks are useful, especially if they include strategies that are specific enough so that they can be readily used (such as the most specific ones for summarizing in reading, as in Figure 2.1). This way the practitioners and learners can judge for themselves the level of abstraction of each strategy on the list and so be better able to make functional use of it if so desired.

2.3.2   Strategies for language learning as conscious or unconscious

The second problematic issue pertains to the absence of consensus as to whether strategies need to be *conscious* in order for them to be considered strategies. Basing her argument on the case of young children who seem to behave strategically without being conscious of their strategizing, Bialystok (1990: 4) refers to making choices without conscious consideration. The implication is that children, especially young ones, are not really capable of describing their strategy use. A three-year research project to describe the strategies used by pupils in Japanese, French, and Spanish immersion programs and to help them improve their strategy use, however, demonstrated that even young children were capable of describing their strategies (Chamot, 1996; Chamot, Barnhardt, El-Dinary and Robbins 1996; Chamot and El-Dinary, 1996; Chamot, Keatley, Barnhardt, El-Dinary, Nagano and Newman, 1996). The investigators found that the pupils could not only indicate the strategies that they were using, but showed improvement in their performance in the immersion programs as a result of the training that they received.

A recent discussion of the role of consciousness in second language learning would suggest terminology that may be useful in discussing this issue of consciousness about strategy use, even though the terms were meant to refer to attention to language material and **not** to language strategies. Drawing on Schmidt (1994), we could stipulate that language learning strategies are either within the *focal attention* of the learners or within their *peripheral attention*, in that learners can identify them if asked about what they have just done or thought. If the behavior is so unconscious that the learners are not able to identify any strategies associated with it, then the behavior would simply be referred to as a *process*, not a *strategy*. For example, learners may skim a portion of text in order to avoid a lengthy illustration. If the learners are at all conscious (even if peripherally) as to why the skip is taking place, then it would be termed a strategy. Ellis (1994) points out that if strategies become so automatic that the learners are no longer conscious of employing them, they are no longer accessible for description through verbal report by the learners and thus lose their significance as strategies. This approach to dealing with strategies has appeal for researchers who conduct empirical research on strategies in order to arrive at descriptions to be used in strategies-based instruction.

2.3.3 Differing criteria for classifying language learning strategies

The third problem results from the fact that different criteria are used to classify language learning strategies, causing inconsistencies and mismatches across existing taxonomies and other categorizations. As we indicated in the above definitions, some strategies contribute directly to **learning**, such as memorization strategies for learning vocabulary items (e.g. the use of keyword mnemonics) or organizational strategies for remembering grammatical structures (e.g. the use of charts which emphasize and contrast the key features of the structures to be learned). Other strategies, perhaps the bulk of them, have as their main goal that of **using** the language – for example, verifying that an intended meaning for a given vocabulary item was conveyed or checking to see if a certain grammatical inflection is appropriate in a given context. Some strategies are *behavioral* and can be directly observed (e.g. asking a question for clarification), others are behavioral but not easily observable (e.g. paraphrasing in cases where the product is not obviously a paraphrase of something else), and others are purely *mentalistic* and not directly observable (e.g. making mental translations into the native language for clarification while reading). In order to identify them, such mentalistic strategies must be accessed through means other than observation, such as through verbal report. Strategy frameworks have also been developed on the basis of degree of explicitness of knowledge and the kind of knowledge (e.g. linguistic v. world knowledge, and form-focused v. meaning-focused knowledge) (Bialystok, 1978; Ellis, 1985).

In addition, strategies are sometimes labeled as belonging to 'successful' or 'unsuccessful' learners, when, in fact, the effectiveness of a strategy may depend largely on the characteristics of the given learner, the given language structure(s), the given context, or the interaction of these. Moreover, the very same learner may find that a given reading strategy (such as writing ongoing, marginal summaries while reading a text) works very well for the fifth paragraph of a given text but not for the sixth. The difficulty could result from the learner's lack of vocabulary or grammatical knowledge, from the fact that the material is summarizer-unfriendly in that paragraph, or from some distraction in the reader's environment (the classroom, the home. or the library).

Strategies have also been distinguished from each other according to whether they are cognitive, metacognitive, affective, or social (as defined above). The problem is that the distinctions are not so clear-cut. In other words, the same strategy of ongoing text summarization may be interpretable as either cognitive or metacognitive. It might not be possible to neatly draw the line between *metacognitive strategies* aimed at planning a summary and evaluating the results both during the process of constructing the summary and after finishing the writing of it, and *cognitive strategies* associated with summarizing, such as that of reconceptualizing a paragraph at a higher level of abstraction. It is likely that both types of strategies may be utilized, and delineating whether the strategy is one or the other is what is problematic. In fact, the same strategy may function at different levels of abstraction. For instance, skipping an example in the text so as not to lose the train of thought may reflect a metacognitive strategy (i.e. part of a conscious plan to not get distracted by detail) as well as a cognitive strategy to avoid material that would not assist in writing, say, a gist statement for the text.

So given these dichotomies and continua in the classification of learning strategies (as well as others not mentioned here), what solution might there be for the learners, practitioners, and researchers? Ellis (1994: 539) takes the somewhat upbeat attitude that 'considerable progress has been made in classifying learning strategies . . . from the early beginnings when researchers did little more than list strategies.' He notes that there are now comprehensive, multi-leveled, and theoretically motivated taxonomies (e.g. O'Malley and Chamot, 1990; Oxford, 1990; Wenden, 1991). Ellis notes that high inference is still called for in order to interpret which strategy is being used when, and that strategies belonging to one type frequently vary on a number of dimensions such as specificity (as illustrated in Figure 2.1 with the example of summarizing) and the extent to which they are observable.

It would seem that researchers and developers of materials for learner training would want to identify as accurately as possible those strategies that are likely to be relevant for the given learners in the given context. It would also seem advisable to make an effort to identify non-observable strategy use through various research methods, such as through learner strategy interviews and written questionnaires, observation, verbal report, diaries and dialog journals, recollective studies, and computer tracking (see Chapter 3). At the present time, no single assessment method prevails in the field. Certain research methods (e.g. surveys and observation) are well established but have failed in some cases to generate useful data on learners' strategy use. Other methods (e.g. computer tracking[8]) are emerging as new research tools, but their potential has not yet been fully explored by researchers. While the use of verbal report as a research tool has come under criticism, it nonetheless has provided numerous insights about the strategies used before, during, and after tasks involving language learning and language use.

2.3.4   Broadening the concept of strategic competence

A fourth issue involves the fact that the term *strategic competence* has broadened well beyond its original meaning. While early reference to strategic competence as a component of communicative language use (Canale and Swain, 1980; Canale, 1983) put the emphasis on *compensatory strategies* (i.e. strategies used to compensate for a lack in some language area),[9] Bachman (1990) provided a broader theoretical model for viewing strategic competence, which was recently refined by Bachman and Palmer

(1996). The authors conceive of strategic competence as 'a set of metacognitive components, or strategies, which can be thought of as higher order executive processes that provide a cognitive management function in language use' (Bachman and Palmer, 1996: 70). The areas of metacognitive strategy use include the following:

(1) a *goal-setting component*, wherein the respondents identify the tasks and decide what they are going to do;
(2) an *assessment component*, whereby the the speakers (listeners, readers, or writers[10]) determine what is needed, what one has to work with, and how well one has done; and
(3) a *planning component*, whereby the respondents decide how to use their knowledge of the topic and their language knowledge.

Within this broader framework offered by Bachman and Palmer, it may still be the case that a fair number of strategies are, in fact, compensatory. Non-native speakers (and even some native speakers in some situations) may omit material because they do not know it when put on the spot, or may produce different material from what they would like to in the hope that it will be acceptable in the given context. They may use lexical avoidance, simplification, or approximation when the exact word escapes them under pressure or possibly because they simply do not know the word that well or at all. Yet much of the strategic behavior that falls under the rubric of strategic competence in Bachman and Palmer's model is not compensatory. Such non-compensatory strategies include, for example, metacognitive strategies for determining the language needed to perform the given task, cognitive strategies for selecting appropriate language structures (when the necessary or desired structures **are**, in fact, available to the non-native), strategies for planning how to accomplish the task, and finally post-task assessment strategies.

As in the case of any theoretical model, non-natives may make differential use of the components of this model when performing specific communicative tasks. For example, many learners may not adequately assess a situation before engaging in communication, and because of this they may violate certain sociocultural conventions. In addition, learners vary according to their conversational style. There are those who tend to plan out the specifics of their utterances before producing them, consistent with the above model, while there are others who tend to start talking immediately with the intention of working things out on an on-line basis. A study conducted by Olshtain and myself (see 7.3), involving the use of verbal report directly after the performance of oral role-play interaction, obtained empirical data regarding the extent of strategic assessment and planning actually taking place before the completion of role-play inter-actions for the speech acts of apologizing, complaining, and requesting.

The fact that the concept of strategic competence has been broadened to encompass not only compensatory but also non-compensatory behaviors clearly suggests that the previous definition was too restrictive. It may be beneficial to conduct more empirical studies to determine the extent to which such models actually reflect the strategic behavior of the non-natives they are intended to describe. It is not so much an issue of validating the theoretical model as much as it is one of determining the degree to which one or another component of the model tends to be favored or ignored by a cross-section of learners.

2.3.5 Linking learning strategies to learning styles and other personality-related variables

The fifth, and final problematic issue to be discussed in this chapter involves what is perceived by some as an inadequate linking of learning strategies and learning styles in the language learning field. Learning strategies do not operate by themselves, but rather are directly tied to the learner's underlying *learning styles* (i.e. their general approaches to learning) and other personality-related variables (such as anxiety and self-concept) in the learner (Brown, 1991). They are also related to demographic factors such as sex, age, and ethnic differences (Politzer, 1983; Oxford, 1989). Schmeck (1988) underscored the need to understand learning strategies in the context of learning styles, which he defined as the expression of personality specifically in the learning situation. Schmeck encouraged researchers to view learning styles and learning strategies in the context of general personality factors such as reflectiveness/impulsiveness, field independence/dependence, self-confidence, self-concept, self-efficacy, creativity, anxiety, and motivation (intrinsic/extrinsic) (Oxford and Cohen, 1992). According to Schmeck (1988: 179), a learning strategy disembedded from personality-related factors is 'only a short-term prop for learning.'

Oxford (1993b) identifies five learning style contrasts in her *Style Analysis Survey* (*SAS*). She makes the point that each style preference offers significant benefits for learning and that the important thing is for learners to identify the style preferences for that work and to apply them whenever possible. She notes that learners' 'comfort zone' is their favorite style. In addition, she feels that learners can stretch their comfort zone through practice. The following is a description of the style contrasts that appear on the *SAS*:

(1) *the use of physical senses for study and work*: <u>visual</u> (learning best through visual means – books, video, graphics) v. <u>auditory</u> (preferring

listening and speaking activities – discussion, debates, audiotapes, role-plays, lectures, meetings) v. *hands-on* (benefiting from doing projects, conducting experiments, playing active games, working with objects, moving around the room);

(2) *dealing with other people*: extroversion (enjoying a wide range of social, interactive learning tasks such as discussions, debates, and role-plays) v. introversion (preferring to do more independent learning or working alone or with another person they know well);

(3) *handling possibilities*: intuitive–random (future-oriented, able to find the major principles of the topic, valuing speculation about possibilities, enjoying abstract thinking, and avoiding step-by-step instruction) v. concrete–sequential (oriented to the present, preferring one-step-at-a-time learning activities, wanting to know where they are going in their learning at every moment);

(4) *approaching tasks*: closure-oriented (focusing carefully on all tasks, meeting deadlines, planning ahead, preferring neatness and structure, and wanting rapid decisions) v. open (enjoying discovery learning in which they pick up information in an unstructured way, accepting messiness, putting off decisions, preferring to learn or work without deadlines or rules);

(5) *dealing with ideas*: global (concerned about getting the main idea, guessing meanings, predicting what will come next in a story or in an activity, and communicating even if they do not know all the words or concepts) v. analytic (focusing more on details, logical analysis, and contrasts while they are learning; they like to break broad concepts into units and prefer to have specific rules).[11]

Once learners have a sense of their style preferences, it may be easier for them to see why it is they prefer using certain strategies and not others. For example, if the learners are more global in their style preference, they may enjoy using reading strategies which assist them in getting the gist of an article – such as using inference when things are not spelled out in the text. If they are more inclined to focus on details, they may feel uncomfortable when using a global approach, and may prefer to have the meaning of particular items in the text spelled out clearly before they attempt to put it all together into a gist. Research has begun to document how the teacher's instructional style preferences and the learning styles that the students benefit most from may be at odds. Oxford and Lavine (1992), for example, provide empirical descriptions of potential or actual style conflicts in the classroom. An alert teacher may defuse such potential conflicts by balancing structured with unstructured activities and inductive with deductive course material presentations, as well as by making liberal use of visuals for the benefit of those who learn best by seeing, by carefully moderating the use of repetitive drills for vocabulary and grammar practice, by allowing students the option of cooperating on homework, and by other means (Felder and Henriques, 1995). A diagnostic approach to the issue would call for assessing the learners' style preferences and those of the teacher before determining the appropriate instructional approaches for the given class.

With respect to learner strategy studies, the focus until somewhat recently has tended to be on cognitive and metacognitive strategy use without providing much in the way of personality-related, social, and demographic information about the subjects. Factors such as learning styles, world knowledge and beliefs, attitudes toward the language and motivation to learn it, anxiety, sex, and ethnicity have received lesser emphasis (Oxford and Cohen, 1992). The O'Malley and Chamot (1990) taxonomy focused on cognitive and metacognitive strategies, for instance, and only touched the surface of social and especially affective strategies. Likewise, affective aspects of language learning were generally left out of the Faerch and Kasper (1983a) taxonomy. The situation has improved somewhat through the *personological* work of some strategy investigators (Ely, 1989; Ehrman and Oxford, 1990; Galloway and Labarca, 1991; Oxford, 1996b). It may be beneficial to learners, teachers, and program evaluators, however, to collect on a more routine basis some information on learning styles, beliefs and attitudes, language learning motivation, and the other variables listed above, along with data on the learning environment and teacher variables.

2.4 Dealing with the problematic issues in a strategies-based instructional program

In order to illustrate how the problematic issues discussed above might be dealt with in the real world, a project in strategies-based instruction at the University of Minnesota will be used. At present, there are numerous means available for strategy instruction, such as general study skills courses, peer tutoring, research-oriented training, videotaped mini-courses, awareness training, strategy workshops, insertion of strategies into language textbooks, and integration of strategies into foreign language instruction (see 4.2.3). Since past experience at the University of Minnesota and elsewhere had indicated that various short-term interventions had only short-term effects at best, it was determined that the most effective program would most likely be one of *strategy-based instruction* – that is, explicit classroom instruction directed at learners regarding their language learning and language use strategies, and provided alongside instruction in the foreign language itself. The provision of strategies-based instruction for learners usually depends on intensive teacher development, as a result of which the teachers then provide strategy awareness training to their learners as a regular feature of their instruction (see 4.2).

A series of seminars of up to thirty hours of instruction, entitled 'Strategies-Based Foreign Language Learning,' was developed at the University of Minnesota for teachers from different foreign language programs. The seminars have focused on training the participating teachers in how to create their own strategy-based instructional materials.[12] The teachers are thus responsible for applying the strategies to their own curricular needs, and, when possible, are paired with teachers from their own language department to share lesson plan ideas. For the less commonly taught languages (e.g. Hebrew, Hindi, Irish, Norwegian, and Portuguese[13]), the teachers are asked to form cross-language strategy support teams. After the teachers have had opportunities to create strategies-based materials and to practice integrating strategies into typical language learning tasks, they present micro-teaching strategy/language sessions to their peers in order to practice strategy instruction techniques before introducing the activities into their own classrooms. The sessions are videotaped and critiqued by all the participants.

2.4.1   Using the term *strategy*

For the purposes of the teacher seminars in strategies-based instruction, the term *strategy* has not been distinguished from *substrategy*, *technique*, *tactic*, or any other terms, even though a good deal of subcategorizing has taken place. The emphasis has been on generating lists of strategies relevant to specific tasks at hand, drawing as much as possible on the literature, as well as on the insights of the teachers in the seminars and those of their students as well. In addition, a more rigorous classification scheme for speaking strategies was developed for an experimental treatment administered by three of the teachers who completed the seminar on strategies-based instruction – two intermediate French teachers and one intermediate Norwegian teacher. The details of the experiment appear in Chapter 5. The classification included strategies used before, during, and after speaking (Weaver, *et al.* 1994; see Appendix 5). Just with respect to the before-speaking strategies, there were four levels of specificity. The first was the category of pre-speaking strategies itself, the most general category. Then this category was subdivided into strategies for lowering anxiety (e.g. relaxation techniques and positive self-talk) and those for preparing and planning (e.g. identifying the goal and purpose of the task, activating background knowledge, predicting what is going to happen, and planning possible responses). The prediction and planning strategies were each in turn subdivided, producing seven prediction strategies and six planning strategies. The purpose of this example is to show that during efforts to make strategy options explicit, the metalinguistic labels and sub-labels are less important than the descriptive labels for each level of specificity. These descriptive labels take much time and thought to develop adequately, and depend greatly on empirical investigations for their authenticity and applicability to the given language tasks.

2.4.2 Conscious use of strategies

In the University of Minnesota research study, an effort was made to describe the actual strategies that the French and Norwegian inter-mediate learners in both the experimental and control classrooms used in performing speaking tasks. Accordingly, the focus was exclusively on the strategies that would be within the students' sphere of consciousness, whether the students were giving them peripheral or focal attention at the time. Thus, the approach concurred with Ellis' (1994) position that strat-egies no longer accessible for description through verbal report by the learner lose their significance as strategies. The emphasis in this study was on those strategies that could be explicitly identified by experimental and control subjects before, during, and after the three speaking tasks that they were asked to perform.

The findings of the study would suggest that explicitly describing, discussing, and reinforcing strategies in the classroom – and thus raising them to the level of conscious awareness – can have a direct payoff on student outcomes (see Chapter 5). If instructors systematically introduce and reinforce strategies that can help students speak the target language more effectively, their students may well improve their performance on language tasks. By preserving the explicit and overt nature of the strategy training teachers better enable students to consciously transfer specific strategies to new contexts. The study also seems to endorse the notion of integrating strategy training directly into the instructional plan and of embedding strategies into daily language tasks. In this way, the students get accustomed to having the teacher teach both the language content and the language learning and language use strategies at the same time.

2.4.3 Classifying the strategies

The University of Minnesota strategies-based instruction project received direct input from Oxford and from Chamot, and the general strategy categorization used reflected a combination of the taxonomy upon which Oxford's *Strategy Inventory for Language Learning* (*SILL*) was based and that used by Chamot in her research. The strategies used in explicit training and assessed through strategy checklists designed for that purpose, combined different types of strategies (metacognitive, cognitive, affective, and social), observable and mental strategies, and a combination of learning and use strategies. The three speaking tasks selected for pre- and post-testing were purposely designed so as to elicit somewhat different kinds of strategies, and the checklists accompanying the different tasks were thus somewhat different from one another (again see Chapter 5).

2.4.4   The broader concept of strategic competence

The series of University of Minnesota seminars for language instructors on how to conduct strategies-based instruction and the accompanying research project would fit within the broader definition of strategic competence developed by Bachman and Palmer (1996) (see 2.3.4). Just as this framework calls for a description of how non-native users of a language determine what they need to do in a given task, plan the specific action that they will take, execute their plan, and then assess their success at the task, the seminars and the research study gave importance to the different stages in language strategy use – before, during, and after listening, speaking, reading, and writing. The research study focused specifically on the speaking process (before, during, and after) through the strategy checklists filled out immediately following the completion of each task.

2.4.5   Linking strategies to learning styles and other personality-related variables

In the University of Minnesota study, learners were asked questions about their learning preferences, their reasons for studying the target language, and a series of demographic questions. Although their responses were related to the frequency of use of particular strategies on a given task, there were few significant correlations and the limited number of subjects (55) did not allow us to pursue the analysis by subdividing students according to demographic and other categories. Such an analysis would be intended to determine the extent to which strategy use is conditioned by personal variables. Ultimately, the questionnaire data were used to determine the comparability of the demographics for the experimental and comparison groups, and the preliminary analysis performed on the data indicated that there were indeed few differences between these groups. Fortunately, a series of studies have been conducted by

Oxford and colleagues in this area (see, for example, Oxford, 1996b). Among the studies are one on the influence of gender and motivation on EFL learning strategies (Kaylani, 1996) and one on the influence of cultural factors on strategy use (Levine *et al.*, 1996).

2.5 Conclusions

This chapter has provided working definitions of second language learning and second language use terminology, has considered five problematic issues relating to the conceptualization and use of these terms, and has briefly demonstrated ways that one program for strategies-based instruction has dealt with these issues in the field.

While the terminological issues are in no way settled, there does appear to be a greater movement towards consensus. The growing demand for strategy taxonomies to use in teacher and learner seminars has put a premium on generating strategy lists that are comprehensive, comprehensible, and functional. As more field work takes place, lists such as that of speaking strategies in this chapter and the ones that it was based on will become far more common. Already books are beginning to appear which take one of the areas where strategies are so important, such as listening (Mendelsohn, 1994) or vocabulary (Tréville and Duquette, 1996), and develop it fully at both a theoretical and a practical level. This is a most promising trend at a time when language learning and language use strategies can have a major role in helping to shift the responsibility for learning off the shoulders of the teachers and on to those of the learners.

2.6 Discussion questions and activities

1. Define for yourself *language learner strategies*. Then compare your definition with the one provided in the chapter. You have a colleague who insists that a strategy is still a strategy even if learners use it unconsciously – in other words, without any awareness that they are using it. If you were to endorse this view, what would your reasoning be? If you were to take exception to the view, what would your reasoning be then?

2. With a partner, perform some L2 task, such as reading an unseen text for comprehension (e.g. an article in the newspaper) or writing a short note to a colleague requesting a professional favor. As you are doing the task, have your partner ask you about the language learning and language use strategies that you are using or used to accomplish the

task. (You may wish to use verbal report, as described in 3.1.3.) See if you can identify the category that each of those strategies represents (i.e. which are language use strategies such as retrieval strategies or communication strategies, and which are learning strategies).

3. Assume that you are a foreign language instructor at an institution that for years has referred to 'language learning strategies' without distinguishing among the different categories. They have all been lumped into one general pool. On the basis of this chapter, you now have some handy distinctions to make. Prepare a mini-lecture on these distinctions. Then do an exercise with your colleagues (or with the fellow students in your class). Divide them up into small groups so that each group is dealing with one of the categories of strategies. Have each group identify at least five examples of strategies within that category. Then compare results across groups to see if the examples seem to work. Which examples seem to overlap categories? Find ways for explaining this overlap.

4. At your high school, you overhear your colleagues talking about 'good' and 'bad' strategies, and about the need for students to use more strategies and to use them more frequently. You have become informed on this topic and prepare a few remarks to present at the next staff meeting. What would your main points be in setting the record straight for your colleagues (or your fellow students)?

5. As a staff project or homework assignment, fill out Oxford's *SAS* and her *SILL* or some other instruments which assess both learning style and learner strategies. As you fill out each item, make marginal notes or tape-recorded comments when you have reactions to what you think particular items are assessing. Compare your reactions to these two instruments with the reactions of your colleagues or fellow students. What do you see as the strengths of each instrument? What would you consider to be its weaknesses? Would you recommend administering them to students in your second or foreign language classes? If not, what alternatives would you recommend?

Notes

1. Portions of this chapter are taken from a paper originally presented at the Symposium on Strategies of Language Learning and Use, Seville, Spain, December 13–16, 1994. Those portions have been revised extensively.
2. See Cohen (1987b) and Hulstijn (1997) for reviews of the research literature on keyword mnemonics and Cohen (1990) for a sample training exercise.
3. Retrieval strategies have appeared primarily in the communication strategies literature, with the focus on the retrieval of vocabulary rather than grammatical forms. Faerch and

Kasper (1983b), for example, included at least six strategies for retrieving vocabulary words from memory: just waiting for the word to appear, appealing to formal similarities, retrieving the word through its link to other words in the same semantic field, searching for the word via other languages, thinking back to the language learning situation, and using sensory memories.

4. I am most grateful to Tim McNamara for suggesting to me the term *cover strategy* (Personal Communication, July 9, 1996) since it expresses the concept so well.

5. In language use situations, there may be no intention to communicate, such as in totally mechanical drills or even in meaningful but non–communicative drills. In other words, it is probably meaningful for students to ask each other how to get to the nearest library on campus, but it may not be a communicative act to do so if both students already know where the nearest library is.

6. See Naiman *et al.* (1975), Rubin (1975), Stern (1975), Hosenfeld (1976), and Naiman *et al.* (1978), often collectively known as the 'good language learner' studies. Nation and McLaughlin (1986), among others, have addressed the difficulties associated with the 'good' strategies approach to learner strategy research.

7. This discussion of the five problematic issues is based in part on Oxford and Cohen (1992). For the most part, when reference is made to *language learning strategies* without mention of *language use strategies*, the latter is implied as well.

8. As will be further described in 3.1.6, tracking programs can unobtrusively create a log of learners' uses for various resource functions contained within the computerized language program, whether in writing tasks, reading tasks, or grammar drills.

9. There is a somewhat pejorative ring to the term *compensatory*, suggesting something remedial. A more positive term might be that of *complementary strategies*, which suggests strategies that are meant to complement other existing means of communication.

10. Whereas strategic competence was initially linked primarily to speaking, researchers have expanded its coverage to include listening (Tarone and Yule, 1989), reading, and writing (Oxford, 1990) as well.

11. Recently, an effort has been made to revise some of the terms for learning style to make them more accurate. So, for example, it has been noted that the more appropriate opposite of *global* is *particular*, rather than *analytic*. Learners may focus on the global picture or on particulars. Since *analytic* actually describes the process whereby learners break down or disassemble material in order to deal with it, the opposite process is that of *synthesis*, referring to the process of assembly. Ehrman and Leaver (1997) refer to these two processes as *synoptic* (perception of phenomena as wholes) and *ectenic* (perception of phenomena as composites). Likewise, these researchers are dissatisfied with the term *random* as used for some time in the *sequential* v. *random* distinction (*intuitive–random* v. *concrete–sequential* in Oxford's inventory). They note that an ordering determined by a learner may look random, but may not be so in the mind of the learner. Hence, they are looking for a new term.

12. These seminars have been funded through a National Language Resource Center grant awarded by the Center for International Education, US Office of Education, to the University of Minnesota.

13. What is deemed a less commonly taught language (LCTL) varies from context to context. So whereas Portuguese may be a LCTL in Minnesota, it would probably be a most commonly taught language in parts of Spain.

3 Methods for investigating language learning and language use strategies

Let us assume that a group of foreign language teachers have become convinced that it is not enough for them to focus on their instructional curriculum, but rather they need to pay more attention to what their learners are doing with the curriculum and to ways to assist them in being more effective learners. How do they gather information from the learners as to what they are and are not doing? How can they go about this in a systematic way? Let us also assume that a team of researchers is concerned with the difficulties that a particular group of language learners is having with the given foreign language since, based on their backgrounds, they are clearly under-achieving. They suspect that the problem lies with the strategies that the learners are or are not using, and with the way that they use the strategies that they employ.

If teachers or researchers wish to gather information regarding language learner strategies, what means of assessment are there for them to use? While there are actually a number of possible approaches and a series of methods within each approach, a given study will usually select only one or two of these methods. Selection is made in part according to:

(1) the objectives of the study as expressed through the specific research questions;
(2) the language modalities involved: the receptive ones of listening and reading, and the productive ones of speaking and writing;
(3) the language learning environment;
(4) concerns about the reliability and validity of the given instrument;
(5) time constraints;
(6) budgetary considerations.

The first half of this chapter (3.1) consists of an analysis of six different approaches to assessing language strategies: learning strategy interviews and written questionnaires, observation, verbal report, diaries and dialog journals, recollective studies, and computer tracking. The strengths and weaknesses of each strategy assessment method are discussed. One point to be stressed in the discussion below is that while certain research methods (e.g. questionnaire surveys and classroom/out-of-class observation) are well established, the data that they yield are not necessarily very informative about learners' strategy use. Other methods are not so well established but are gaining ground. One of these is verbal report, which has come under criticism as a research tool, but which has nonetheless provided numerous insights about the strategies used before, during, and after performing language learning or language use tasks. Still other methods (e.g. computer tracking) have yet to emerge as research tools in strategy research except in limited cases, so it is fair to say that their potential has not yet been fully explored by researchers.

The second part of the chapter provides an in-depth discussion of one of the six methods, namely, verbal report, in light of its rising popularity as a research tool. The section starts by contrasting the three forms of verbal report – self-report, self-observation, and self-revelation. Next, ways in which verbal report has contributed to the understanding of language learning and language use strategies is addressed. Then, some concerns about the appropriate use of such measures in research are offered. The issues include: the immediacy of the verbal report, the respondents' role in interpreting the data, prompting for specifics in verbal report, guidance in providing verbal reporting, and the effects of verbal report on task performance. Finally, attention is given to the elements which need to be included in the write ups on verbal reports so that others will understand fully what was done, be able to make comparisons with other studies, and also be able to replicate the procedures. The following areas are addressed: (1) the subjects' characteristics, (2) the characteristics of the materials, (3) the nature of the criterion task, (4) guidance in verbal reporting, (5) methods of analysis, (6) categories used to score verbal report protocols, (7) interrater reliability checks, (8) selection of verbal report excerpts for inclusion in research reports, and (9) theories used in framing the verbal report study.

The point is made that care in the write-up can help to dispel arguments that such methodological approaches are not adequately rigorous. Since by now there have appeared a number of studies using verbal report techniques to better understand the processes involved in language learning and language use, it would seem that the time has come to provide greater systematicity both in the collection of such data and in the reporting of such studies through the research literature. It is noted that such information on verbal report methods could: (1) assist researchers in making comparisons across studies, (2) facilitate efforts at replicating studies which have used verbal report, and (3) help investigators to identify language learning and language use strategies on various language tasks and to relate the use of these strategies to success on the tasks.

3.1   A synthesis of approaches to assessing language learning strategies

Andrew Cohen and Kimberly Scott[1]

Today we are visiting an intermediate Japanese foreign language class. The teacher has just set up a role-play situation between students and their professor in which the students need to request a postponement of the due date for a written assignment. The students are struggling in their minds to find the appropriate language for making this request to their professor, a person of higher status. They make a rapid scan through their knowledge base to identify vocabulary and structures that may be suitable. They then worry about how to deliver this material. As they are delivering it, they realize that mid-course corrections in what they have said are necessary.

This activity also happens to be the subject of research. The researcher is faced with the task of describing the language use strategies that the students utilized in this role-play situation. The problem is how to capture this information. How much can be obtained through oral interview or written questionnaire? How much of it might be revealed through systematic observation? Would it be possible to reconstruct the use of strategies through retrospective verbal report? Might the learners make helpful, informative entries into their diaries or dialog journals that evening? This chapter is about the choices the researcher makes in trying to collect data on language learning and language use strategies.

Since language learning strategies are generally internal or mentalistic processes, certain research approaches may fail to provide adequate data on learners' strategy use. Thus, designing a study that assesses strategy use with some accuracy is a challenge. In the body of research on language learning strategies, researchers have used numerous assessment methods to determine patterns of strategy use among learners. In this chapter, six of those methods are described: oral interviews and written questionnaires, observation, verbal report, diaries and dialog journals, recollective studies, and computer tracking.

For each assessment method, there are a number of issues that the individuals doing the research must consider, whether they are trained researchers or teachers without much or any research training. First, not all assessment methods are suitable for studying every type of language learning strategy, and differences in assessment according to the language skill areas being studied (e.g. listening, speaking, reading, writing, and vocabulary learning) are an added consideration. Furthermore, each method of assessment has a certain number of options which can be manipulated by the researcher depending on the aims of the study.

In this section, some options relevant to language learning strategy research will be described for each method, and in several instances, suggestions for innovations in the use of these methods are provided. In addition, the advantages and disadvantages of each assessment method will be offered.

3.1.1 Oral interviews and written questionnaires

While in many ways oral interviews and written questionnaires are distinct strategy assessment methods, they are similar in that they both elicit learner responses to a set of questions or probes. In addition, they both require the researcher to make choices regarding question format and research procedures.

ADVANTAGES AND DISADVANTAGES OF STRUCTURED INTERVIEWS AND QUESTIONNAIRES

A major dimension of both oral interviews and written questionnaires is the degree of structure in the questions or probes. Questions can range from those that ask for yes–no responses or indications of frequency (e.g. 'never,' 'seldom,' 'sometimes,' 'often,' and 'always') to less structured questions asking respondents to describe or discuss language learning strategy behavior in detail. In the latter case, the respondents clearly have more control over the information that is included in the answer.

In *highly structured interviews* and *questionnaires*, the researcher has a specific set of questions that are to be answered by the respondent in a set order. In this case the researcher has complete control over the questioning, and the respondent usually does not have an opportunity to elaborate on the answers. The data obtained from this type of interview or questionnaire are uniformly organized for all respondents and lend themselves to statistical analysis. An example of a structured language strategy questionnaire survey is Oxford's *Strategy Inventory for Language Learning* (*SILL*) (Oxford, 1990, 1996a; see also Oxford and Burry-Stock, 1995; Bedell and Oxford, 1996; Dreyer and Oxford, 1996). (See Chapter 5 for a description of the instrument and for sample items from the 80-item version.)

At the other end of the spectrum are *unstructured questions* or *probes* that simply ask the respondents to discuss a certain area of interest. The duration and depth of the response and the choice of the focus are left largely to the respondent's discretion. Thus, the respondents have the freedom to pursue areas of personal interest with only minimal guidance from the interviewer.

There is also the possibility of *semi-structured interviews* or *questionnaires*. In such cases there is most likely a prompt which requests certain information (e.g. 'How did you go about reading the short essay that was assigned as homework yesterday?'), but the exact shape of the response is not predetermined. The respondents are free to give any description they may wish. In a more structured situation, there may be multiple-choice alternatives or a list of strategies for reading the essay, and the students are to rate each according to the extent to which they used them (e.g. 'pre-read the text to get an idea of its general meaning,' 'looked for headings and subheadings as a clue to the meaning of the text,' 'checked for a description of the topic at the outset or a summary at the end,' 'used a dictionary when unknown words were encountered,' 'guessed words from context,' and so forth).

The responses to structured instruments may be simplistic or contain only brief information about any one learning strategy. For example, a question that merely asks students whether or not they use mnemonics does not get at some of the more interesting issues: how often they use mnemonics, in what language learning and language use situations they think mnemonics are helpful, or (for those who have been trained in the use of keyword mnemonics) whether they use mnemonics in their current studies. Furthermore, predetermined questions – especially those that are not carefully piloted – may have ambiguities in their wording which could lead to problems of interpretation on the part of the respondents. In addition, if researchers are too explicit about what they mean in a given question (e.g. with the inclusion of specific examples), the question by its nature may motivate the respondents to select a certain response, thus making the instrument less objective.

Unstructured and semi-structured interviews and questionnaires have the advantage of allowing the researcher and learners to pursue topics of interest which may not have been foreseen when the questions were originally drawn up. Yet the reduction of structure also means that the volume of data is increased and the data themselves are likely to be more highly individualized, which could prevent the researcher from determining overall patterns. Sometimes the data from semi-structured and unstructured instruments can be used effectively to identify dimensions that can then be used profitably in structured interviews or questionnaires.

ADVANTAGES AND DISADVANTAGES OF LARGER NUMBERS OF RESPONDENTS

Another important dimension in oral interviews and written questionnaires is the number of participants. Using just one subject allows the interviewer to develop a detailed case study of that learner. In some such studies, the subject is actually the investigator as well, obviating the problem of finding a willing subject (see, for example, Schmidt and Frota, 1986; Altman, 1997; Cohen, in press(a)). Whether or not the researcher and the subject are one and the same, the case study approach can yield insights which are useful in describing, for example, the learner's strategy use. One way to strengthen the impact of case studies is to gather a number of them, as was done in the early days of child language acquisition work. It is difficult to generalize from a single case study, but when a series of them produces similar results with respect to one or another dimension, then generalizations may begin to emerge from the data.

In addition to one-on-one interviews, a researcher could conduct a group interview or administer a questionnaire to learners. In a small group interview, the interviewer can introduce a topic such as 'the use of paraphrasing and gesturing during role plays' and ask the students to comment. One problem with small group interviews is that some subjects' responses may be affected by social desirability. In that type of situation, with their peers listening, respondents may be fearful of producing a socially unacceptable answer. In addition, if certain subjects are unwilling to volunteer information in group settings, the information obtained is likely to be biased in favor of students who are more outspoken. However, small group interviews may be more effective in terms of cost and time than individual interviews.

In contrast to interviews, written questionnaires are usually administered to large groups of learners and/or to groups at various sites. A major benefit of large-scale surveys is the potential for generating and testing hypotheses because of the large number of respondents. On the other hand, a given survey may not transfer well from one setting to another, either because there are significant differences in the way that the questionnaire is administered or because the respondents in the different sites differ in how they interpret the items. This could be especially true if the measure is translated and used in different cultures around the world (see Oxford, 1996b).

ADVANTAGES AND DISADVANTAGES OF FORMALITY

Yet another factor of concern in the design of interviews and questionnaires is that of degree of formality. Of concern here is the manner in which questions are asked of learners, and the extent to which the questions and the setting encourage the learners to relax and provide accurate, honest answers. To a degree, formality is affected by the rapport established between the interviewer and the subjects and is independent of the degree of structure. It is possible to have an interviewer conduct a highly structured interview in a friendly and informal manner. On the other hand, in an unstructured interview, the interviewer could have a highly formal manner for asking questions or following up on interesting topics. A manner that is too informal may not be desirable if the researcher wants to keep enough distance from the students to maintain objectivity and the ability to pursue topics that are crucial to the research. Yet, the subjects should feel comfortable talking at length about their learning, including affective aspects. If the interviewer is too formal in manner, then the students may be reluctant to discuss the learning environment, especially in describing some of their social and affective strategies which may touch on their rapport with the teacher or with other learners.

TOWARDS MORE ACCURATE STRATEGY DESCRIPTIONS

One of the main problems with oral interviews and written questionnaires as a whole is that much of the data constitutes self-report or the learners' generalized statements about their strategy use (see 3.1.3 for definitions of the terms). Once learners move away from instances of language learning or language use behavior, they may also tend to become less accurate about their actual strategy behavior (Cohen, 1987a). Learners may overestimate or underestimate the frequency of use of certain strategies. They may also be unaware of when they are using a given strategy, and even more importantly, how they are using it. To avoid this problem, the researcher may wish to have respondents focus on recent language strategy use. The questions would attempt to have the respondents think of specific learning events as opposed to more generalized behavior patterns. For example, the researcher could interview students or have them fill out written questionnaires immediately following a language task and ask questions specific to that task. For instance, the learners could perform the task seated at a booth in the language laboratory, and could record their verbal report data directly into the microphone at their console. This type of information would most likely constitute self-revelation (think aloud) and self-observation. The next section discusses another widely-used research method, that of systematic observation by the researcher, whether in or out of the classroom.

3.1.2   Observation

Observational methods rely on participant or non-participant observers to produce the data – whether from structured observation schedules, from ethnographic field notes, or from other methods. A major challenge in attempting to apply observational techniques to language learners is that many of the language use and language use strategies cannot be observed since they are mentalistic and not behavioristic. Is it possible, for example, to determine through observation whether a learner is in the process of circumlocuting in order to describe an object (e.g. a bookend) when the vocabulary word is not available? Is it possible to observe a learner's efforts to retrieve a word by means of a keyword mnemonic? Access to such language use strategies most likely must come from interviews, written questionnaires, and verbal report (see below), wherein the learners generate the data. In planning an observational study, the researcher needs to consider a variety of factors: the number of observers and observed, the frequency and duration of observations, and how the observational data are collected, tabulated, and analyzed.

With regard to the number of observers, an investigator may choose to observe a language learning activity alone or with other observers, each observing the same or different learners, at the same or at different times. There will be trade offs if the observations focus on one learner as opposed to focusing on a small group or on an entire class of language learners. Especially in the observation of language learning strategies, observing the entire class may be most profitable in that waiting for one learner or a small group to reveal their use of strategies may not provide much useful data. Of course, it is possible to record non-verbal behavior (e.g. students' facial expressions, gestures, signs of alertness, and so forth), as well as to observe written behavior by sitting next to learners and taking note of what they write in their notebook.

Another factor is the frequency and duration of the observations. First, the investigator has to determine the number of observations over time. If meaningful data are to be obtained from observation of learning strategy behavior, then it is likely that the investigator will need to visit the same class over an extended period. A more limited observational framework may work best if the objectives of the observation are limited – e.g. just getting a feeling for the classroom climate in which the language learner strategies are being employed or making use of the observational data simply to jog the learners' memory as to classroom events during those specific lessons. Secondly, researchers need to make choices as to their focus – whether, for example, to focus on a 15-minute role-play activity or to observe an entire class period in order to collect data on the use of speaking strategies.

Yet another factor concerns how the observation is conducted. It is likely that the investigator(s) will be present in the room while the learning activity is taking place. In addition, audio- and videotapes may also be made of the class session in order to create a more permanent record of what took place. Although there now exist sophisticated means of collecting video- and audiotaped data, there are countless instances of key events that somehow do not get captured by the available technology, so that the presence of live observers may play a crucial role in both the collection and the interpretation of the language strategy data. Note that if the activity is videotaped, the investigator would also be able to replay the tapes for the learners and thereby use the tapes not just for observational data but as an aid in the collection of verbal report data as well (to be discussed below). In other words, the tapes could be used to jog the memory of the learners as to what they were thinking and doing in the classroom at that time.

The final factor concerns the investigator's method for recording strategy use. One option is that of note-taking, which can be more or less structured. The investigator has a choice of taking broader, more impressionistic notes of everything of relevance that occurs, or of taking notes that focus on a few types of strategies or behaviors (Oxford, 1990). The researcher may be able to take more complete notes if the observation is recorded on audio- or videotape. Another option is to use some sort of observation scale or checklist. An example of an observation scale that was used for collecting learning strategy data is the *Class Observation Guide* (O'Malley, Chamot, Stewner-Manzanares, Küpper, and Russo, 1985; O'Malley, Chamot, Stewner-Manzanares Russo, and Küpper, 1985). Finally, the investigator may wish to combine the use of an observation scale with note-taking in order to obtain more complete data.

DISADVANTAGES OF OBSERVATION

The key drawback of the observational method is its inability to produce descriptions of internal or mentalistic strategies such as reasoning or self-talk, as suggested above. Investigators can note behavior such as asking for clarification, but many strategies never result in an obvious behavior. Thus, an observational study may yield a description of a learner's use of strategies, but this description may reflect a largely incomplete view of the learner's actual strategy use. Researchers who have used observations for investigating learner strategies have experienced frustrations in deriving descriptions of even those strategies which may be thought to be most observable. For example, Naiman, Frölich, Stern, and Todesco (1978) had difficulty determining when high-school students of French were using circumlocutions. Furthermore, on teachers' solicitations from students, Fanselow (1979) noted that seemingly obvious questions that teachers ask may have implicit messages that students cannot interpret easily, even after asking the speaker for clarification. Neither the implicit motives of the teachers in asking such questions, nor the strategies that the students use to try to understand the solicitations may be readily observable by the outside investigator.

Another drawback is that researchers are likely to collect data only on the students who are more verbal during the class session, and this may limit the data to only a subset of language learners – namely, the outspoken or extroverted. In fact, many students may be left out of the strategy descriptions altogether even though these students may be some of the most interesting in terms of the strategies they use and the results they obtain.

Yet another problem associated with observation methods is the bias inherent in an observer's descriptions of the strategies. The observer is always affected by prior expectations, and any observational scale or checklist will limit how the observer views the students' strategy use. With student-generated data, there is less chance that the descriptions will be limited by or reflect the researcher's expectations, though even in this case there is that possibility. Finally, some students' behavior may change when a researcher or video camera is present in the classroom. For example, if an observer is present, some students may be less willing to make mistakes and consequently become less talkative. This problem, however, may be a factor in all assessment methods, to differing degrees. For example, students who know they will be asked to give a verbal report following a role play may become more deliberate in their mental planning for the role play. With regard to observation methods, the problem of students' altering their normal behavior could be mitigated by repeated observations. If the observer or video camera is present during several lessons, students may become accustomed and consequently revert back to their normal classroom behavior.

ADVANTAGES OF OBSERVATION

Observational methods may also have benefits – when used to describe learning strategies that are clearly observable. In such instances, the data obtained are likely to be uniform, assuming the researcher uses the same terms to describe the same phenomena. Second, external observational records may help to lend a more impartial, objective perspective to the research study, rather than having the study rely solely on data provided by learners. In fact, learners may sometimes alter strategy descriptions according to what they think are socially acceptable answers. Furthermore, if the observation information is collected in a structured form (such as an observation scale), the resulting data are likely to be more quantitative in nature. Thus, they will lend themselves more readily to statistical analysis and can be used to generate or test hypotheses. In spite of these potential advantages, though, observation will continue to have limited applications to learning strategy research because so much of language learning strategy behavior is unobservable.

3.1.3   Verbal report

Often methods such as classroom observation produce indications or clues as to the strategies that learners use, rather than instances of actual strategy use, since what is usually obtained is some language product rather than information regarding the processes used to arrive at that product. Hence, researchers have had to rely to some extent on their own intuitions in order to produce descriptions of strategy use – such as a description of the strategies used by a classroom learner to make a request for an item whose name they cannot remember. We would suggest that verbal report measures provide a more viable – perhaps the most viable – means of obtaining empirical evidence as to strategy use than do other means.

TYPES OF VERBAL REPORT

Verbal report measures have played a role in many of the research studies on language learner strategies. Numerous insights about the strategies that learners use have been obtained from them as they provided verbal report data before, during, and after performing language learning or language using tasks. It is important to note that verbal report is not one measure, but rather encompasses a variety of measures intended to provide mentalistic data regarding cognitive processing.

Verbal reports include data that reflect:

(1) *self-report*: learners' descriptions of what they do, characterized by generalized statements about learning behavior – e.g. 'I tend to be a speed listener,'

(2) *self-observation*: the inspection of specific, not generalized, language behavior, either introspectively, i.e. within 20 seconds of the mental event, or retrospectively – e.g. 'What I just did was to skim through the incoming oral text as I listened, picking out key words and phrases,' and

(3) *self-revelation*: 'think-aloud,' stream-of-consciousness disclosure of thought processes while the information is being attended to – e.g. 'Who does the "they" refer to here?'

Verbal reports can and usually do comprise some combination of these (Radford, 1974; Cohen and Hosenfeld, 1981; Cohen, 1987a). Self-report data tend to appear frequently on questionnaires which ask learners to describe the way they usually learn and use language. Self-observation implies reference to some actual instance(s) of language learning or language use. For example, entries in journals or diaries which retrospectively describe some language learning or language use event involving the subjunctive would count as retrospective self-observation. Self-revelational or think-aloud data are only available at the time that the language learning or language use events are taking place, and are generated when the respondents are simply describing, say, their efforts to use the correct form of the subjunctive, and not attempting to analyze this effort. Thoughts which are immediately analyzed would constitute introspective self-observation – for example, 'Now, does this utterance call for the present or imperfect subjunctive? Let me see . . .'

We note that the use of verbal report protocols in L2 learning strategy investigations has benefited greatly from the extensive use of this research methodology in the native language. Such work, especially in reading and writing (e.g. Garner, 1982; Flower and Hayes, 1984), has paved the way for much of the L2 work. Even though a recent book by Pressley and Afflerbach (1995), for example, focuses on the use of verbal reports of first language (L1) reading, it constitutes an excellent compendium of ideas for L2 researchers. The authors refer to verbal reports as 'a maturing methodology with much interesting work already accomplished and considerable work to be done' (Pressley and Afflerbach, 1995: 1). In their book, the authors demonstrate how the use of verbal report (whether as an exploratory methodology or as a means for testing hypotheses about reading) has yielded an elegant description of reading. They provide a description of what they refer to as *before-reading*, *during-reading*, *after-reading*, *monitoring* and *evaluating strategies*, based on a review of 38 primary-data studies. As the authors put it, 'The think-alouds were extremely revealing about the dynamics of comprehension difficulties and how understandings of text shift in reaction to comprehension difficulties and surprises in text' (Pressley and Afflerbach, 1995: 38).

Examples of L2 learner strategy studies where verbal report has consisted of self-report interviews and questionnaires are numerous (see, for example, Naiman, Fröhlich, Stern, and Todesco, 1978; O'Malley, Chamot, Stewner-Manzanares, Russo and Küpper, 1985; Wenden, 1985; Ramírez, 1986; Oxford *et al.*, 1987). In such studies, the respondents answer oral interview questions or complete written questionnaires about their language strategies. Since self-report has been shown to be somewhat removed from the cognitive events being described, this approach may produce data which are of somewhat questionable validity. Questionnaire items referring to general behavior (i.e. 'what you tend to do . . .') may elicit learners' **beliefs** about what they do, rather than what they actually do. Efforts are often made by investigators to increase the extent to which respondents provide self-observational and self-revelational data and to decrease the amount of self-report data. The purpose is to obtain data that describe the language learning or language use event at or near the moment it occurs. Such data might be expected to more accurately reflect what learners actually do than might the response to a questionnaire item calling for a description of generalized behavior. In effect, self-revelation and self-observation are intended to complement self-report – to produce convergent assessment of learner strategies.

Verbal report methods primarily reflecting self-revelation and self-observation have been employed as a means of describing strategies in the learning and use of L2 vocabulary (e.g. Cohen and Aphek 1979, 1981; Neubach and Cohen, 1988; Chern, 1993; Huckin and Bloch, 1993; Gu, 1994), L2 listening (e.g. Murphy, 1987; Vandergrift, 1992; Anderson and Vandergrift, 1996), L2 speaking (e.g. Robinson, 1991; Cohen and Olshtain, 1993; Cohen *et al.*, 1995), L2 reading (e.g. Hosenfeld, 1984; Block, 1986; Cavalcanti, 1987; Kern, 1994), L2 writing (e.g. Zamel, 1983; Raimes, 1987; Cohen and Cavalcanti, 1987, 1990; Skibniewski, 1990), and in the processing of entries in bilingual dictionaries (Neubach and Cohen, 1988).

Verbal report has also been used for investigating the subset of L2 language use strategies referred to in Chapter 2 as *communication strategies*, especially those used in compensating for gaps in communicative ability (e.g. Poulisse, Bongaerts, and Kellerman, 1986; Poulisse, 1990). In addition, verbal report is used with tasks which combine most or all of the strategy areas, such as in investigating the strategies used in language learning and language use overall (see, for example, Cyr, 1996, Chapter 5, for a description of a retrospective study of immigrants to Montreal), in the translation of texts (Faerch and Kasper, 1986; Borsch, 1986; Gerloff, 1987; Krings, 1987), and in taking L2 tests (Cohen, 1984, 1994a, 1994b; Feldman and Stemmer, 1987; Stemmer, 1991; Gordon, 1987; Anderson, 1989, 1991; Nevo, 1989; A. Brown, 1993; Hill, 1994; Warren, 1996; Abraham and Vann, 1996).

Let us now take a look at issues of controversy regarding this method of data collection.

DISADVANTAGES OF VERBAL REPORT

Critics of verbal report methods note that much of cognitive processing is inaccessible because it is unconscious (see, for example, Seliger, 1983). Critics among second language researchers have contended that whereas verbal report methods may help to describe language use strategies, it remains to be demonstrated whether they can inform us about language knowledge or skill learning, as this information is more likely to be unconscious (Seliger, 1983). Even if the processing is not unconscious, it has been considered either as too complex to capture in protocols (Dobrin, 1986), or as putting too great a burden on learners' memories for them to report mental processing with any accuracy. Thus, researchers who use such measures either have to somehow raise the level of conscious awareness of processing or make do with insights regarding those processes to which respondents have conscious access. The use of such measures may also require respondents to unravel some of the complexity inherent in a given set of cognitive processes and/or improve their recall skills.

In addition, there exists the possibility that if the information is not directly accessible (i.e. the tasks involved are largely automatic), probes may force the subject to produce a verbal response that is not closely related to the actual thought processes (Ericsson and Simon, 1980). It has also been pointed out that verbal reports may be too dependent on retrospection – in that it can take 20 minutes to report on $1\frac{1}{2}$ seconds of mental processing (Boring, 1953). Hence, what may have begun as an introspective account quickly turns into a retrospective one. Critics likewise refer to the tendency to repress data – to supply socially acceptable data (Bakan, 1954). Thus, protocols may be systematically contaminated by an indulgence in shared assumptions (Dobrin, 1986). In fact, protocols have been depicted as an edited replay of the respondents' perception, an invention of the respondents' folk psychology (Lyons, 1986). Not only the cultural background of the respondent, but also the background knowledge or schemata that the respondent has about the performance of such verbal report tasks might play a role (Cavalcanti, 1984).

Furthermore, verbal report methods have been criticized for their potentially intrusive effect. For example, in reading research, attention is drawn to the possibility that immediate retrospection may distort the process of reading if the readers read more closely than normal, read sentence by sentence, or concentrate on the additional cognitive and meta-cognitive task (Mann, 1982). Not only is there the possibility that the verbal report task may cause reactive effects, and thus produce data no longer reflecting the processes intended to be investigated (see under 3.2 below); there is also the possibility that the results will vary according to the type of instructions given, the characteristics of the participating subjects (some more informative than others), the types of material used in collecting protocols, and the nature of the data analysis (Olson *et al.*, 1984).

For example, the respondents may differ with respect to their verbal skills. Some may be more adept than others at providing the appropriate amount of verbal report data, at the appropriate level of specificity. Also, respondents may use different terms to describe similar processes or the same terms for different processes. A way of getting around this problem would be to train the respondents in the terms to use in their responses. However, such a form of intervention may distort the data in cases where respondents are meant to supply their own labels for their cognitive processes. In addition, differences may exist between spoken and written verbal report so that studies which combine both sources of data may ultimately find the two types of data to be incompatible (Afflerbach and Johnston, 1984).

Finally, there is the potential problem that could arise when respondents do a task in a target language and report on it in their L1 or another language. The problem is that the respondents are likely to be recoding the information, which may in itself cause information to get lost due to limits of memory capacity as well as other factors such as inaccuracy during the translation of thoughts. The reporting (especially in on-line, self-revelation) may alter the original thought processes more than when no recoding takes place (Faerch and Kasper, 1987: 19).

ADVANTAGES OF VERBAL REPORT

While the critics would suggest that these numerous problems with verbal report measures seriously limit the degree to which findings can be generalized and might even preclude their use, proponents of verbal report would argue that cognizance of these problems in planning the research design may help to avoid some of them.

What may be said to characterize many of the verbal report studies across the different activity areas is their dependency on the information processing model (see Ericsson and Simon, 1993: 11–24). These verbal report studies reflect a theoretical framework whereby for the most part only information which is processed in a serial, controlled fashion is reported – a notable departure from verbal report data collected in the past (see Titchener, 1912). Perhaps the major purpose for using verbal report protocols is to reveal in detail what information is attended to while performing tasks – information that is otherwise lost to the investigator (Ericsson, 1988; Ericsson and Simon, 1993). Whereas the neurological origin of cognitive processes may not be available for inspection, the cognitive events themselves are often available through verbal report (Steinberg, 1986: 699). It is suggested that language learners underestimate the extent of conscious (or potentially conscious) processing because they are not attending to it. Furthermore, the directness of introspection gives it a character not found in any other investigation of psychological phenomena (Bakan, 1954).

Whereas the reliability of mentalistic measures has been questioned in comparison with behavioristic measures, research has demonstrated that verbal reports, elicited with care and interpreted with full understanding of the circumstances under which they were obtained, are, in fact, a valuable and a thoroughly reliable source of information about cognitive processes (Ericsson and Simon, 1980; Pressley and Afflerbach, 1995). In a number of settings, for example, subjects' reports of their hypotheses and strategies have proved to be highly correlated with their subsequent behavior – and are often the most accurate predictors available (Lieberman, 1979).

As noted at the outset of this section, verbal reports have been used as a source of data for understanding the learning and use of language in numerous ways. With respect to second language **learning**, the uses of verbal report have been admittedly limited. Immediate retrospective verbal report has, for example, helped to describe strategies in learning vocabulary by association, such as through mnemonic keywords (Cohen, 1990: 134–40; Cohen and Aphek, 1981). Such strategy data provide at least partial information regarding vocabulary learning processes, regardless of whether the learner subsequently produces a correct retrieval of the vocabulary item. With respect to language **use**, the research literature is more extensive. For example, the think-aloud method has broadened the scope of what is described in text processing by providing insights as to the use of prior knowledge in text comprehension and as to the monitoring of this and other comprehension processes (Waern, 1988). Furthermore, helpful information about the writing process has been derived from protocol analysis without having to account for every mental process (Smagorinsky, 1989).

While critics have often referred to verbal report data as too qualitative in nature, Hillocks (1994) reminds us that quantitative studies, while taking the stance of being dispassionate and objective, inherently involve biased interpretations. In addition, he notes that verbal report often relies on counting instances of activity in order to arrive at conclusions, and so he would argue against categorically labeling verbal report data as qualitative. Those who have collected and analyzed verbal report protocols will attest to the fact that much of the analysis can be quantitative in nature.

Finally, it needs to be pointed out that verbal report is not seen as a replacement for other means of research but rather as a complement to them, as all research measures have their potential strengths and weaknesses. (We will return to verbal report in 3.2 below.)

3.1.4   Diaries and dialog journals

DIARIES

In an effort to collect data on learners' strategy use over a period of time, some researchers have turned to diaries as a research tool. Even though diaries are described as 'first-person journals' (Bailey and Ochsner, 1983), they often contain longer narratives and other information that are not in the first person. Despite this, we will continue to use the term *diary* rather than *journal* for an individual's written reflections on language learning.

DIALOG JOURNALS

A second way to collect learners' thoughts and emotions in written form is through a *dialog journal* which adds an important element to diaries: a reader who responds (and, ideally, at length) to the learners' writing. Such journals often take the form of a notebook with the right-hand page saved for some writing or reading assignments which the students perform and for which they receive feedback directly on that page. The left-hand page is reserved for the student journalists to ask questions or make comments before, during, and after they do the assignment. The teacher responds to these comments also on the left-hand page, without 'correcting' the language used by the student journalist. Another approach would be not to have any assignments written in the journal, but simply entries by the students when they have something to ask about or comment on. In classroom settings, the reader is generally the teacher, but other students or classroom aides may participate as readers. In theory, the dialog journal is supposed to be an ongoing, written conversation between the student and the reader about topics that have been generated by the student (Peyton and Reed, 1990). In reality, however, the teacher or student readers may make only brief – often one-sentence – comments on what the owner of the journal has written, rather than participating equally in the dialog. Dialog journals have been used widely in L1 and L2 classrooms to encourage students to write frequently on topics of interest to them. It appears that dialog journals have yet to be used widely as a research tool in studies on language learning strategies.

FORM AND CONTENT

Since diaries and dialog journals are learner-generated and usually unstructured, the entries may cover a wide range of themes and issues. For example, the entries may include learners' written verbal report of the cognitive, metacognitive, and social strategies that they use daily in their language learning. For the most part, the verbal report in diaries and dialog journals constitutes retrospective self-report or self-observation since learners generally write their entries after the learning event has taken place. For example, learners could describe what they usually do when they do not understand the teacher's instructions (an example of self-report) or could describe a specific incident in that day's class session during which they requested clarification of the teacher's instructions (self-observation).

Depending on the nature of the language learning strategies being studied, the researcher may be able to elicit from learners self-revelational data in diary and dialog journal entries. Perhaps the simplest way to obtain entries with self-revelation is to have students take notes during the language learning task and then transcribe their notes into diaries or dialog journals later that day. (These notes could be interspersed among the regular class notes involving new vocabulary, grammar, or whatever.) If the students take good notes, they may be able to reconstruct their thoughts at the time of the learning task with some accuracy.

There is another option for using diaries to obtain self-revelation during the writing process. While performing reading or writing tasks in the target language, learners could keep a separate page (e.g. the left-hand page in a dialog journal) or use a wide margin on the composition page to make comments about the difficulties that they are encountering in strategy use or in finding strategies to use during their reading and writing tasks. For example, learners could – at the moment of uncertainty – make a note when they are not sure if they have correctly understood or used a verb tense in a particular sentence. This way, they would be sure to record the problem before they forgot about it. In addition to hearing from the students about their reading problems or reading a particular composition, a teacher could review the learners' notes and respond to their specific reading or writing problems. The result would be a dialog journal that provides self-revelational and self-observational data specific to the reading or writing process.

DISADVANTAGES OF DIARIES AND DIALOG JOURNALS

Two of the serious drawbacks to using diaries and dialog journals as research tools are the volume of data produced and the potentially random nature of the entries. If learners write on self-chosen topics, the data are cumbersome to read and may not suggest or support any hypotheses regarding language strategies. In fact, many learners may not even mention learning strategies at all. To avoid this problem, some researchers have directed students to write about specific language learning strategies. For example, in one instance the diary writer/learner focused on specific cognitive strategies, namely, inductive and deductive inferencing (Rubin and Henze, 1981). In the Oxford *et al.* (1996) study, students were asked to focus more broadly on their approaches to listening comprehension, grammar, and vocabulary. Yet requesting that students write only about specific strategies may make them less cooperative than if they are given an outlet for describing concerns they have about their language learning experience in general.

The dialog journal may offer an even easier way to concentrate students' writing on learning strategies. If learners provide insufficient information regarding the use of strategies, teachers (as researchers) could, in response to the entries, ask them to provide more detail retrospectively. Even if the learners provide more detail, the resulting data may be difficult to use for research purposes. First, the resulting information is likely to be more qualitative than quantitative, and the techniques available for summarizing and analyzing qualitative data may not be as applicable (Bailey, 1991) unless these data lend themselves to transformation into quantitative data through content analysis procedures (Oxford *et al.*, 1996).

Second, the typically small number of subjects in diary studies restricts the ability of researchers to generalize the findings to all language learners (Bailey, 1991; Nunan, 1992). We should also note that diaries and dialog journals are subject to the criticisms directed at verbal report since the data on learning strategies mostly constitute self-report and self-observation.

ADVANTAGE OF DIARIES AND DIALOG JOURNALS

In spite of the above limitations, diaries and dialog journals can be useful research tools. The aim of most diary studies is not to produce rigorous quantitative results which can be generalized to language learners as a whole; instead, diaries have been used to find out what is significant to the learners, a very important area of concern now that much research is turning away from teaching to learners and learner variables (Bailey, 1991). Furthermore, much of the data that are collected in a diary or dialog journal may be inaccessible through other research techniques (Nunan, 1992). In addition, diary and journal writing may be of benefit to the students themselves because regular writing can help them become more aware of their strategies.

A final plus with regard to diaries is that they can be kept anywhere by anyone. Learners have the option of writing for even several months before giving their diaries to a researcher for analysis. Therefore, diaries may be more conducive than dialog journals to research on learning in less structured learning environments (e.g. a learner who visits the target culture and lives with a family for three months during summer vacation from school). One such diary was kept by Rivers (1979) during a trip she made to Chile.

In the case of dialog journals, the learners and reader(s) must be able to correspond with each other easily and frequently. So, for this reason, most dialog journals are kept by people who see each other on a regular basis. On the other hand, it would be possible to set up a dialog journal arrangement between learners in one location and readers in another, using electronic mail as the link.

3.1.5 Recollective studies

Recollective studies involve thinking back to some prior language experience and attempting to reconstruct what it was like. Such studies constitute a distinct method of strategy assessment. While journals reflect a learner's periodic, ongoing record of strategy use while participating in the learning process, a recollective account refers to a learner's description and interpretation of a language learning experience that took place months or even years before. Although a recollective study may contain information about specific strategies or problems the learner encountered, given the time lapse the learner is more likely to recollect about the experience as a whole, possibly comparing two or more language learning experiences. Journals, on the other hand, often focus on the specific language learning setting that the learner is involved in at the time and can be limited to a certain set of strategies that are of interest to the researcher.

Recollective studies can take a variety of forms, depending on the preferences of the subjects or the researchers. The information could be in the form of written narratives or poems (see Oxford *et al.*, 1996), or as responses to an oral interview, where the information is tape-recorded and then transcribed. The recollections often consist of a description of significant events in the learner's experience studying the language, such as going through a silent period and getting over it or dealing with the differing sets of emotions that emerge in different language learning environments. If interviews are used as a means of getting the learners to recollect, the emphasis would presumably be on creating an environment in which the learners feel comfortable about describing language learning events from the sometimes distant past. A key element here would be to ensure the learners' freedom to retell the significant aspects of their personal language learning experiences in any appropriate form, most likely unstructured.

DISADVANTAGES OF RECOLLECTIVE STUDIES

The major drawback of this assessment method is the inevitable memory deterioration between the language learning experience and the study.

The time lapse creates several problems. First, much detail will be lost over time, and the resulting data will, as noted above, be general in nature. Learners will tend to make generalizations about the strategies used or problems encountered in the entire learning experience rather than providing detailed descriptions of strategy use for a single event or task. Second, the time lapse opens the possibility of the subjects' creative reinterpretation of what took place during the learning experience. Not only will the statements tend to be generalized to the entire experience, but also such statements may get distorted in the learner's later reconstruction of the experience. Consequently, the results of any recollective study should be viewed as anecdotal, highly individualistic and possibly distorted accounts of students' learning experiences.

ADVANTAGES OF THE RECOLLECTIVE STUDIES

In spite of these problems, there are advantages of recollective studies. First, this type of study may be more objective because of the learner's distance from the experience. Second, the learner can provide an overall summary of the learning experience because their recollections are unlikely to be burdened with details. Third, the subjects may gain important personal insights as to learning strategies that have tended to work for them (e.g. setting specific goals, such as ordering a meal in the target language) and as to settings that they have tended to prefer (e.g. chatting in a cafe v. discussing a topic with a partner in class). This self-awareness of personal learning preferences can be of significant value to students who want to take an active role in managing their own future learning experiences.

As the number of recollective studies increases, it may become possible to discern patterns in the recollections themselves. In other words, it may be found that certain types of strategies are more likely to be recollected than others. For example, a strategy for dealing with an emotional upset around a language goof may come to mind more readily than a strategy for remembering certain grammar points.

3.1.6   Computer tracking

Researchers are now starting to explore the potential of computer tracking in assessing language strategy use. This may turn out to be a promising tool for certain areas of research. Such programs can be used to collect information either with or without the learner's awareness (but presumably with their full consent). Such tracking could get at language learning strategies associated with the use of resource functions accompanying word processing programs, the order of processing of elements in reading text for comprehension or in producing written text, and the choice of speed for reading and writing tasks. It appears that as of the present time, the computer tracking technology has been applied in only a limited way to researching language strategies. The strategies investigated are those supplied by the computer programs in the form of resource functions.

Tracking programs can unobtrusively create a log of learners' uses for various resource functions contained within the computerized language program, whether in writing tasks (e.g. word processing, filling out forms, and the like), reading tasks (a summarization exercise, a cloze completion task, a multiple-choice reading comprehension task), or grammar drills. These resource functions could include a dictionary, a thesaurus, a reference grammar, a style checker, a spell-checker, tutorials on how to complete given language tasks (e.g. formation of verb tenses), and background knowledge on a given topic (see Chapelle and Mizuno, 1989).

With the exception of the observational method, the research methods discussed so far have relied on the learner's self-generated descriptions of strategy use, either through written or oral assessment techniques, and, as noted above, the results from these assessments can be problematic for various reasons. For example, the learner may be totally unaware of having used a given strategy or may be aware but unable to accurately remember a specific instance of strategy use. By automatically recording a learner's use of a resource function, the computer eliminates the problem of data distortion through human inaccuracy or unawareness. Chapelle and Mizuno (1989), for example, studied the extent of use of resource functions by 34 high- and low-proficiency ESL students doing computerized grammar lessons. Baily (1996) reports a study using a French word processing program, *Système-D*, to record individual students' use of resource functions while the students worked on essays. These resource functions included a dictionary, sets of vocabulary and phrase groups, a reference grammar, and a spell-checker. In this study, adult learners of French used the program to compose essays, and then the computer's log of the essay composing process was compared with the final compositions. Baily looked for evidence of four strategies used to compensate for problems in vocabulary and sentence structure: use of synonyms, use of circumlocutions, coining of new words, and approximating the message.

DISADVANTAGES OF COMPUTER TRACKING

One limitation of computer tracking is its inability to describe language learning and language use strategies which do not result in the use of a resource function on the computer. For example, a computer would be unable to detect a learner's use of inferencing to determine a word's meaning. In other words, the strategy must result in a concrete manipulation of the computer program; otherwise, the computer will be unable to detect the use of that strategy. Thus, computers may be better able to provide a comprehensive picture of strategy use when used in tandem with another method, such as verbal report, which can capture mentalistic strategies.

Another limitation of computer tracking research is that its very on-line nature may interfere with the collecting of the data. So, for example, it is easier to collect such data from reading and writing tasks than from listening tasks, and next to impossible to collect such data from speaking tasks without disrupting the task altogether.

Use of computer tracking as an assessment method is also affected by other practical matters. As Baily (1996) notes, some students are more comfortable using computer technology, which can affect how often they use the various resource functions. Second, inferring strategy use by comparing computer logs with final compositions or reading comprehension tests may be difficult in certain circumstances. There is always the danger that the researcher will either infer a strategy that has not been used by the learner or misinterpret the type of strategy used due to incomplete information. Third, research might be limited by the lack of commercial availability of programs. This may limit the languages that are used for research unless suitable programs become more widely available. Finally, the resources in the computer programs themselves may be limited, causing some students to use other dictionaries or reference grammars.

ADVANTAGES OF COMPUTER TRACKING

Despite the above limitations, it would appear that computer tracking has a potential use in certain types of research. In fact, such programs are quite suitable for studying strategies for producing written language while lacking adequate linguistic knowledge. To a more limited extent, computers can also track strategies for forming concepts and hypotheses by keeping a log of the learner's use of resource functions to look up unknown words/phrases during the composition or reading process.

3.1.7   Concluding comments on instruments for assessing strategies

Every assessment method offers unique advantages as well as disadvantages. The challenge for researchers is to choose an assessment method that will provide the desired type of information for the given study. In a field as fledgling as that of L2 strategy use, there is as yet no fully established set of assessment procedures so it is necessary to try out different approaches and to evaluate their effectiveness.

Issues that may impact the choice of assessment method and selection of options within the method include the following: the purpose of the study (to generate hypotheses or to conduct a detailed case study of one learner), the number of learners and researchers, the resources available, the strategies to be studied, the types of language tasks for which the strategies are used (e.g. speaking or reading), and the context in which the language learning takes place (e.g. a university class or a three-month visit to a foreign country). Ehrman (1996) has recently written a book intended to assist foreign language teachers in diagnosing the learning styles and strategies of their students, especially those who are not doing well. She discusses how to do observations and interviews, and how to use the results of questionnaires, tests, and language aptitude instruments in assisting the learners. The book includes case study information on some 35 teenagers and adults learning a foreign language or English as a second language. Such volumes are helpful for busy practitioners who want concrete examples of how to assess language learning styles and strategies, and then apply the results in the classroom.

While some approaches to assessment such as questionnaires have been widely used, other assessment methods have yet to be extensively employed by researchers. For example, computer technology has been used in only a limited number of studies on language learning strategies to date. As researchers become more familiar with computers and other assessment options, new assessment methods will surely be developed.

Given the problems inherent in any assessment method, researchers may want to consider using a combination of assessment methods. So, returning to the example with which we opened the chapter, namely, that of wanting to describe the speaking strategies used in role playing in an intermediate-level university course in Japanese, we could ask the question, 'How best might we describe the speaking strategies of these students?' We could start by asking how much could be obtained through oral interview or written questionnaire. If written questionnaire data would not be appropriate in this case, it would be possible to interview the learners and to include verbal report techniques in this interview. Since the learners are usually given a few minutes to think about the role play before starting, the researcher could request that they provide self-revelational data (think-aloud) during this time. These data are likely to include planning and rehearsal strategies such as searching for patterned (prefabricated) phrases and attempting to paraphrase in the case of unknown words.

Next, we could utilize retrospective verbal report to reconstruct the use of strategies just after the generating of the utterances. For example, the researcher may wish to ask a student about the usage of a certain phrase in order to determine whether it is an instance of *approximation* – i.e. when learners are unable to find a particular foreign language word and substitute a similar, perhaps more general word instead, such as 'tool' when they would have liked to say 'wrench.' The greater the time lapse between the role play and the follow-up interview, the greater the likelihood that memory deterioration will take place. Then we could determine whether any of the data could be collected by means of observing the learners and videotaping the conversations. As mentioned above, not many strategies are actually observable, but the researcher may see evidence of strategy use, such as with regard to vocabulary: translating words into the native language to better understand them aurally or in print, avoiding translation by trying to understand words from the context, gesturing when unsure of the vocabulary in speaking, appealing for assistance from someone else, and coining new words in the target language. As a backup to observations, the investigators could check the videotapes to see whether the use of any of these targeted strategies was captured on video.

In addition, we could show the videotape of the speaking task to the learners to prompt their memory. If the learners are to view the videotape, the timing of the interview may be an issue to consider. On one hand, we may want to replay the videotape for the learners soon after the actual speaking task in order to avoid the effects of memory deterioration as much as possible. On the other hand, the researcher may wish to view the videotape first in order to formulate questions that would be asked in a subsequent session with the learners.

Finally, the learners could be encouraged to make entries into a dialog journal which the teacher would collect and respond to from time to time. Special permission could be obtained in order to allow researchers access to these journals as well. The learner entries could well provide more insights regarding strategy use, in some cases clarifying or elaborating on points made during the verbal report interviews. As an incentive to the learners, the teachers could offer extra credit for those students who maintain their dialog journals for the duration of the language course (and, possibly, beyond the termination of the course). Ideally, the teachers would be knowledgeable enough about the research that their replies to the learners would help to provide more focus to future entries.

In conclusion, it would seem that researchers have a variety of assessment methods at their disposal, and these methods may be combined in any number of ways in order to collect the most useful data for the given

study. The field of language learning strategies may benefit most from a
wide application of assessment methods in multiple research contexts. In
the next section, we will focus more in depth on the use of verbal report
in collecting language learning and language use strategy data.

3.2 Verbal reports as a source of insights into second language learner strategies[2]

In this section, we return to verbal report and consider this methodology in greater detail. We will note ways to refine verbal report methods
and will also indicate the types of information that researchers may wish
to include in their write ups so that others might better understand the
particular verbal report method utilized. Such information should assist
in the making of comparisons across studies and will facilitate researchers
in replicating studies that have appeared in the literature. Hence, this
section ends not by focusing on a justification of verbal report methods,
but rather by considering the fine-tuning of such methods. Points taken
up in this discussion may apply to the use of other methods for researching learner strategies as well.

As indicated in section 3.1.3 above, the reason why verbal report has
gained popularity in the last several decades despite frequent criticism,
is that this research methodology provides data on cognitive processes
and learner responses that otherwise would have to be investigated only
indirectly. Furthermore, verbal report has at times provided access to the
reasoning processes underlying cognition, response, and decision making.

Despite the extensive use of verbal report methods in what now amounts
to a host of recent studies, consumers of research using verbal report are
still sometimes uncertain as to the inferences that they can legitimately
make on the basis of these reports. At the same time that Pressley and
Afflerbach refer to verbal reports as a maturing method, they also rightly
refer to it as an 'underdeveloped' one (1995: 119). For this reason, we will
now consider a series of problematic areas regarding the methodology,
with an eye to where development needs to take place in order for the
methodology to be more fully developed and hence to lend itself more
readily to easier interpretation.

3.2.1 Issues in verbal report methodology

IMMEDIACY OF VERBAL REPORT

A distinction has been made in the literature between self-revelational
data in the form of immediate, on-line think-aloud protocols which involve

no editing or analysis on the one hand and self-observational data in the form of introspective or retrospective self-observation on the other. Ericsson and Simon (1993) have advocated the collection of self-revelational data over other approaches to verbal report because asking questions only about what is likely to be accessible in short-term memory is seen as a means of making such reports more reliable in that there is no strain on the memory to reconstruct past thoughts.[3] In sharp contrast to this methodological position, the Pressley and Afflerbach survey of studies in L1 reading found considerable variation as to the immediacy of the reporting and the amount of interpretation respondents were asked to provide (1995: 22).

The researchers discovered not only self-revelational protocols but also self-observational reports which were collected after each sentence, after each episode, at signaled spots in the text (usually two or more sentences), after every two minutes, at the end of the text, or whenever the readers wanted. The investigators found fluctuation both within and across studies as to whether subjects were asked to provide think-aloud, introspective (i.e. within 20 seconds of the event), or retrospective reports (separated somewhat in time from the actual reading). Pressley and Afflerbach give one explanation for this departure from exclusive use of the think-aloud approach, namely, that in order to obtain verbal report of otherwise automatized cognition, there is a need to slow down the process, for example through the interruptive methods listed above (Pressley and Afflerbach, 1995: 9).

Not only did Pressley and Afflerbach have difficulty in determining if verbal reports in the studies that they reviewed actually reflected traces remaining in short-term memory or rather reflected the subjects' recon-structions of what happened as they read. They were also unable to determine whether there was substantive difference in quality between think-aloud data produced when subjects performed no analysis and the self-observational data when they analyzed what they were thinking (1995: 128). The reasons they gave for their inability to make a comparison were: (1) there was too little systematic study of this issue in the given research reports, and (2) the verbal reporting itself was influenced dif-ferentially by the nature of the training, coaching, or prompting that the respondents received before and during the reporting phase.

One recent study considered the issue of delay in the case of retro-spective verbal report after completing the writing task (Greene and Higgins, 1994). The investigators offered four suggestions for improving the reliability and validity of such data: (1) minimizing the time between the process and report by obtaining a report immediately after a writer completes a task, (2) designing prompts that can help writers better access detailed information from their short- and long-term memory (e.g. through the use of concrete examples and contextual cues), (3) making clear to the respondents the purpose of the retrospective accounts,[4] and (4) reporting one's findings in ways that enable readers to see how the conclusions have been derived from the data (e.g. by including enough data in a report so that readers are able to make their own assessments about the value of research based on, say, retrospection).

RESPONDENTS' ROLE IN INTERPRETING THE DATA

There are researchers who are wary about having subjects interpret why they are doing something. The rationale given is that a request to provide interpretation is more likely to influence how the respondents perform continuing phases of the same task. In addition, they see the asking of a 'why' question as likely to produce unreliable answers if at the time the respondents are not thinking about why they are doing the action (Ericsson and Simon, 1993: 7).[5] Thus, it is recommended by some that interpretation of verbal report be left to researchers, rather than, say, getting the respondents to categorize their cognitions. Despite these recommendations, Pressley and Afflerbach's review of 38 primary-data studies of L1 reading found that many studies went beyond having readers simply report their thoughts, and requested them to interpret their processes as well (1995: 21). Presumably, the insights from self-observation offer a rich enough source of information not available through think-aloud protocols alone that researchers are willing to risk threats to the reliability of the verbal report tasks in order to obtain the data.

PROMPTING FOR SPECIFICS IN VERBAL REPORT

Early descriptions of verbal report methods usually included the stipulation that respondents should not be given instructions as to what to provide verbal reports about. They were to be left to their own devices since any instructions might lead to biased processing. But anyone who has been faced with analyzing transcriptions of **undirected** verbal report protocols has seen how such data are likely to be too general and incomplete. So, even methodological hard-liners such as Ericsson and Simon are in favor of giving instructions to the respondents so as to make the verbal reports more complete (1993: 11).

Not so surprisingly, then, we see that many studies now do include instructions to elicit particular cognitive behaviors. For example, reading researchers have cued different processes in the different studies. Pressley and Afflerbach found one study which requested that subjects create a summary of what they read and in which the respondents were informed about the importance of summarization, a second study which asked respondents to attend to content and style when reading, and others which required subjects to make inferences. The authors conclude that prompting respondents to use particular processes may be necessary: 'it is reasonable to prompt [processes] in order to assure that a sample of the target processes will, in fact, be observed' (Pressley and Afflerbach, 1995: 133). With regard to post-experimental assessment, Cantor *et al.* (1985) have found that more valid information is produced if the cues involve specific items from the experiment (in their case, animal episodes and geometric form episodes).

GUIDANCE IN PROVIDING VERBAL REPORTS

Not only has it proven effective to have respondents receive specific prompts as to what to verbal report about, but it has also been seen that instruction in how to provide verbal report for a given task improves the quality of the data. Ericsson and Simon have found that in order to assure that the verbal report does not interfere with the task at hand, after the instructions there must be warm-up trials with tasks that yield easy-to-analyze think-aloud, introspective, and retrospective reports that are easy to analyze. The researchers suggest that subjects be given trials on these warm-up tasks until they are able to make verbal reports without confounding them with explanations and justifications (Ericsson and Simon, 1993: xxxii). This is to ensure consistency across subjects: 'In some studies, more extensive warm-up procedures are used explicitly to **train** the subjects to conform to the think-aloud instructions' (Ericsson and Simon, 1993: 82). In a study in which subjects were asked not only to think aloud but also to try to give a reason for each response they made before keyboarding it into the computer, the respondents who provided verbal report after receiving training improved more on the computerized cognitive task than those who did not receive the training (Berry and Broadbent, 1984). In the review of 38 primary studies of verbal report in L1 reading, it was found that while in some studies the respondents were given an opportunity to practice, in others they were not (Pressley and Afflerbach, 1995: 22)

THE EFFECTS OF VERBAL REPORT ON TASK PERFORMANCE

There are a series of issues relating to the effects of verbal report on task performance. We will now look at four of them: reactive effects, positive effects, the choice of language for verbal reporting, and the authenticity of the assessment task once verbal reporting has been added to it.

Reactive effects of verbal report

Verbal report that involves intervening during the performance of a task has been criticized for the reactive effects that such intervention may cause. Stratman and Hamp–Lyons, for example, conducted an exploratory study to determine the extent of reactivity in writing. They had eight writers engage in two revision tasks eight weeks apart, one with think-aloud verbal reports. All subjects were trained in how to provide think-aloud protocols. The researchers found for the subjects in their study that thinking aloud increased the number of new word-level errors (morphological, tense, and spelling) (Stratman and Hamp-Lyons, 1994: 103). Contrary to the investigators' expectations, thinking aloud was found to inhibit word or phrase additions in the revision process. They also found that while thinking aloud did not have an impact on complex meaning changes at the micro-structural level, it stimulated the production of entirely new sentences (Stratman and Hamp-Lyons, 1994: 107). They concluded that thinking aloud **does** alter the nature of processing in the revision phase of writing. They posited that think-aloud protocols may systematically influence the correction of organizational-level errors (i.e. the reordering of displaced sentences, the adjusting of faulty paragraph boundaries, the detection of faulty pronoun references, the detection of redundancies, the detection of word-level errors – in morphology, tense, and spelling, and the introduction of new word-level errors) and may also influence the amount and kind of micro-structural meaning changes as well.

Positive effects of verbal report

While the study by Stratman and Hamp-Lyons on the use of verbal report during the revision phase of writing produced reactive results of a presumably negative nature, a series of other studies would suggest that there may be positive consequences of verbal report. Collecting retrospection verbal report (termed *intervention protocols*) at various points during the writing has also been found to improve the reliability of the data collection task. Swanson-Owens and Newell (1994) found that the interruption of writing for the purpose of reflecting on process served as a supportive measure in helping writers learn about composing, and thus provided scaffolding for a subject's learning during data collection. Similarly positive outcomes of verbal report have been reported for studies in the areas of vocabulary learning and reading as well. For example, Crutcher (1990) conducted a study of vocabulary learning with keywords and obtained retrospective reports for half of the items. He found that retention of the words was better for those items.

With regard to verbal reports in L2 reading, Nyhus (1994) looked at the attitudes of non-native speakers of English toward the use of verbal report to elicit their reading comprehension strategies. The respondents were seven learners studying in a ten-week course through the Command English Program in General College at the University of Minnesota – a bridge program for refugee and immigrant non-native speakers of English. Five of the respondents were Vietnamese, one Chinese, and one Russian. Most had been in the US for only two or three years. The study looked at their attitudes toward the effects of think-aloud and retrospective verbal report on their reading. They were also asked to assess verbal report as a research methodology.

The respondents were shown a videotape of the researcher reading aloud and providing think-aloud verbal report from a sociology text. Three excerpts from a sociology text were chosen for use with the respondents. Two were for practice readings and the third for the data collection. Red dots were placed between sentences to remind the respondents to verbalize their thoughts. Two sets of interview questions were developed, the first twelve questions to be asked following the respondents' initial think-aloud verbal report and the second eleven questions to be asked following the respondents' retrospective verbal report. The respondents were asked to read the text as they normally would but to say out loud, in English, all of their thoughts. They were told that they could read the text silently, but all chose to read it out loud. The respondent and the researcher then listened to the recording of the verbal report, and the respondents provided a retrospective verbal report by pausing the tape when they wanted to make additional comments about thoughts which had occurred to them while reading the text. The researcher also had the respondents report on what they had been thinking but not verbalizing. Next, the researcher interviewed the respondents regarding their views about the think-aloud methodology. In addition, there was a second interview to elicit attitudes toward the retrospective methodology after the task had been completed.

For the most part, the respondents viewed the effects that they attributed to verbal report as beneficial. Most felt that think-aloud verbal report affected their thinking about their reading in a positive way. It was reported to enhance their awareness and assessment of various aspects of the reading process, including an awareness of themselves as readers and of their interaction with the given text. Only two of the seven had negative comments about verbal report, and these were the students whose English was the most limited. Since all verbal report was conducted in English, performing the verbal report in English was most likely to the detriment of those with poorer English skills.

Despite several cases of difficulty in verbal reporting in English, all respondents viewed verbal report as useful in various ways. They saw it as a means for placing students at a given level, as a diagnostic tool for determining their specific reading needs at a given level, and as a study technique to be used alone or in small groups. The students saw the group approach as a particularly beneficial method for discovering alternative ways of thinking about a text. Retrospective verbal report through having readers listen to and comment on a playback of their think-aloud verbal report provided still more insights. It was seen as a means of helping readers, instructors, and researchers gain further insight into readers' thinking and reading processes.

Choice of language for reporting

An issue that the Nyhus study calls up is that there may, in fact, be a second language threshold below which attempts to provide verbal report in the target language will be counterproductive. Upton (1993), for example, found that when given a choice as to language for verbal reporting, the more advanced native Japanese-speaking EFL subjects were likely to choose to provide verbal report on English reading comprehension tasks in English, while the less proficient respondents preferred to use Japanese. Researchers may prefer at times to have the verbal report in the target language, such as when the respondents are speakers of a variety of languages or when the language of the respondent group is not known to the researchers and obtaining translations is unfeasible. However, researchers need to be aware that the practice of requiring verbal reports to be in the target language may be at the expense of collecting adequate data.

Authenticity of the task

Other issues of reactivity aside, there is still the one regarding the authenticity of the task when verbal report is involved. Almost without question, the introduction of verbal reporting techniques alters the nature of the task so that it is no longer the task that it was, regardless of whether its inclusion has a beneficial or detrimental influence on the performance of the task. In fact, respondents may well be told that the task they are engaged in will not count for credit in order to ensure their willingness to participate in the data collection process. The challenge for researchers, then, is to simulate task conditions as they would be if the instrument were administered without the addition of verbal report and, furthermore, to ask respondents to perform the tasks as much as possible in the way that they would if they were not providing verbal report. For some assessment tasks, this is easier to do than for others.

For example, some forms of verbal report are less intrusive than others. If respondents are simply to check off from an attached list those strategies that they used on a given item just after responding to the item, the activity may have a minimal influence on performance on that item. If, on the other hand, the respondent is to give an oral explanation of processing strategies whatever they may be and without the use of a checklist, then the verbal reporting may be more intrusive, possibly detracting from performance on the testing task itself.

3.2.2   Towards more robust verbal report methods and more complete write ups

What seems to emerge from this discussion of methodological issues in verbal report is the need for both more refined measures and more details about the verbal report methods employed in each given study. This more detailed information would facilitate comparison across studies. So, for example, Pressley and Afflerbach propose a study of reading strategies which would call for a carefully detailed comparison between think-aloud verbal reports and delayed reports. The study would assess the extent to which ongoing verbal report might interfere with on-line reading and distort the natural reading processes, and the extent to which stopping after every sentence or few sentences might shift the nature of subsequent reading, if at all. They would also wish to investigate the question as to how long reports can be delayed before they are altered by the delay (Pressley and Afflerbach, 1995: 13). In making their plea for greater completeness in the description of verbal report methods, Pressley and Afflerbach include a listing of variables for which more complete and systematic information is desirable (1995: 120–3). Let us now relate Pressley and Afflerbach's listing of variables to studies of L2 assessment. The following list 'includes areas in which verbal report methods can be refined and in which methods can be described in more detail to facilitate comparison across studies':

Subjects' characteristics

For the purpose of comparison across studies, the educational background of the respondents, their knowledge of the task at hand, and their motivation to do the task should be made clear. In addition, their level of language proficiency (especially in the case of L2 studies) and their age should be indicated. Pressley and Afflerbach (1995) also suggest that their short-term memory capacity and their spatial ability be noted, but this would entail special psychological testing which is usually not conducted in L2 assessment. Pressley and Afflerbach also stress the need for studies with larger numbers of subjects, since most studies are of individual cases or of small groups. Their point is that while the accumulation of small-scale studies using verbal report does help to generate a large-scale picture, comparison across them can be somewhat problematic, especially if the approaches to data collection are different. The problem is that most researchers do not have the budget to conduct verbal report work with large groups.

Whereas Pressley and Afflerbach limit themselves to respondents who were performing a task in their native language and providing verbal report in that language, research into L2 test-taking strategies is faced with the issue of choice of language for verbal reporting, as indicated above. When dealing with groups of speakers of numerous languages, the verbal report protocols may need to be in the target language for the sake of expediency. In cases where the respondents share the same native language or speak a limited number of languages, it would then be advisable to give them a choice as to language of verbal report, since the less proficient they are in the target language, the more difficulty they may experience trying to do the task in the target language and also provide verbal report in that language at the same time. As noted above, the study by Nyhus (1994) found that the two weaker non-native readers of English L2 were the ones reporting difficulty providing the verbal report, which had to be in the second language. In light of this discussion, it is important that researchers indicate the extent to which their respondents used the target language, their native language, or some other language in their verbal reporting in studies where a choice was given and the respondents took advantage of it.

Characteristics of the materials

When textual material serves as a stimulus for verbal report data, it would be helpful if the investigator specified the genre of the material, its topic, its length, and its difficulty level for the given respondents. While some or most of these variables may be provided as a matter of course (especially if texts are included in the appendix of the study), Pressley and Afflerbach would request that investigators indicate the fit between the task and the characteristics of the given respondents. Any such details could help other researchers to interpret the findings with greater ease, as well as to attempt replication of the study, if so desired. Perhaps more so in foreign than in native language reading, the genre of the text can make a big difference in the ease of reading. Even if the readers feel comfortable with the genre (e.g. journalistic writing), still they may have difficulty with the specific topic transmitted by means of that genre (e.g. an account of a festival which does not exist in the reader's home culture and with which the reader is completely unfamiliar).

Criterion task

It is imperative for the purpose of comparison that the researcher provide a clear indication of the tasks that the respondents were asked to perform (e.g. in reading research, whether it was free recall, recognition, question answering, summarization, or some combination of these), plus the directions given to the subjects. Pressley and Afflerbach found in the studies that they reviewed that the instructions were either not provided or that reference to them was vague. The reason that the instructions are considered so crucial in verbal report work is expressly because of the orientation to the task that can be given through them. It is also important to have a clear description of any technical equipment employed in the study (e.g. a multimedia program on CD ROM). Likewise the goals of the language task should be clear, as well as the modalities utilized.

Guidance in verbal reporting

It is valuable both for comparison across studies and for replication that information be given as to the nature and extent of guidance that the subjects received in verbal reporting. It is useful to know, for example, whether the subjects received feedback in practice sessions, whether they were coached during the data collection sessions and, if so, the length of the guidance – for example, until they had performed the verbal report in a way that produced the desired type(s) of data. As indicated above, it has become more common to instruct respondents in how to provide verbal report, as well as to coach them as they are providing it (e.g. requesting that they not report on the basis of what they **usually** do, but rather that they stick to what they are actually doing at the given instance).

Methods of analysis

In order for other researchers to interpret the findings, it may prove beneficial to include details as to the development of the categories and coding schemes used in interpreting the verbal report data that were obtained. It may also be beneficial to include the codes and symbols used in the transcriptions of the verbal report protocols – for example, symbols for suprasegmental features, such as tone of voice. Of course, verbal report data may also be collected in the written modality, as has been done in various studies (e.g. Robinson, 1991). In such cases, there would be no suprasegmentals. In any event, Pressley and Afflerbach found that there was usually incomplete reporting of any scoring codes that may have been developed for the purpose of analyzing the data.

Categories used to score verbal report protocols

It is helpful for researchers to indicate how the actual scoring of verbal report protocols is done, since there is so much interpretive work involved. If the respondents themselves listen to their verbal report in order to assist in the interpretation of protocols, as Nyhus (1994) did in her study on the effects of verbal report on L2 reading, it would be important to highlight this feature and to describe it fully in the write-up phase. Such a procedure has the value of improving the validity of the measure, since the respondents themselves are verifying the accuracy of what they reported, editing what was reported so that it is more intelligible to others, and possibly adding what they had neglected to mention the first time around. It might even pay to have researchers provide verbal report while they are engaged in the task of making their decisions about how to score given instances of behavior appearing in the protocols. Verbal report protocols of raters of second language, for instance, reveal instances where the raters do not understand the categories that they are supposed to be using in their ratings (e.g. 'style,' 'register,' and so forth).

Interrater reliability checks

In cases where two or more investigators score the data, it would be advisable to run interrater reliability checks to determine the extent to which the investigators are using similar criteria in arriving at scores. Information about such interrater reliability checks should be provided in the research report.

Selection of verbal report excerpts for inclusion in research reports

A somewhat subtle issue is that of how the data are chosen for inclusion in reports. Other researchers would want to know how representative such excerpts are of the data set as a whole. There is a concern that the investigators may slant the findings according to the excerpts from the data that they choose to include in their reports. It is for this reason that Greene and Higgins (1994) go to some lengths to demonstrate how to represent verbal report data in an equitable way in their study of retrospective verbal report of L1 writing processes. It may be useful to indicate the percentage of the data set that is represented in the report – e.g. all the examples of X that were collected, 20% of the examples, and so forth.

Theories used in framing verbal report study

The researchers are asked to identify the theoretical principles that the verbal report techniques were intended to investigate. In order to help validate the verbal report measures utilized in the study, Pressley and Afflerbach consider it the researchers' responsibility to provide information as to whether the verbal report measures really reflect the cognitive processes that are being reported. They contend that the researchers should indicate the relationship between the verbal report and the performance outcomes, much as they do in their own book by demonstrating that theoretical models of reading including their own model of constructively responsive reading were supported by verbal report data obtained from reading studies (Pressley and Afflerbach, 1995: Chapter 4). As Pressley and Afflerbach put it, 'As validation efforts proceed, we urge careful attention to the establishment of clear linkages between theory, verbal process reports, and other measures that can be complementary to verbal self-reports. We believe this work will do much to bring verbal reports from the status of a "bootstrap operation" (Ericsson and Simon, 1993) to a maturing methodology' (1995: 126).

Most published studies of second language acquisition include a statement of the research questions with the rationale for each. If the verbal report measures are simply aimed at exploring some aspect(s) of these research questions, then the theoretical underpinnings are probably provided. It is possible, however, that the theoretical rationale for a given verbal report procedure is not overtly clear to the reader of the report. In such cases, the request would be to provide this rationale.

THE VALIDITY OF VERBAL REPORTS

While the above discussion of nine issues related to more robust verbal report methods and more complete write ups focused mostly on the reliability of the verbal report measures, their validity also comes into play in each and every issue. Although larger samples help to make the results more valid, an alternative to increasing the sample size would be to amass a series of well-planned and well-executed small-scale studies. As for the role played by the materials and the tasks in the determination of validity, it is imperative that the consumers of the research results have adequate information about the nature of the materials and about the specific instructions that the respondents were given for performing the task. Such information is crucial in interpreting the verbal report responses received. By the same token, the consumers of the reports need to know the extent to which the respondents were coached in how to perform the task.

Once the data are collected, the analysis procedures also have direct impact on whether the data measure what they purport to measure – i.e. the rationale for the construction of the analysis categories and then the actual process of data analysis. Did the raters understand and properly use all of the rating categories? With regard to interrater reliability, if there is more than one rater, a low interrater reliability coefficient would call into question not only the reliability of the ratings but their validity as well.

Furthermore, there is the issue of whether the reported data are comprehensive or selective, and, if selective, what this says about the validity of the reporting process. Finally, there is concern that the study not simply be using verbal report for its own sake but rather because the data collection method does, in fact, help to gather data bearing on the theoretical issue(s) at hand.

3.3   Summary and conclusions

The first half of this chapter consisted of an analysis of six different approaches to assessing language learner strategies: oral interviews and written questionnaires on learner strategies, observation, verbal report, diaries and dialog journals, recollective studies, and computer tracking. The strengths and weaknesses of each strategy assessment method were discussed and then suggestions were given regarding possible ways to use the various approaches and the benefits of doing so. In essence, considering a panoply of assessment measures and possibly adopting more than one in any given strategies study would allow for greater rigor than if only one approach is used. In any case, any research method needs to be adequately piloted with the intended sample in the local context before being used in data collection.

The last portion of the chapter contrasted the three forms of verbal report – self-report, self-observation, and self-revelation – and briefly indicated the contribution that verbal report methods have made to the understanding of language learning and language use strategies. The section then focused on concerns about the appropriate use of such measures and about the nature of the write ups which include mention of verbal report measures. The issues included the immediacy of the verbal reporting, the respondents' role in interpreting the data, prompting for specifics in verbal report, guidance in verbal reporting, and the effects of verbal report on task performance.

The lengthy focus on both refining verbal report methods and on improving the write up of verbal report procedures was intended to underscore the importance of being rigorous both in design and in description. The purpose would be not only to improve the data, but also to make it possible for other researchers to understand fully what was done, to be able to make comparisons with other studies, and to be able to replicate the studies. In addition, the point was made that care in the write up can help to dispel arguments that such methodological approaches are not adequately rigorous.

While previous discussions of verbal report in the second language literature have tended to focus on justifying verbal report in the face of criticism from those opposed to it, this discussion has instead focused on the fine-tuning of verbal report methods. Since by now so many studies using verbal report techniques have emerged, the time has come to provide greater systematicity both in the collection of such data and in the reporting of such studies through the research literature. This close scrutiny of verbal report was intended to help raise awareness as to key dimensions concerning its use as a research tool so that the already valuable findings from verbal report studies will be even more greatly enhanced by the extra methodological rigor.

3.4   Discussion questions and activities

1. If teachers or researchers wish to gather information regarding language learner strategies, there are various means of assessment available for doing so. This chapter describes six of them. To make these approaches of assessment more real for you, divide yourselves into groups of three or more (depending on the size of the total staff or class). Each group will consider one of the six means of assessment. In each group, one person would be responsible for giving a sales pitch for that method of data collection, a second for shooting it down, and the third for pointing out the conditions under which the approach may be beneficial. In effect, there would be six mini-debates going on. The third participant would have the option of rejecting the approach if he or she determined that the arguments against use outweighed those in favor. Then, the third person from each group is responsible for reporting back to all eighteen or more people in the total group regarding the outcomes of the exercise.

2. You have been invited to give a presentation to prospective classroom researchers on verbal report and how to utilize it in collecting data from learners regarding their strategies. The audience is somewhat knowledgeable about verbal report – enough so that they are confused about what to do. They have heard that if the reports are to reliable and valid, various 'shoulds' must be observed: verbal reports should be collected at the moment the thoughts arise, the respondents should have no part in interpreting their protocols, the respondents should not be directed in what to report about or how and therefore should certainly not receive any training in how to do it, and they should not engage in verbal report in the first place if there is any chance that the data collection method will interfere in any way with the carrying out of the language task. On the basis of the research literature and your own thinking on the matter, prepare a brief set of comments intended to set the record straight or at least to lay out more flexible guidelines than those prescribed by means of all the 'shoulds.'

3. The chapter offers a listing of information that is necessary for write ups of verbal report in the research literature so that consumers of the reports can better interpret the results and so that replication of the studies is facilitated as well. Find at least two sources in the literature which include write ups of verbal report and check to see which of those items they include and exclude. Report back to the your class or group of colleagues with the results of your investigation. Based on your own experience and your sense of what is realistic to expect authors to actually write down regarding their research methods, rank the items according to high priority, medium priority, and low priority.

4. Design your own instrument for measuring strategy use on some task(s). Describe the instrument in detail: its specific purpose, its length and make up, instructions, and the means for analyzing the results. Try it out with colleagues or fellow students. Analyze the results and see what they think about the instrument that you have designed and constructed.

Notes

1. This section is a much revised and modified version of Cohen and Scott, 1996. Kimberly Scott teaches Japanese at the Folwell Middle School in Minneapolis.
2. This is a revised version of a paper which appeared in *Applied Language Learning* 1996 7(1): 7–26. The original version of this paper was presented at the Colloquium on Issues in the Assessment of L2 Learner Strategies, AAAL Annual Conference, Long Beach, CA, March 25–28, 1995.

3. The Ericsson and Simon book was originally written in 1984 and was reissued intact in 1993 with a 53-page preface, intended to update the book. The 1984 volume has served for many as the authority on how verbal reports are supposed to be conducted. The Pressley and Afflerbach (1995) volume constitutes perhaps the first effort to determine the fit between Ericsson and Simon's methodological recommendations and actual uses made of the methodology in the field.

4. Current research policies at many institutions now require that respondents be fully informed as to what they will be asked to do and that they give their written consent. So, in essence, the days of concealing the true motives from the respondents are waning. Furthermore, it may be counterproductive for the purposes of the study to have the subjects distracted for even a portion of the time by anxieties concerning the uses to be made of their responses.

5. Actually both reliability and validity are of concern here. First, there is the concern that the measure produce data that are both consistent within any given verbal report session, as well as being consistent across sessions of a similar nature. The second concern is that the data be valid – i.e. that they actually constitute examples of what they purport to measure. Hence, reliability is a contributing factor in the determination of validity.

4 Strategy training for learners and the role of the teacher

4.1 Introduction

This chapter will focus on strategy training, starting with a broad-ranging discussion of the various forms it can take and then considering the possible roles that the teacher can play. In the next chapter, we will look at the research literature on strategy training and consider an experimental study which investigated the impact of stategies-based instruction on speaking a foreign language.

The underlying premise is that language learning will be facilitated if students become more aware of the range of possible strategies that they can consciously select during language learning and language use. The view taken is that the most efficient way for learner awareness to be heightened is by having teachers provide strategies-based instruction to students as a part of the foreign language curriculum. A variety of approaches to providing student-directed language learning and language use strategy instruction are discussed. Suggestions are given for developing in-service strategy training seminars for foreign language instructors, and a step-by-step approach to the design of strategy training programs is presented.

Section 4.3 focuses on the role of the teacher in strategies-based instruction. The position taken is that teacher training institutions may wish to reconsider language teacher roles for the twenty-first century in their teacher education programs. Given this modest but growing tendency among language educators to view teachers not only as language instructors but also as learner trainers, teacher training programs may benefit from a unit on the effective use of language learning and language use strategies. In this section, attention is given to roles that language teachers might wish to consider assuming in the classroom if they are interested in improving the learners' use of strategies for learning and using the language. Such roles could include: diagnostician, learner trainer, coach, coordinator, language learner, and researcher.

4.2   Making strategy training a reality in the foreign language curriculum

Susan J. Weaver and Andrew Cohen[1]

During the last few decades, there has been a marked shift in the focus of language instruction, toward the needs of individual learners. Language teachers have begun to accommodate individual learners in the classroom by attempting to meet their various linguistic, communicative, and socio-cultural goals, while at the same time adapting their instruction to meet the students' differing language learning needs. In general, the philosophy of foreign language instruction has changed to one which is more interactive and communicative, and less static and teacher-centered. The 'domain' of language teaching has thus been broadened (Tarone and Yule, 1989: 20).

Inherent in this shift in focus is also a shift in the responsibilities of both teachers and students in the foreign language classroom. No longer does the teacher act as the locus of all instruction, controlling every aspect of the learning process. Rather, the learners themselves now, more than ever, are sharing the responsibility for successful language acquisition and, in doing so, are becoming less dependent on the language teacher for meeting their own individual language learning needs. By giving the students more responsibility for their own language development, language programs are inviting the learners to become more autonomous, to diagnose some of their own learning strengths and weaknesses, and to self-direct the process of language development. In other words, learners are being encouraged to 'learn how to learn' and 'learn how to use' a foreign language in a variety of instructional programs around the world.

Given these changes, should language learners be left to their own devices or should they receive some form of training in how to learn a foreign language? Our point of view is that learning will be facilitated if students are explicitly trained to become more aware of and proficient in the use of a broad range of strategies that can be utilized throughout the language learning process. When strategy training is included in the instructional package, students can learn how to learn a foreign language while they are learning the language content. Students can improve both their learning skills and their language skills when they are provided with the necessary tools to:

(1) self-diagnose their strengths and weaknesses in language learning;
(2) become more aware of what helps them to learn the language they are studying most efficiently;
(3) develop a broad range of problem-solving skills;
(4) experiment with both familiar and unfamiliar learning strategies;

(5) make decisions about how to approach a language task;
(6) monitor and self-evaluate their performance; and
(7) transfer successful strategies to new learning contexts.

The process is one of having learners take responsibility for their own learning. The language instructor is then in the role of supporting the learners as they reach their personal learning goals, and language learning really becomes a team effort.

Foreign language program administrators can contribute to this effort by offering strategy training to students as part of the foreign language curriculum. *Strategy training*, i.e. explicitly teaching students how to apply language learning and language use strategies,[2] can enhance students' efforts to reach language program goals because it encourages students to find their own pathways to success, and thus it promotes learner autonomy and self-direction. Strategy training is now practiced in many locations around the world, in programs with both ample and with limited resources, in programs that cater to learners at all levels of the curriculum, and in a variety of formats with differing degrees of integration into the regular curriculum (see Oxford and Leaver, 1996).

Not only are the results of research now indicating that both more successful and less successful learners at any level of proficiency can learn how to improve their comprehension and production of a foreign language,[3] but in addition it would appear that – at least at the outset – **explicit** instruction in the development, application, and transfer of language learning strategies is preferable to implicit instruction. In this section of the chapter we will examine several aspects of explicit strategy training that can be applied to the context of university-level foreign language programs. We will:

(1) describe the goals of strategy training for foreign languages;
(2) discuss insights from L1 and L2 research regarding strategy training;
(3) outline seven ways to provide strategy training;
(4) present suggestions for developing strategies-based instruction (SBI) seminars for foreign language teachers;
(5) consider evaluative research on strategy training programs; and
(6) conclude with a step-by-step approach to the design of strategy training programs.

4.2.1 Goals of strategy training for foreign languages

Strategies for foreign languages can be categorized according to their intended function as either language **learning** strategies and language **use** strategies. In Chapter 2, language learner strategies were defined as those processes which are consciously selected by learners and which may result in actions taken to enhance the learning or use of a foreign language, through the storage, retention, recall, and application of information about the target language. Strategies include those thoughts and actions that are clearly intended for language learning, as well as those that may well lead to learning but which do not ostensibly include learning as the primary goal. They are at least partially conscious, can be transferred to new language tasks, and can be utilized by learners in unique and creative ways to personalize the language learning process.

Language learning strategies are the conscious thoughts and behaviors used by learners with the explicit goal of improving their knowledge and understanding of a target language. The language learning strategy repertoire includes cognitive strategies for memorizing and manipulating target language structures, metacognitive strategies for managing and supervising their strategy use, affective strategies for gauging their emotional reactions to learning and lower anxieties, and social strategies for enhancing learning, such as though cooperating with other learners and seeking opportunities to interact with native speakers. If learners have a well-functioning repertoire, then these strategies will facilitate the language learning process by promoting successful and efficient completion of language learning tasks, as well as by allowing the learners to develop their own individualized approaches to learning.

Language use strategies come into play once the language material is already accessible, even in some preliminary form. Whereas language learning strategies are used with an explicit goal of improving learners' knowledge of a given language, language use strategies focus primarily on helping students utilize the language that they have already learned to whatever degree. As described in Chapter 2, language use strategies include strategies for retrieving information about the language already stored in memory, strategies for rehearsing target language structures, strategies for covering oneself in the language classroom, and strategies for communicating in the language despite gaps in target language knowledge.

For example, given the task of orally re-telling a story read in the foreign language, Learner A may prepare for the task by visualizing the story, either mentally or by actually sketching out pictures in sequence, while Learner B may prefer to remember the key words and phrases of the story using mnemonic devices or by taking notes. Learner C may utilize her background knowledge of a similar story that she has read and apply this knowledge when attempting to re-tell the new story. Learner D may focus on rehearsing what he will say (mentally, orally, or in writing) and try to relax by using positive self-talk or deep-breathing exercises. Learners E, F and G may choose to collaborate with each other by pooling their resources, and Learner H may self-monitor her performance throughout the task and reflect on areas in which she needs improvement. The specific strategy chosen is not the issue here; rather, what counts is that the learners can successfully complete the task by utilizing the strategies that they find useful.

Again as pointed out in Chapter 2, strategies are not inherently 'good' or 'effective,' but rather need to be evaluated in terms of their effectiveness for the individual learner in the completion of the language task at hand. Choosing an effective strategy depends on many factors, including the nature of the language task (its structure, purpose, and demands), individual learner differences (such as age, gender, learning style preferences, language learning aptitude, prior experience in learning other foreign languages, career orientation, and personality characteristics), and the current and intended levels of language proficiency. No single strategy will be appropriate for all learners or for all tasks, and individual learners can and should apply the various strategies in different ways, according to their personal language learning needs.

The goal of strategy training is to explicitly teach students how, when, and why strategies can be used to facilitate their efforts at learning and using a foreign language. By explicitly teaching students how to develop their own individualized strategy systems, strategy training is intended to help students explore ways that they can learn the target language more effectively, as well as to encourage students to self-evaluate and self-direct their learning. The first step in this process is to help learners recognize which strategies they already use, and then to develop a wide range of strategies, so that they can select appropriate and effective strategies within the context of particular language tasks. Ellis and Sinclair (1989: 2) describe this aim as one of providing learners with 'the alternatives from which to make informed choices about what, how, why, when, and where they learn.' Carrell (1996) emphasizes that teachers need to be explicit about **what** the strategy consists of, **how, when,** and **why** it might be used, and how its effectiveness can be evaluated.

An empirical study by Vogely (1995) explored the strategies that 83 college students of Spanish perceived themselves to use while performing an authentic listening comprehension task, and compared the relationship between their reported strategy use and their listening ability. She found that while students had the knowledge and the strategies necessary to be successful listeners in the foreign language, they did not seem to mobilize these resources as effectively as they could have. Her conclusion was that being strategic was not simply a matter of knowing what strategy to use, but also how to use it successfully. She concluded that teachers could help learners bridge the gap between 'knowing what' and 'knowing how.'

A further goal of strategy training is to promote learner autonomy and learner self-direction by allowing students to choose their own strategies and to do so spontaneously, without continued prompting from the language teacher. Learners should be able to monitor and evaluate the relative effectiveness of their strategy use, and more fully develop their problem-solving skills. Strategy training can thus be used to help learners achieve learner autonomy as well as linguistic autonomy. 'Students need to know what their abilities are, how much progress they are making, and what they can (or cannot yet) do with the skills they have acquired. Without such knowledge, it [will] not be easy for them to learn efficiently' (Blanche and Merino, 1989: 313).

While the classroom teacher can provide instruction and opportunities for practice with the various strategies, the ultimate responsibility for choosing and implementing appropriate strategies lies with the individual student. 'Learner training aims to help learners consider the factors that affect their learning and discover the learning strategies that suit them best. It focuses their attention on the process of learning so that the emphasis is on *how* to learn rather than *what* to learn' (Ellis and Sinclair, 1989: 2). Oxford (1990: 201) further emphasizes that 'the general goals of [strategy] training are to help make language learning more meaningful, to encourage a collaborative spirit between learner and teacher, to learn about options for language learning, and to learn and practice strategies that facilitate self-reliance.'

The strategy training movement is predicated on the assumption that if learners are conscious about and become responsible for the selection, use, and evaluation of their learning strategies, they will become more successful language learners by improving their use of classroom time, completing homework assignments and in-class language tasks more efficiently, becoming more aware of their individual learning needs, taking more responsibility for their own language learning, and enhancing their use of the target language out of class. In other words, the ultimate goal of strategy training is to empower students by allowing them to take control of the language learning process.

4.2.2   Insights from the literature regarding explicit strategy training

Explicit training in the use of a broad range of strategies for learning foreign language vocabulary, and for grammar, reading, writing, listening, and speaking skills has become a prominent issue in language acquisition research. Efforts in strategy training have been undertaken and researched for some time in first language pedagogy, especially with regard to reading strategies (e.g. Belmont and Butterfield, 1977; Brown *et al.*, 1980; Ryan, 1981; Duffy *et al.*, 1983; Pressley and Levin, 1983; Brown *et al.*, 1984; Garner, 1987, 1990), and parallel efforts in assessing foreign language strategy training have also appeared in the literature (see O'Malley and Chamot, 1990; Fujiwara, 1990; Wenden, 1991; Oxford, 1992a; Cohen *et al.*, 1995; Dörnyei, 1995; McDonough, 1995; Oxford, 1996b; Thompson and Rubin, 1996).

Most of the research in the area of foreign language learning strategies has focused on the identification, description, and classification of useful learning strategies.[4] This research has been aimed at learners who have successfully or unsuccessfully utilized their knowledge of learning strategies to complete various language tasks or to describe their own learning processes. In recent years, the literature on interventionist studies aimed at training learners to be better at the learning and use of language has been growing (see Chapter 5 for a review). While no empirical evidence has yet been provided to determine the best overall method for conducting strategy training, at least three different instructional frameworks have been identified. They have been designed to raise student awareness as to the purpose and rationale of strategy use, to give students opportunities to practice the strategies that they are being taught, and to help them understand how to use the strategies in new learning contexts. Each of the three approaches outlined below contains the necessary components of explicit strategy training: it emphasizes discussions about the use and value of strategies, encourages conscious and purposeful strategy use and transfer of those strategies to other contexts, and allows students to monitor their performance and evaluate the effectiveness of the strategies they are using.

The first approach to strategy training has been suggested by Pearson and Dole (1987) with reference to first language, but it can also be applied to the study of second and foreign languages as well. This model targets isolated strategies by including explicit modeling and explanation of the benefits of applying a specific strategy, extensive functional practice with the strategy (ranging from highly structured practice to independent strategy selection and use), and then an opportunity for transfer of the strategy to new learning contexts. Students may better understand the applications of the various strategies if they are first modeled by the teacher and then practiced individually. After a range or set of strategies have been introduced and practiced, the teacher can further encourage independent strategy use and promote learner autonomy by encouraging learners to take responsibility for the selection, use, and evaluation of the various strategies that they have been taught. Peasson and Dole's sequence includes:

(1) initial modeling of the strategy by the teacher, with direct explanation of the strategy's use and importance;

(2) guided practice with the strategy;

(3) consolidation where teachers help students identify the strategy and decide when it might be used;

(4) independent practice with the strategy; and

(5) application of the strategy to new tasks.

As for the second approach to strategy training, Oxford *et al.* (1990) outline a useful sequence for the introduction of strategies that emphasizes explicit strategy awareness, discussion of the benefits of strategy use, functional and contextualized practice with the strategies, self-evaluation and monitoring of language performance, and suggestions for or demonstrations of the transferability of the strategies to new language tasks. This sequence is not prescriptive regarding strategies that the learners are supposed to use, but rather descriptive of the various strategies that they could use for a broad range of learning tasks. The sequence they suggest is the following:

(1) ask learners to do a language activity without any strategy training;

(2) have them discuss how they did it, praise any useful strategies and self-directed attitudes that they mention, and ask them to reflect on how the strategies they selected may have facilitated the learning process;

(3) suggest and demonstrate other helpful strategies, mentioning the need for greater self-direction and expected benefits, and making sure that the students are aware of the rationale for strategy use. Learners can also be asked to identify those strategies that they do not currently use, and consider ways that they could include new strategies in their learning repertoires;

(4) allow learners plenty of time to practice the new strategies with language tasks;

(5) show how the strategies can be transferred to other tasks;

(6) provide practice using the techniques with new tasks and allow learners to make choices about the strategies they will use to complete the language learning task;

(7) help students understand how to evaluate the success of their strategy use and to gauge their progress as more responsible and self-directed learners.

After a range or set of strategies have been introduced and practiced, the teacher can further encourage independent strategy use and promote learner autonomy by helping learners take responsibility for the selection, use, and evaluation of the various strategies that they have been taught.

With regard to the third approach to strategy training, Chamot and O'Malley's (1994) sequence is especially useful after students have already had practice applying a broad range of strategies in a variety of contexts. Their approach to helping students complete language learning tasks can be described as a four-stage problem-solving process:

1. *Planning*: The instructor presents the students with a language task and explains the rationale behind it. Students are then asked to plan their own approaches to the task, choosing strategies that they think will facilitate its completion. For example, they can set goals for the task, activate prior knowledge by recalling their approaches to similar tasks, predict potential difficulties, and selectively attend to elements of language input/output.
2. *Monitoring*: During the task, the students are asked to 'self-monitor' their performance by paying attention to their strategy use and checking comprehension. For example, they can use imagery, personalize the language task by relating information to background knowledge, reduce anxiety with positive self-talk, and cooperate with peers for practice opportunities.
3. *Problem-solving*: As they encounter difficulties, the students are expected to find their own solutions. For example, they can draw inferences, ask for clarification, and compensate for lack of target language knowledge by using communication strategies such as substitution or paraphrase.
4. *Evaluation*: After the task has been completed, the learners are then given time to 'de-brief' the activity, i.e. evaluate the effectiveness of the strategies they used during the task. They can also be given time to verify their predictions, assess whether their initial goals were met, give summaries of their performance, and reflect on how they could transfer their strategies to similar language tasks or across language skills.

Each of these stages helps students become more aware of their strategy use, have a chance to practice using and transferring the strategies, engage in self-monitoring and evaluation of strategy use, and take part in discussions about the rationale behind the strategies. These instructional frameworks can be used in various combinations to complement each other and add variety to a strategy training program. When these sequences are used in the classroom, teachers should be encouraged to provide suggestive, rather than corrective, feedback to allow students to consider alternative ways of approaching different learning tasks, and to focus on student self-evaluation of the effectiveness and efficiency of strategy applications.

4.2.3   Options for providing strategy training

A variety of instructional models for foreign language strategy training programs have already been developed and put into practice in various educational settings. The options to be described below include: general study-skills training which is separate from the language course, awareness training both through lectures and through workshops, peer tutoring, the insertion of strategy discussions directly into the textbooks, videotaped mini-courses, and strategies-based instruction in which strategy training is fully integrated into the language curriculum under the guidance of the teacher. Each option differs in the level of explicitness of the training, the level of student awareness of the practical applications and transferability of the strategies, and the level of integration into the foreign language curriculum.

GENERAL STUDY-SKILLS COURSES

Most universities offer programs which help students to develop general study skills, to clarify their educational goals and values, and to diagnose individual learning preferences. These programs are sometimes intended for students who are on academic probation, but can also target successful students who want to further improve their study habits. Many of these general academic skills can be transferred to the process of learning a foreign language, such as using flash cards, overcoming anxiety, and developing good note-taking skills. The courses are sometimes designed to include language learning as a specific topic of focus in order to highlight how learning a foreign language may differ from other types of academic course work. Foreign language students can be encouraged to participate in these courses in order to develop general learning strategies.

These kinds of programs are especially helpful for more motivated students, who have experience in transferring learning skills across class subjects, and can also assist learners in the development of a general awareness of the learning process. Participating students may become more efficient language learners even though the training is not provided within a contextualized language learning setting. However, general study-skills courses may not be sufficient training for the task demands of learning a foreign language, although they may be the answer for universities without the funding necessary to provide specialized learning strategy training for learners of foreign languages.

AWARENESS TRAINING: LECTURES AND DISCUSSION

Also known as consciousness-raising or familiarization training, this kind of training consists most often of isolated lectures and discussions and is usually provided apart from regular language classroom instruction. Oxford

(1990: 202) describes awareness training as a program in which 'participants become aware of and familiar with the general idea of language learning strategies and the way such strategies can help them accomplish various language tasks. In awareness training, however, participants do not have to use strategies in actual, on-the-spot language tasks.' Dickenson (1992) emphasizes two kinds of learner awareness necessary for effective foreign language learning strategy instruction: language awareness (knowledge that makes it possible to talk about and describe language) and language learning awareness (knowledge about some of the factors that influence the learning process). Oxford and Cohen (1992: 13) refer to the latter as 'strategy' awareness: 'When one talks about strategy awareness, one is referring to the learner's understanding of his or her own strategy applications – how he or she takes in new language material, encodes it, and transforms it to make it usable for actual communication.' This kind of awareness training should preferably take place within the individual classroom setting, but it can also be provided by language learning 'experts' for large numbers of students.

For example, for a number of years I would give talks once a month to groups of beginners and more advanced learners of Hebrew at an intensive language center in Netanya, Israel. The purpose of the strategy training was to help language learners of all ages to take greater responsibility for their own progress. The training could be characterized as a 'wake-up call' to learners, in which a combination of new information, humor, and friendly cajoling was used, to get learners to shift from a more passive, even apathetic, role to a more active one with regard to their language learning. My greatest challenge was in coaching senior citizens in their learning of Hebrew, given their hearing, sight, and memory problems, not to mention various kinds of psychological considerations. The presentations concerned various aspects of strategy use and self-directed learning, including topics such as paying attention, vocabulary learning, speaking, writing, and reading. The focus was always highly practical so that if the topic were on vocabulary, learners were, for example, given tips on how to create mnemonic devices for remembering new words. If the topic was on speaking or writing, the learners were given concrete examples of useful and dysfunctional error correction, so they would have a sense of the kinds of feedback that would be most beneficial to them. In some cases the talks prompted the students to be more vocal in negotiating classroom activities with their teachers, as opposed to having the teachers make all of the decisions – including ones that might have been of little or no benefit to the given learners.

I would stay at the language teaching center over the weekend and would lead an informal rap session Saturday mornings or afternoons, entitled 'Everything you ever wanted to know about language learning but were afraid to ask.' In effect, I functioned in the role of language learning therapist at the center. The Hebrew language teachers would frequently eavesdrop on the student-oriented sessions (including the informal therapeutic ones) to clarify (and in some instances change) their perspective on the role of the learner in the language learning process and to gather information on specific learning strategies. As a result of the awareness training sessions, it appeared that both learners and teachers increasingly saw the value of learner self-direction.[5]

As another example of awareness training, starting with the 1993–94 academic year, all elementary language classes at Carnegie Mellon University have been required to have an additional module entitled 'Learning about Language Learning,' which accounts for 15% of the grade in the language course. The students must attend three lectures on language learning given by scholars such as Dick Tucker and Herb Simon, read sections excerpted from Lightbown and Spada's (1993) book, *How languages are learned*, complete Oxford's *Strategy Inventory for Language Learning (SILL)* (Oxford, 1990), fill out a short questionnaire on their language learning background and motivation, have occasional discussions in their language classes in which they reflect on the process of second language learning and their strategy use, and write two papers during the semester reflecting on their experiences. The syllabus explains the rationale for this training: 'In the course of this class, you will be asked to reflect on how you are learning and whether you are using the most appropriate strategies for your own learning styles and needs' (Harrington *et al.*, 1994). Feedback from students' diaries seemed to indicate benefits from the enhanced awareness of learning that this approach encouraged.

Another example of general awareness training was the Foreign Language Learning Strategy Symposium at the University of Minnesota in April, 1994. The two featured speakers, Anna Chamot and Rebecca Oxford, gave a joint lecture entitled 'Foreign language learning strategies: practical ways to enhance the language learning process.' Students of foreign language from various language programs heard about the historical development of strategy training, about the theoretical and research contexts for such strategy training, about comprehension and production strategies, and also about ways to learn vocabulary. Chamot and Oxford also gave the participants a hands-on activity which called for the use of several learning strategies and thus provided the participants first-hand experience at practicing the strategies. The lecture served as a general introduction to those kinds of strategies that can be used when learning a foreign language. The brief question-and-answer session that followed the lecture gave students opportunities to address issues related to their particular language learning needs.

Although awareness-raising is a crucial aspect of strategy training, it may not provide the learners with enough information and strategy practice to allow them to fully self-direct the learning process. Because this training is often not contextualized or related to the particular language tasks the students will be asked to perform in their own classrooms, many students may have difficulty knowing how and when to use the strategies they have been exposed to, organizing and planning their strategy use, finding language-specific strategies, and transferring strategies across skills or tasks. On the other hand, some students may find that this kind of training is sufficient to encourage independent (and appropriate) strategy use. Such learners seem to intuitively grasp the broader applications of language learning strategies. This approach to strategy training provides students with a general introduction to strategy applications, does not take time away from classroom language instruction, and allows for collaboration across foreign language programs in the development of general strategy training because it does not require language-specific strategy instruction.

AWARENESS TRAINING: STRATEGY WORKSHOPS

Short workshops constitute another, usually more intensive, way of increasing overall learner awareness of strategies through various consciousness-raising and strategy assessment activities. They may, for example, address the improvement of specific language skills (e.g. delivering oral speech acts, writing business letters in a more native-like style, and learning large quantities of vocabulary quickly) or ideas for learning some aspect(s) of a specific foreign language. These courses can be offered as non-credit classes for anyone interested in language learning, whether or not enrolled in a language course, or can be required as part of a language or academic skills course. Often these workshops offer a combination of lecture, hands-on practice with specific strategies for various language tasks, and discussions about the general effectiveness of systematic strategy use.

An example of such a workshop was the 'Workshop Series in Language Learner Training' offered during the 1994–95 academic year in consultation with the Learning and Academic Skills Center at the University of Minnesota. All University students were invited to attend one or more of the sessions, each of which focused on distinct aspects of the language learning process. The series included topics such as 'Vocabulary learning,' 'Attending to ensure learning and speaking to communicate,' and 'Reading for comprehension.' These workshops provided students with theoretical and empirical bases for the employment of language learning and language use strategies, hands-on activities utilizing general and specific strategies, and a bibliography of resources for further self-study. The participants also had opportunities for extensive small-group discussions concerning problems students often face in the university-level language classroom, ways to improve overall strategy use, the transfer of strategies to other language tasks, and goal-setting suggestions. Response to these workshops was positive, and the students themselves requested that more workshops be provided on a regular basis. The students were able to work with specific language skills, practice the strategies with direct feedback from the workshop leader, and ask for advice about improving strategy use.

The main advantage of having available a series of workshops is that each workshop can be devoted to a specific topic or skill and that they can be offered on an ongoing basis. These workshops can be offered to address general strategy applications, and thus be useful across language programs, or they can be language-specific if there are special needs for a particular language program (e.g. suggestions for learning *kanji* in a beginning Japanese class). Taken together, the set of workshops serves to reinforce in the minds of the learners the notion that strategy use may genuinely enhance their learning.

PEER TUTORING

Tandem programs, as they have been referred to, began in the 1970s in Europe and have begun to flourish in many universities across the United States. Holec (1988) describes this system as a 'direct language exchange' program that pairs students of different native language backgrounds together for mutual tutoring sessions. Thus, for example, an American student of Italian would be paired with a student from Italy who is studying English as a second language. The principle requirements of the tutoring sessions are that the students have regular meetings, that they alternate the roles of both learner and teacher, that the two languages be practiced separately, and that equal amounts of time be devoted to both languages. Often, the students exchange suggestions about the kinds of language learning strategies that they typically use, thus providing an *ad hoc* form of strategy training.

Feedback from students participating in European *tandem* programs has been positive (Holec, 1988), with the majority of the participants finding the meetings to be less stressful than regular class sessions, a welcome change from more academic sources of language learning, and an excellent opportunity to take more responsibility for learning. Some students also pointed out the obvious benefits of the opportunity for cultural exchange, and others focused on the advantages of authentic target language practice. Negative reactions voiced by participants focused primarily on the lack of structured learning materials, since the meetings were often quite informal and thus did not provide the students with an organized approach to improving target language skills.

Another approach to peer sessions would be to encourage students who are studying the same language (at the same or different levels of proficiency) to organize regular target language study groups or tutoring sessions. Students who have already completed the language course may also be invited to attend these meetings to maintain their fluency in the language. The less proficient students can benefit from the language skills of the more advanced students, and the advanced students also tend to benefit from the extra language practice. In addition, the students themselves may have more insights into the particular difficulties of the target language than their own language teachers.

The peer-tutoring approach to strategies training is inexpensive and easy to organize, although in terms of the strategy training itself, few students have the background necessary to provide each other with suggestions for systematic strategy use. Further, students may not be fully aware of how to transfer strategies across language skills and tasks. If the students are also receiving some other form of strategy training, then the peer tutoring sessions could be devoted to discussions of the students' reactions to the various strategies.

STRATEGIES INSERTED INTO LANGUAGE TEXTBOOKS

Many foreign language textbooks have begun to appear that (implicitly or explicitly) 'embed' strategies into the class activities and thus into the language curriculum. When the strategies are **implicit** and thus not explained, modeled, or reinforced by the classroom teacher or the textbook itself, strategy training may not actually take place, and students may not be aware that they have been using the strategies at all. Sometimes the rationale for these activities is only explained in the teacher's manual and the teachers do not have sufficient training to explain the strategies' importance or value as language learning tools. At other times, a strategy may be described briefly in English (e.g. an explanation is given of how 'reflecting on the title of a reading passage' can improve comprehension by activating background knowledge), but the strategy is not subsequently reinforced through other activities in the book. Experienced language learners may recognize the usefulness of these strategies and find ways to transfer them to similar tasks, but the average or beginning student may either not understand that these strategies can be transferred to new tasks or they may simply forget to use them. Thus, the language instructor will have to explicitly debrief learners about the strategies and reinforce those that appear in the textbook, making sure that the students are aware of the purpose of systematic strategy use.

There are also a few language textbooks that are expressly devoted to overt strategy training and 'spiraling' (or progressive reinforcement) of the strategies as part of the language course itself (see Hajer, Messtringa, Park and Oxford, 1996). These books have strategy-embedded activities as well as explicit explanations of the benefits and applications of the various strategies they address. Because the focus of the activities is contextualized language learning, learners can develop their learning strategy repertoires while learning the target language at the same time. Although most of these textbooks have been written for learners of English as a second language (e.g. Heinle & Heinle's *Tapestry* series, co-edited by Robin Scarcela and Rebecca Oxford), foreign language textbooks are also now becoming available (e.g. *¿Sabías que . . . ?: beginning Spanish*, developed by Bill VanPatten and colleagues [1996]).

There are several advantages to using textbooks with explicit strategy training and reinforcement, the most obvious of which is that students do not then need extracurricular training because the strategies are already included as part of the regular language course. In addition, these textbooks reinforce strategy use across both tasks and skills, and thus encourage students to continue applying the strategies on their own. However, given the results of an empirical study conducted by Nyikos (1996), the teachers themselves may still require strategy training in order to utilize the materials appropriately.[6] This can be accomplished by providing in-service foreign language teacher development programs specifically designed to allow teachers to become aware of the applications of strategies and to promote extensive strategy use in their classes. (See section 4.2.5 below.)

VIDEOTAPED MINI-COURSES

Joan Rubin developed an interactive videodisc program and accompanying instructional manual designed for adults (high school and above) to use before beginning an introductory-level foreign language course. The one-hour *Language learning disc* was designed to raise students' awareness of learning strategies and of the learning process in general, to show students how to transfer strategies to new tasks, and to help students take charge of their own progress while learning the language (Rubin, 1996). Using authentic language situations, the instructional program includes 20 different foreign languages, and offers learners an opportunity to select the language, topic, and level of difficulty they wish to focus on. The materials are structured to expose the students to various strategies in many different contexts, and the videodisc is divided into three main sections: (1) an introduction, (2) general language learning strategies, and (3) strategies related to reading, active listening, or conversation.[7]

Although the benefits of this highly interactive and individualized program are considerable, the videodisc has had very limited circulation within university-level foreign language programs. However, videodisc technology and equipment, as well as computerized language programs, are now becoming more widely available to both teachers and learners. The main advantages of Rubin's videodisc are that students can adapt the program to meet their individual language learning needs and that it can be used in conjunction with other forms of strategy training. Students can use the multimedia package to explore several different aspects of the language learning process in order to prepare them for the study of a foreign language.

STRATEGIES–BASED INSTRUCTION

Strategies-based instruction (SBI) is a learner-centered approach to teaching that extends classroom strategy training to include both explicit and implicit integration of strategies into the course content. Students experience the advantages of systematically applying strategies to the learning and use of the language they are studying. In addition, they have opportunities to share their own preferred strategies with the other students in the class and to increase their strategy repertoires within the context of the typical language tasks that they are asked to perform. The teachers can individualize the strategy training, suggest language-specific strategies, and reinforce strategies at the same time that they are presenting the regular course content.

In a typical SBI classroom strategy training situation, the teachers:

(1) describe, model, and give examples of potentially useful strategies;
(2) elicit additional examples from students based on the students' own learning experiences;
(3) lead small-group / whole-class discussions about strategies (e.g. reflecting on the rationale behind strategy use, planning an approach to a specific activity, evaluating the effectiveness of chosen strategies);
(4) encourage their students to experiment with a broad range of strategies; and
(5) integrate strategies into everyday class materials, explicitly and implicitly embedding them into the language tasks to provide for contextualized strategy practice.

The first four of these components have often stood alone as the approach when strategies are included in the language classroom. The field has referred to this approach as 'strategy training,' 'strategies instruction,' or 'learner training' (cf. Chamot and Rubin, 1994: 771, with regard to these three terms). The component that makes it *strategies-based instruction* is the added element of **explicit** (as well as implicit) integration of the training into the very fabric of the instructional program.

Teachers have at least three options for how to conduct SBI:

1. They start with the established course materials and then determine which strategies to insert and where.
2. They start with a set of strategies that they wish to focus on and design activities around them.
3. They insert strategies spontaneously into the lessons whenever it seems appropriate (e.g. to help students overcome problems with difficult material or to speed up the lesson).

They also allow students to choose their own strategies and do so spontaneously, without continued prompting from the language teacher. In all likelihood, teachers will be engaged in SBI with an explicit focus on strategies only part of the time, while the rest of the time the strategies will be implicitly embedded into the language tasks. Whether or not strategies are embedded into the textbooks, classroom teachers are always to integrate the strategy training into the regular language course work, thus providing the students with contextualized strategy practice.

The goal of this kind of instruction is to help foreign language students become more aware of:

(1) how they learn most effectively;
(2) how they can enhance their own comprehension and production of the target language; and
(3) how they can continue to learn on their own and communicate in the target language after they leave the language classroom.

In other words, strategies-based instruction aims to assist learners in becoming more responsible for their efforts in learning and using the target language. It also aims to assist them in becoming more effective learners by allowing them to individualize the language learning experience. For example, strategies such as 'rehearsing structures' are gone over in class and practiced so that in 'real' speaking situations, the learners would select the strategies as a regular part of their functioning.

In principle, SBI is not specific to any given teaching methodology or culture. It is possible that a given teaching method might favor certain strategies over others – for example, not translating material or, to the contrary, putting an emphasis on translation. Also, certain cultures may favor or refrain from certain practices such as public correction of spoken errors in class. SBI is not prescriptive, but rather provides a panoply of strategies, and students must determine which to use, when, for what purposes, and how to use them.

Although it may seem that in-class strategy training takes valuable time away from teaching the language content, teachers who have used this approach have reported that their students become more efficient in completing classroom language tasks, take more responsibility for self-directing their learning outside of class, and gain more confidence in their ability to learn and use the target language. Further, after the language teachers have been taught how to provide strategies-based instruction, they can apply this training to all of the classes that they teach. In addition, these teachers then become 'strategy experts' themselves and thus can offer valuable feedback on the effectiveness of an integrated strategies approach.

4.2.4 Conducting evaluative research on strategy training programs

Researchers at several major universities are developing projects designed to assess the results of strategy training on student performance. Generally, an experimental group of foreign language students receives strategy training, such as through SBI, and is compared with one or more control groups. Whereas it used to be the researcher, and not the regular classroom teacher, who provided the training, the classroom teachers are increasingly being trained themselves to conduct strategy training programs with their students (see, for example, Weinstein and Underwood, 1985; Chamot and O'Malley, 1994; Cohen *et al.*, 1995).

While a fair number of learners receiving strategy training have shown greater improvement in language performance than those who were not trained in strategy use, Oxford (1990) reports that potentially more convincing results are mitigated by several factors associated with doing strategy training for research purposes. First, for the sake of parsimony in research design, researchers often choose to focus only on certain strategies for specific language skills, rather than conducting extensive training both across tasks and across language skills. This approach does not provide the learners with sufficiently broad strategy training, although some students may be able to develop new strategy applications on their own. Second, the strategy training is not always contextualized, so students may not see how a particular strategy for monitoring the verb ending in an isolated sentence-level task might apply to verb formation in extended written discourse. Because the transferability of strategies is an important aspect of any training program, students will not fully benefit from the strategy training until they are able to use the strategies effectively across language tasks. In this case, the more 'aware' students will benefit most from the training.

Despite the problems, training with a research component does provide university foreign language program administrators and strategy researchers with empirical data related to the effectiveness of strategy training in authentic language classrooms. (For a comprehensive review of research studies on the effectiveness of strategy training, see Derry and Murphy, 1986; O'Malley and Chamot, 1990; Oxford, 1990; McDonough, 1995; and Oxford, 1996b. In addition, at least one teacher participating in the strategies-based instruction study described in Chapter 5 has produced a written description of her experiences and reactions to training her students in the use of strategies [Lybeck, 1996]).

4.2.5 · Suggestions for developing SBI seminars for language teachers

There are various ways that program administrators can furnish language teachers with the tools to provide their own strategy training for students, ranging from general awareness training to full-scale SBI training seminars. For example, the director of language instruction or an associate could provide short awareness-raising workshops and lectures. Secondly, language instructors could be asked to attend any of the numerous presentations, colloquia, and workshops on strategy training at professional conferences. Thirdly, in-service SBI seminars could be developed.

Of these options, in-service seminars provide the most extensive and efficient means for training classroom teachers in how to conduct their own strategy training in the form of strategies-based instruction. O'Malley and Chamot (1990: 154) refer to this as 'developing in teachers the understanding and techniques for delivering effective learning strategy instruction to students.' The participating language instructors can gain a better sense of the individual needs of their students and positively reinforce effective strategy use as the language course progresses. In addition, they can learn how to embed the strategies into everyday class activities and how to help students choose strategies related to specific curricular guidelines. Teacher training in strategies-based instruction can also prepare language teachers for the spontaneous introduction of strategies in their classes, thus providing both individualized and contextualized strategy training for all of their students.

These seminars could be offered as part of the pre-service orientation program for incoming foreign language instructors within specific language departments or be provided as in-service training across language programs. This kind of training would ideally include several different methods of instruction: lectures, outside reading of journal articles and book excerpts describing learning/teaching experiences and issues, paired and small-group discussions, hands-on strategy activities, observation of classes taught by teachers who have already implemented strategies-based instruction with their students, interactive sessions to practice the development of strategy-integrated lesson plans, and peer/student micro-teaching.

Lectures and readings on the theoretical and research contexts in which strategy training has developed can provide an important foundation upon which to examine any given set of strategies. However, experience has shown that the amount of theory and the manner in which it is introduced needs to be tailored to the individual needs of the participants in order to assure its effectiveness. For example, it may pay to intersperse the theoretical underpinnings with the practical applications so that teachers can see just how the theory and the practice relate to one another.

Discussions among teachers are likely to focus on the emergence of SBI as a means of integrating diverse teaching philosophies, methodologies, and approaches to learning, as well as on philosophical and methodological issues concerning the language learning process. These discussions (in pairs or small groups) can serve to create a genuinely meaningful classroom context for these instructors. Experience has also shown that these teachers-in-training need numerous opportunities to reflect on the information being presented in the seminar, as well as to discuss their own language learning and teaching experiences, in order to prepare them for their future roles as facilitators of their own students' reactions to the strategy training. In addition, if this part of the training program emphasizes the role of the learner as a source of knowledge about language learning and language use strategies, the instructors may feel more comfortable with these kinds of discussions in their own classes since they will have already had experience sharing similar ideas and suggestions.

A practical hands-on approach, where the participant instructors themselves actively experiment with the strategies presented, will help to prepare them to train their own students and allow them to practice implementing the strategies at the same time. For example, they could take diagnostic surveys (e.g. learning style inventories and strategy assessment surveys), reflect on ways that they themselves may differ from other language learners (e.g. think about and discuss their own language learning experiences and how individual learning style preferences and other factors can affect strategy choice), actively participate in learner training activities (e.g. learn new vocabulary with different mnemonic devices, answer general comprehension questions after skimming a text, rehearse short speeches, selectively attend to short listening passages), and engage in problem-solving or metacognitive discussions (e.g. in small groups or pairs, discuss various ways to approach a particular task, isolate potential difficulties, make strategy choices, implement the selected strategies, and evaluate their effectiveness). By actively engaging in and reacting to authentic strategy use, the teachers-in-training can gain a better understanding of what to expect from their own students, as well as getting first-hand practice with generating multiple problem-solving techniques (i.e. choosing their own strategies). In this way, the instructors will truly **experience** the strategies before actually teaching them.

Participants may also find it useful to keep journals of their experiences during the training sessions to use as a resource when later called upon to present strategy training themselves. These journals could include affective reactions to the training, as well as ideas for the integration of strategies into various kinds of activities. Excerpts from these journal entries could later be compiled into a resource handbook for the teachers to use as support after the training program has ended.

Another useful resource for the teachers is the opportunity to observe authentic class sessions conducted by other language instructors who have already undergone the strategy training program. The teachers can meet to exchange ideas about specific aspects of the presented lessons and discuss how the strategy training fits into the overall language curriculum. It would also be beneficial, if possible, to have the teachers-in-training talk with the students in the class to hear their reactions to being SBI participants. It is the learners themselves who can provide some of the most significant and insightful comments about the realities of classroom strategy training. If there are not enough language classrooms to observe, teachers could also watch videotapes of class sessions taught by colleagues who regularly provide strategies-based instruction. These demonstrations of explicit strategy instruction for students in authentic contexts can be especially helpful in showing the teachers how the strategies are being embedded into a particular course curriculum.

An additional important feature of the teacher-training seminar is the provision of opportunities for teachers to practice integrating strategies into everyday lesson plans and developing strategies-based teaching materials. If the teachers only receive pre-prepared strategy materials to use with their students, they may have difficulty adapting the instruction to the needs of their own students. The seminar could provide the teachers with opportunities to generate their own ideas about how the strategies could be incorporated into their current language curricula by having them adapt existing course materials or create new teaching materials. This can be accomplished by having the teachers bring in actual lessons that they have already prepared, and, in pairs or small groups, they could work together to brainstorm ways in which different strategies could be inserted into the activities, create new materials to fill in any gaps, and then share their ideas with the rest of the class. As a group, the participants could then generate several possibilities for presenting each activity, and by sharing these lesson plans, they would have access to a wide variety of ideas for strategy integration that they could later incorporate into future lessons. In addition, these activity-writing sessions can also serve as a feedback mechanism both for the training coordinator (to assess the effectiveness of the strategy training) and for the teachers themselves (to gauge their ability to apply the content of the seminar in practical ways).

Finally, after the teachers have had opportunities to create new materials, as well as to integrate strategies into their existing lesson plans, they are likely to be willing and able to present short strategies-based language lessons to their peers in order to practice the instructional techniques before introducing them into their own classrooms. These micro-teaching sessions can also be extended to small groups of current language students for additional teaching practice. This would provide authentic responses to strategy training from actual language learners, allowing the teachers to experience a simulated classroom atmosphere much like what they will eventually face. If possible, these sessions could be videotaped so that they could then be used to generate discussions about the effectiveness of the lessons, to allow the teachers to reflect on their teaching skills, and to provide the training coordinator with additional insights into the teachers' needs within and beyond the training sessions. For example, the coordinator of the training may see the need to adjust the current training curriculum, to arrange for follow-up support after the 'official' training has ended, or to plan future training sessions.

As part of an ongoing series of research projects involving the introduction of strategy instruction into foreign language immersion programs, Anna Chamot of George Washington University and her colleagues from the Washington DC area school districts offered training seminars for teachers of Japanese, and separate similar seminars for teachers of French and Spanish respectively over a three-year period. The contents were developed based on informal assessment of teachers' needs (through discussions with teachers and the coordinators). The teachers were given the rationale for teaching strategies, examples of immersion students' strategies use, material in the target language for introducing the concept of strategies to students, suggestions for integrating strategies into the regular instructional program for immersion students, and an opportunity to develop strategies-based lessons. The teachers found that the most useful aspects of the workshops included guidance on how to identify students' strategies, an opportunity to work with a partner to integrate strategies into a lesson, suggestions as to how to explicitly teach strategies, and tips on enabling students to explain their thoughts in the target language (see Chamot, Keatley, Barnhardt, El-Dinary, Nagano and Newman, 1996).

In contrast to the same-language approach, the SBI teacher-training seminars at the University of Minnesota have been created for teachers from different foreign language programs with no pre-packaged teaching materials provided, other than examples from the course itself. The SBI training program, which is contained in a training manual offering 30-, 15-, 6-, and 3-hour courses of instruction (Weaver and Cohen, 1997),[8] focuses on helping the teachers create and adapt their own instructional materials from the very beginning of the program. The teachers are thus responsible for applying the strategies to their own curricular needs, and, when possible, are paired with teachers from their own language department to share lesson plan ideas. For the less commonly taught languages at the University of Minnesota (e.g. Hebrew, Hindi, Irish, Norwegian, Portuguese, and so forth), the teachers are asked to form cross-language strategy support teams. Teaching suggestions are shared throughout the different foreign language programs and teachers thus have contact with a wide variety of instructional materials, teaching philosophies, and performance criteria.

Both of these teacher-training methods have been successful in bringing fully integrated strategy training to a great number of students through the regular classroom language teachers. The administrative decisions regarding the format for each of these seminars are based upon the needs of the individual institutions, as well as the need to provide students with systematic strategy training which has been integrated into everyday classroom activities. The goal of this kind of seminar is to train classroom language teachers (who will eventually train their own students) in the identification, practice, reinforcement, and transfer of language learning and language use strategies via strategies-based instruction.

4.2.6 A step-by-step approach to the design of strategy training for learners

The strategy training approaches outlined above provide language program administrators with options for providing strategy training for large numbers of learners. Based on the needs, resources, and time available to an institution, the next step is to plan the instruction that the students will receive, regardless of the form of training. Many considerations must be taken into account when designing explicit strategy training programs for foreign language learners. The following seven-step approach is largely based on suggestions for strategy training by Oxford (1990). This model is especially valuable because it can easily be adapted according to the needs of various groups of learners, the resources available to a particular institution, and the length of the strategy training, whether short- or long-term. It can be used in the preparation of short workshops and awareness training lectures for students or as a guideline for teachers who have attended SBI seminars.

DETERMINING THE LEARNERS' NEEDS AND THE RESOURCES AVAILABLE FOR TRAINING

The first step in designing any foreign language curriculum is to assess the needs of the learners. This is an especially crucial step when designing a curriculum that will integrate strategy training. The factors involved in this kind of needs assessment include: their current and intended levels of proficiency, their experience with foreign language strategy use or with learning other languages, their learning style preferences and personality characteristics, their beliefs and attitudes about language learning, their expectations regarding the roles of both the classroom teacher and the individual language learner, and the reasons why the students have chosen to study a particular foreign language.

Next, the amount of time to be allotted to the training program must be considered. Will the program consist of short-term intervention or extensive strategy training? How many hours can be dedicated to this kind of training? Will the training be embedded within the course content or will it be provided apart from the language course itself? Scheduling when the strategy training will take place within the particular foreign language curriculum should also be considered in this step.

How much funding is available for the training program? Will individual language programs sponsor the training or would it be a collaborative effort on the part of several departments? Will the training be language-specific or more general in nature? Which kind of training program will be most cost-effective and thus reach the greatest number of students? Is the training to be offered only once a year, or will it be offered on an ongoing basis throughout the year?

Finally, who will conduct the training itself? Does the sponsoring institution have resident 'experts' who can carry out the training program(s) and/or develop the materials needed, or will outside lecturers/trainers need to be brought in? (For further description of decisions related to materials development, see the section on 'Preparing the materials and activities' below.)

SELECTING THE STRATEGIES

First, it is necessary to determine the strategies that the learners already use, and select strategies which are appropriate to the characteristics and needs of the learners. An instrument that has been used for this purpose in numerous language and culture groups around the world is Oxford's (1990) *Strategy Inventory for Language Learning (SILL)*.[9] Since general questionnaires such as the *SILL* are not intended for fine-tuned analysis and description of strategy use on any given task, teachers and administrators may wish to design their own instruments for determining the strategies being used in the performance of tasks specific to their curriculum. (For a detailed description of methods of strategy assessment, refer back to section 3.1.) The following are learner characteristics that may need to be considered in the identification and selection of strategies to be used locally in strategy training: learning style preferences, personality characteristics, cultural or educational background, age, gender, career orientation, previous language study, and levels and types of motivation.[10] In addition, there are the needs-related factors, such as proficiency goals and the kinds of tasks learners will be asked to perform in the language classroom.

Also, the transferability of the strategies to other language learning skills and tasks will need to be considered. For example, the strategy of relating new language information to a meaningful visual image (e.g. a picture of an object or activity, or a mental representation of a word or phrase) is not only useful for learning new vocabulary, but can also be extended to reading, writing, speaking, listening, and grammar tasks. Most strategies can be generalized in this way, although some (such as rote memorization) may have more limited benefits across language tasks, and some (such as skimming a reading passage to get the main idea) may be specific to a particular language skill. In addition, will the strategies be language-specific or more general in nature? For example, there are some strategies that pertain to the learning of a new writing system for languages such as Hindi or Japanese, and there are others that can be used regardless of the target language.

In addition, will the training have a broad or a narrow focus? In other words, will the training focus on multiple clusters of strategies or will it include just a few? Or will it consist of a combination of these approaches such as by first providing the learners with a wide range of strategies and then focusing exclusively on those which the learners themselves have chosen? Because one of the primary goals of strategy instruction is to encourage the learners to use strategies on their own, this last approach may be most beneficial. (See Dansereau [1985] for a description of these different approaches.) This decision may be affected by the amount of time available for strategy training and the proposed structure of the training program, as well as by the immediate and long-term needs of individual learners.

Finally, what is the focus of instruction? Does the course focus on oral production of the target language, emphasize the development of reading skills, or favor an integrated skills approach? The types of strategies chosen and/or spontaneously introduced need to reflect the skills that are emphasized so that there is good fit between the two.

CONSIDERING THE BENEFITS OF INTEGRATED STRATEGY TRAINING

As noted above, there are significant benefits from providing strategy training integrated into the regular class curriculum. SBI is by its very nature contextualized, can be individualized according to the needs of a particular group of learners, and provides hands-on practice with and reinforcement of the strategies during authentic language learning tasks. Wenden (1987b: 161) notes that integrated strategy training 'enables the learner to perceive the relevance of the task, enhances comprehension, and facilitates retention.' However, Wenden also warns that fully integrated strategy training may not necessarily lead to the spontaneous (unprompted) application of strategies by individual learners, nor will it necessarily produce autonomous learners. Such is the case with any innovation. So much depends on how the program is run in the given situation. A justification for engaging in research and evaluation along with program implementation is to have documentation of what worked and what did not in order to make improvements if necessary.

CONSIDERING MOTIVATIONAL ISSUES

Will students be graded on their efforts and/or receive course credit for participation in the strategy training program, or will they be motivated to learn the strategies simply because they want to become more effective language learners? As Oxford *et al.* (1990: 206–7) point out, 'if learners have gone through a strategy assessment phase, their interest in strategies is likely to be heightened, and if you explain how using good strategies can make language learning easier, students will be even more interested in participating in strategy training.' However, inducements such as extra credit may substantially increase enthusiasm in the college classroom, whether the strategy training is integrated in the daily activities or not. Training programs can also be required for students as part of their regular language coursework, using special grading systems.

In addition, motivation can also be increased if the learners have at least some control over the strategies they will learn. Will the learners be able to select their own strategies from the very beginning or will they be asked to learn those that the teacher presents? To what extent will the instruction be adapted to the needs of individual learners? The students themselves may prefer to choose the strategies which will be included in the training program, and because the learners will eventually be expected to select their own strategies when performing language tasks, their input early in the training process can facilitate the transition from explicit instruction and guided practice to self-directed strategy use.

Another factor to be considered is the relative level of resistance to strategy training. Some students may be reluctant to try out new strategies, preferring to rely on the strategies that they already employ, or may not be convinced of the benefits which accompany systematic strategy use. Other learners may have negative reactions to the training because of cultural or personal beliefs about the teacher's role in the classroom and may resist the increased responsibility for learning which accompanies strategy training.

PREPARING THE MATERIALS AND ACTIVITIES

First, it must be determined who will develop the instructional materials. Will teachers receive pre-packaged training materials (from a textbook, curriculum coordinator, or researcher) or will they be expected to produce their own materials (perhaps by adapting the activities in the current curriculum to include strategies)? Will the learners themselves contribute to the development and collection of materials, thereby becoming even more involved in and having more control over the instructional program, or will the trainer (teacher, coordinator, or researcher) alone make decisions regarding the course materials and activities?

Next, will the strategy training be 'flexible' and allow for the spontaneous introduction of new strategies as needed during a classroom activity or will there be a fixed training curriculum? While a fixed curriculum may offer convenience and consistency across training programs, a flexible one allows for more individualized strategy instruction. In any case, in order to conduct spontaneous strategy training in the classroom, the language teachers themselves need to undergo some form of in-service training to ensure that they have received appropriate and sufficient preparation for this kind of strategy instruction. If the goal is to provide the greatest number of students with individualized, contextualized strategy training, the teachers must also be trained.

What kinds of activities do the teachers present during the classroom sessions and assign for homework? Strategies-based materials should reflect the typical kinds of learning tasks that are included in the curriculum. In addition, 'activities must be interesting, varied, and meaningful, and they should deal not just with intellectual aspects of language learning, but with the affective side as well' (Oxford *et al.*, 1990: 209). These materials can include awareness-raising activities, as well as strategy training, practice, and reinforcement activities. In addition to creating new materials specific to a particular training program, another suggestion is to adapt the current curriculum to include strategies-based activities, or to expand the types of activities used in the language classroom to make them more 'strategy-friendly.' For example, teachers can design cooperative learning tasks and small-group discussions that focus on learner reactions to the strategies. Although most foreign language teachers already use a wide variety of 'strategy-friendly' (i.e. strategies-based) activities in their classes, what seems to be missing is an awareness of some or many of those strategies on the part of the students. Thus, the initial strategy training must be explicit and include awareness-raising activities.

CONDUCTING EXPLICIT STRATEGY TRAINING

It is necessary for teachers to inform their learners fully as to the strategies that they are being taught, the value and purpose of employing these strategies, and ways that they can transfer the strategies to other learning tasks. Learners also need to be explicitly trained to select, monitor, and evaluate the strategies that they use (Brown *et al.*, 1980). This kind of explicit strategy training differs from 'blind' strategy training in one important aspect. While both kinds of training can include activities in which strategies are embedded (i.e. structured to elicit the use of specific strategies), the 'blind' approach to strategy training does not provide the learners with explicit information about the strategies that are being used or about why they may be useful. The assumption being made here is that the more students are aware that they are using the strategies that the activity has been designed to practice, the more likely they may be to use them spontaneously in other contexts. The psychological principle involved is that learners better remember material that is reinforced by other material.

Since one of the primary goals of strategy training is to foster learner independence and autonomy, O'Malley and Chamot (1990: 184) conclude that 'strategy training should be direct in addition to being embedded. In other words, students should be apprised of the goals of strategy instruction and should be made aware of the strategies they are being taught.' Thus, explicit strategy training in the language classroom can be as simple as explaining the purpose of the language activity, or calling attention to how the teacher has organized the course materials.

In order to teach students how to strategize, Rubin (1997) would suggest three practical approaches that teachers can take. The first would be to raise the learners' awareness, as suggested above. The means for doing this (adapted from Rubin, 1997) would include:

(1) the use of questionnaires (e.g. style and strategy inventories);
(2) diaries and dialog journals;
(3) focus groups;[11] and
(4) verbal reporting.[12]

The second approach would be through providing the learners practice in the following types of activities:

(1) directing their attention to the need for strategies to accomplish given goals;
(2) writing down problems as they arise so that they are more mindful of areas in which more systematic strategizing may be beneficial;
(3) using a checklist so as to view at a glance the possible range of strategies to choose from;
(4) comparing the potential contribution of strategies on the list and learning to distinguish different strategies from each other (e.g. distinguishing among different mnemonic strategies for remembering vocabulary items);
(5) choosing among alternate strategies for accomplishing the same task;
(6) getting experience in noting the strategies that they actually use, the contexts in which they are used, when they are used, how they are used, and how effectively they are used in those contexts; and
(7) asking themselves questions about their general progress through this more systematic use of strategies.

Rubin (1997) notes the constraints that may come into play when attempting to teach strategy use. One is that the learners may not consider it their role to take so much responsibility for their learning. Secondly, their level of content and strategy knowledge may be less than what the teacher expects it to be. Thirdly, the teacher may not have sufficient knowledge and experience with learner strategies to effectively teach learners how to use them. Finally, the curricular goals may work against the introduction of such explicit instruction about strategies.

If and when students have gained some awareness of and control over their patterns of strategy use, implicitly introduced strategies-based activities may also be appropriate in the classroom. For example, students need not be reminded every time they brainstorm for vocabulary before a reading activity (or answer questions in preparation for a listening task) that they are activating their background knowledge. The teacher can provide explicit strategy training in order to help the students gain expertise in a wide variety of strategies, and then structure the activities to allow the students to insert their own strategies spontaneously. New strategies can be introduced and practiced explicitly, and then further reinforced through activities that implicitly embed the strategies in order to encourage learner autonomy. In addition, when students seem to be having difficulty with a particular aspect of the lesson, they can be given further explicit strategy suggestions. This differs from 'blind' strategy training in one important aspect: the students have already been given explicit strategy training and they are subsequently being asked to take more responsibility for their strategy use.

EVALUATING AND REVISING THE STRATEGY TRAINING

Ongoing evaluation and revision of the training program is necessary to ensure its success. The learners themselves can provide some of the most insightful feedback for the teacher or teacher trainer. Examples of criteria which can be used to evaluate the program include: improved student performance across language tasks and skills, general learning skill improvement (including enhanced problem-solving skills), maintenance of the new strategies over time, effective transfer of strategies to other learning tasks, and a positive change in learner attitudes toward the training program and the language course itself (Wenden, 1987b; Oxford, 1990). Tarone and Yule (1989) emphasize that ongoing needs assessment, based on feedback from the learners themselves, is an important part of any language program. If the focus of instruction is indeed on the learner, then learner input is essential to the successful evaluation and revision of the training.

As noted above, some strategy instruction may be unplanned and spontaneous, based on the immediate needs of learners who are having difficulties with a particular language task. These on-the-spot revisions can provide the learners with highly individualized strategy instruction, as well as additional practice using specific learning strategies. However, as noted above, spontaneous strategy training requires that the classroom teacher also undergo some sort of training to facilitate strategy discussions with students.

Finally, the training program will need to be revised after it has been completed, based on both teacher trainer and student feedback, before it is presented to the next set of learners. This step naturally leads back to the first, in which the learners' specific needs are taken into consideration, thus fully completing the instructional cycle.

4.2.7   Making strategy training a reality: concluding remarks

As can be seen from this presentation, the guidelines for implementing foreign language learning strategy training programs allow administrators a number of options in order to tailor the training to meet the needs of a large number of students, as well as the needs of the individual institution or language program. The most important considerations when designing a strategy training program are the students' needs, the available resources (including time, the costs associated with developing a training program, materials, and the availability of teacher trainers), and, ultimately, the feasibility of providing this kind of instruction.

The overall goal of any strategy training program is to help learners become more successful in their attempts to learn a foreign language. In order to include strategies-based instruction in a foreign language curriculum, it is necessary to choose an instructional model that:

(1) introduces the strategies to the students and raises awareness of their learning preferences;
(2) teaches them to identify, practice, evaluate, and transfer strategies to new learning situations; and
(3) promotes learner autonomy so that students can continue their learning after they leave the language classroom.

Experience has shown that students can be given more responsibility for their own language learning, can make informed choices about how they will learn the target language, and can become more actively involved in the learning process.

In order for strategies-based instruction to reach the students, the teachers need to know how to deliver it – hence the importance of conducting strategy training seminars for language instructors. In such courses, teachers can develop the skills necessary to conduct contextualized strategies training with their own students and can get a clearer understanding of how to encourage their students to use the strategies in and out of class. They also learn how to allow for flexible and highly individualized strategy training and how to provide students with opportunities to learn the strategies while they are learning the language. As these classroom teachers gain expertise in training their own students to use strategies, they can share this expertise with their colleagues and conduct their own strategy training seminars and workshops. It is these teachers who will be the driving force behind making learning strategy training a reality in the foreign language curriculum.

It is also fair to say that strategies-based instruction has appeal to teachers and pupils at all levels of the curriculum. While the program at the University of Minnesota caters primarily to college-level instruction, the one-week SBI teacher training institute provided each summer for credit is attended by teachers at all levels of instruction from elementary schools to adult language institutes.[13] The work conducted by Chamot and colleagues in the Washington DC area has clearly demonstrated that SBI is a valuable innovation even for language immersion education programs and can be introduced even at the kindergarten level, but certainly in the lower elementary grades.

4.3   The role of teachers in strategies-based instruction[14]

Up to this point in the chapter, we have focused mostly on the learners and on facilitating their systematic use of the kinds of strategies that will benefit their learning and use of a second or foreign language. The effect of this effort is likely to be the emergence of a new or an enhanced role for learners, one in which they draw upon previous strategies and ones that are new to them with an extra sense of awareness and purpose. Whereas formerly, their use of strategies may have been more unsystematic and trail-and-error based, now they are more careful strategists, drawing from their strategy options before, during, and after performing language tasks. And what about their teachers? Does this new thrust for learners have an impact on the roles that the teacher assumes? One potentially beneficial shift in teacher roles is from that of being exclusively the manager, controller, and instructor to that of being a *change agent* – a facilitator of learning, whose role is to help their students to become more independent, more responsible for their own learning. In this role, the teachers become partners in the learning process.

It is important to realize that an emphasis on learner strategies and more learner responsibility in the classroom does not in any way put teachers out of work. It may, on the other hand, free teachers to focus more attention on successfully supporting their students' learning. So, for example, let us say that Teacher A has been devoting a good deal of class time to teaching her college students a large group of transitive/intransitive verb pairs in Japanese. The students have been slow to see the rules involved and have also had difficulty remembering the individual vocabulary words for a number of the verbs. She hopes that with enough repetition of the forms in contrast, the learners will get them right. So she keeps drilling the structures, as well as the different verbs themselves ('to open / to be opened,' 'to close / to be closed,' 'to begin,' 'to end,' 'to decide / to be decided,' 'to turn on / to be turned on,' 'to turn off / to be turned off,' and so forth).

In covering the same material, Teacher B has spent time with her students on the learning of grammar rules, especially strategies for isolating the distinguishing features and for employing them effectively in order to make important contrasts. She has also spent time teaching them how to use the mnemonic keyword device in a systematic way. Her students have utilized these and other strategies to both gain control of the transitive/intransitive verb patterns in Japanese and to remember the 20 or so verbs that they were given which followed these patterns. Teacher B has been able to move more quickly from a presentation and drilling phase into the application phase, and into supporting the students in their use of these forms. It is likely that Teacher B's students will also remember these rules and vocabulary items longer than Teacher A's students because of the extra attention given to them in the learning phase and the extra time available for the application phase.

If teachers are willing, in fact, to act as change agents in the classroom – shifting the responsibility for learning more onto the shoulders of the students themselves – they will actually be taking on a series of roles. Sections 4.3.1–6 outline some of the ones that they might assume (based in part on Tyacke, 1991; Oxford, 1990; Willing, 1989) (see Figure 4.1).

4.3.1   Teachers as diagnosticians

First of all, teachers can assume the role of *diagnostician*: identifying the students' current learning strategies and making the learners more aware of them so as to improve the learners' choice and utilization of these and other strategies. As diagnostician, they can heighten learners' awareness as to how they learn best. Suggestions for how to assess the strategies currently being used by learners are provided in Chapter 3, as well as in Oxford (1990), Willing (1989), Wenden (1991). Ideally, the diagnosis is ultimately arrived at by the learners themselves; the teachers serve as catalysts in getting the process going.

R		DIAGNOSTICIAN
E		
S	C	LEARNER TRAINER
E	O	
A	O	
R	R	
C	D	
H	I	COACH
E	N	
R	A	
	T	
	O	
	R	LANGUAGE LEARNER

FIGURE 4.1   Teacher as change agent

4.3.2   Teachers as learner trainers

In the *learner trainer* role, teachers train the learners in the use of strategies, whether explicitly or implicitly. The degree to which the strategies are explicitly presented to learners as opposed to being built implicitly into the language learning material is a matter of teacher choice. For example, a teacher may prefer to train learners explicitly in strategies for learning new vocabulary words rather than simply leaving it to the learners to pick up such strategies.[15] First, it may be a matter of teacher preference – i.e. explicit attention to the given strategy is the most comfortable approach or seems to produce the best results for that teacher. Second, it may be a matter of the complexity of demands put upon the learner in processing the given instructional material – i.e. explicit attention to a given strategy could help to avoid the distraction of associated language processing and may also enhance the transfer of that strategy to use in situations where formal learning is not going on (Willing, 1989). For example, there are a host of possible strategies for performing the reading skill of skimming. Because skimming is such a complex skill, it may pay teachers to describe possible strategies for skimming and then explicitly train the learners in their use.[16]

Thirdly, it may depend on the nature of the strategy itself in that certain strategies may be difficult to learn implicitly. With respect to this last reason for explicit training, let us take the example of the keyword mnemonic for remembering vocabulary words. Although learners sometimes devise these on their own while engaged in vocabulary learning activities, the strategy involved is complex enough that explicit instruction in its use may be advisable. Such instruction may take no more than 15 minutes but could be more beneficial than mere exposure to such a strategy with no explicit training in its use.

4.3.3   Teachers as coaches

In the *coach* role, teachers work with individual learners to develop their language learning strategies. In this case, rather than supplying them with training, teachers are coaching them in areas in which they have already been trained or in areas where coaching alone could enhance either their awareness of possibly useful strategies for the given task or their efficiency at utilizing these strategies. In this role, teachers provide guidance in all areas of concern to the learners on an ongoing basis, whether through periodic conferencing about aspects of the learners' oral or written work, or through other means, such as responding to queries and comments in dialog journals which are kept by the learners.[17]

4.3.4   Teachers as coordinators

There is another teacher role related to the smooth functioning of the learning process, that of *coordinator*, whereby teachers oversee the learners' individual study program – supporting changes in direction as necessary, allowing a fluid syllabus with the appropriate degree of structure in it. This may be a large-scale shift for teachers, since many focus on coordinating the teaching, not coordinating the learning. The role needs to be built on a partnership between the teacher and the learner. For example, each learner needs to keep track of his or her individual study program: the homework assignments attempted and completed, the relative success encountered, the amount of time spent in studying the language, the areas not causing problems and those that are problematic, and so forth. Then, through dialog journaling or conferencing, it is possible for the teacher as coordinator to suggest some mid-course corrections so that the student arrives at a study plan that works – presumably one that makes use of the strategies that the student can utilize most effectively to achieve the maximum benefit.

4.3.5   Teachers as language learners

An additional and most useful role for teachers is that of *language learner*. This role is not a natural consequence of shifting the burden for language learning onto the shoulders of the students. Rather, it is a role that teachers would have to agree to take on, largely in order to better empathize with the trials and tribulations of being a language student in a classroom. If during the process of learner training, the teachers themselves are willing and able to put themselves in the role of language learner, they most likely will become more acutely aware of the kinds of challenges and problems confronting the learners, more sensitive to the learners' needs, and thus better able to train and/or coach them. Some prominent language teacher development programs actually require of their teacher trainees that they take a semester or more of a foreign language, ideally one that is completely unlike any that they have already studied.

There is another function teachers can play as language learner, that of being 'expert language learners' sharing their learning experiences with their students, for example through introspection and retrospection (Dickenson, 1992). In other words, teachers who are non-natives of the target language and have mastered it, or teachers who have successfully learned the native language of their students or some other language, could demonstrate strategies that they have used in order to achieve the level of proficiency that they now have. So, for example, teachers can demonstrate how they have generated useful mnemonic devices for remembering words in the students' native language or strategies that they have used to read difficult texts in that language with a high level of comprehension. If they, too, are highly advanced learners of the language that they are teaching to their students, then there is an opportunity to suggest strategies that could be directly applied by the students if they so wish. The teachers then need to externalize their thinking processes in such a way that the students see how the strategy works.

Let us say that the learners are all English-speaking learners of Japanese and the teacher is a native speaker of English as well. The teacher could share his or her own experiences in using mnemonics. The following are two of my own examples from recent accelerated study of Japanese, and, if I were the teacher, I could share them:

1. I needed to remember the Japanese word for 'vending machine,' *jidohanbaiki*. My first reaction was that it was too long to simply remember by rote and I had not had enough exposure to the word to simply acquire it without effort. So I decided to construct a phrase that would include enough English words to help me to retrieve the Japanese word. After a bit of deliberation, I came up with the thought of using **judo** to get my money back from the vending machine, and if that did not work then using my **hand** or **by** means of a **key**. I realized that 'judo' and *jido~* were not identical in sound, but it was the closest I could get and would thus call for some adjustment at the moment of retrieval of the word. The fact that it was a rather absurd

image seemed to help me to remember it. I had never tried to use a key to unjam a vending machine, but I had used my hand a few times. In fact, this keyword phrase worked both in helping me to identify the meaning of *jidohanbaiki* when I encountered it orally or in writing, and also in production when I had to say or write it, which I needed to do on several occasions.

2. I sometimes look to other languages that I know when I cannot think of a mnemonic device for remembering a word in a language, such as Japanese, which has numerous sound combinations that are not like English. I learned *shukudai* 'homework' by means of a Hebrew mnemonic keyword phrase using *shuk* 'market' and *dai* 'enough.' I thought of being assigned enough (= so much) homework that I did not have time to go to the market.

4.3.6   Teachers as researchers

Finally, teachers can assume the role of *researchers* regarding all the other roles. For example, they can check to make sure that the diagnoses of learners' needs are on track and that the coordination of the learning process is functioning smoothly – perhaps by keeping records as to learning strategy preferences, choice of activities, and outcomes (if this is feasible in the given situation). With respect to the roles of learner trainer and coach, teachers can analyze the learning along with the learners, pointing up the changes. Teachers can also research their own language learning, to determine where they are experiencing success and failure, and why.

4.3.7   Concluding remarks about the roles for teachers in strategies-based instruction

The message to teachers in this section is that the shift in the teachers' set of roles in no way diminishes the need for the teacher. The teachers in these programs are in no way out of work. It is true, however, that the weight on their shoulders is lightened. They are no longer responsible for any and all language learning that goes on in the classroom. This responsibility is shared more with the learners. The teachers are now busy in new ways, given this shift to the role of supporting the learner in more effective learning from the role of 'fountain of knowledge.' It now remains for language teaching programs around the world to pay more heed to the contributions that strategies-based instruction has made to language learning in those sites that have been willing to endorse it in one or another form. It is also important for researchers to look at the ways in which these roles work most effectively.

4.4 General conclusions

This chapter has focused on a technology that is gaining in refinement and fine-tuning, namely, that of enhancing language learners' awareness of how they learn language(s) and how they can learn more effectively. In its most ambitious form, this new technology is intrusive – it moves right into classrooms and makes its appearance either within or between activities aimed at the learning and use of language. It introduces some meta-talk about language learning and using processes. It challenges learners to be more systematic in their use of strategies. It challenges teachers to embrace new roles that ultimately may make their job of teaching more satisfying and productive. The chapter has included a number of suggestions for how to conduct strategy training, as well as suggestions for roles that the classroom teacher may wish to assume in facilitating this effort.

There are obviously educational policy and planning consequences at the program and the classroom levels if strategies-based instruction is adopted. Teachers will need to be trained first and foremost. Yet the content of the instructional program need not be altered. The current program simply receives this SBI overlay, and ideally it will function more effectively as a result. Undoubtedly, the introduction of SBI in the classroom will be time-consuming but then ideally the learners will move through the curriculum more expediently, so this should make up for the outlay of time in training them. How a given SBI program is set up will depend to a great extent on the local context. After an initial effort, SBI is then woven into the fabric of the instructional program.

The next chapter provides an example of an experimental study conducted to determine the effects of strategies-based instruction on the learners' speaking ability. While it is important to recommend innovations for improving language learning and language use, it is also necessary to maintain a research program aimed at validating whatever innovations are being recommended. This research project constitutes one such effort.

4.5 Discussion questions and activities

1. An administrator director of your college program has heard about strategy training and would like to do something to support learners beyond simply having teachers teach at them with the hope that learning will go on. She comes up with a description of the three approaches to strategy training (appearing in section 4.2.2 of the chapter) and asks you to prepare a brief presentation to the foreign language instructional team in which you compare the three approaches,

indicating their commonalities, their differences, and expressing an opinion as to what combination of ingredients you think would make for a beneficial learner training program at your institution.

2. You are the supervisor of the foreign language teaching unit at your high school and are now convinced that strategies-based instruction would make sense in your foreign language classes. The problem is that there just is not very much time for teacher training – perhaps two days at best. With this constraint in mind, read through the suggestions for design of SBI seminars for language teachers (4.2.5) and select those features that you think are crucial. Prepare a list of features for presentation to your staff, along with a rationale for each.

3. A seven-step approach to designing strategy training is presented (4.2.6). Your boss at the high-school foreign language unit requested suggestions from you as to how to design an SBI program. Using as your context for SBI a language program you have taught or studied in, go through the section as if you were actually designing the program. Determine the questions that you already have answers for, and for those that you do not, choose a method that you would use to gather the data. If possible, do this exercise with a partner and take turns with your partner going through the series of questions.

4. Several of your colleagues at work have voiced a number of concerns with regard to the SBI program that you are advocating. While some of them are ardent traditionalists, you think that the time has come to move on. They have three main concerns:

   (a) that they have so little time to do all the teaching they need to do that having to worry about training their students in how to learn would be almost out of the question;

   (b) that shifting the responsibility for learning onto the students may actually constitute an abrogation of their assigned role as teacher;

   (c) that their students will be embarrassed by all the attention focused on them and will consider it a waste of time as well.

Prepare a brief response that relates to each of these concerns.

Notes

1. This section is revised and modified version of Weaver and Cohen (1994). Susan Weaver is currently a doctoral student in applied linguistics at the University of Minnesota.

2. There are those who consider the term *training* as inappropriate for humans, and would prefer terms such as *development*. In this volume, the term *training* is used because it seems to encompass better than any other term the notions of educating, instructing,

and tutoring in an integrated fashion. What is implied is separate training or instruction which is superimposed over the regular language instruction. It is a form of meta-instruction.

3. See, for example, Hosenfeld (1977), Rubin (1981), O'Malley, Chamot, Stewner-Manzanares, Russo and Küpper (1985), Abraham and Vann (1987), Chamot *et al.* (1987), Bacon and Finnemann (1990), Ehrman and Oxford (1990), and Oxford (1996b).

4. For reviews of research literature dealing with the description, identification, and classification of strategies for foreign languages, see Dansereau (1985), Oxford and Cohen (1992), Oxford (1993a), McDonough (1995), Gu and Johnson (1996), and Oxford (1996b).

5. See Oxford *et al.* (1990) and Oxford (1990) for more on this and on other learner awareness training interventions.

6. Nyikos trained 47 junior and senior high school and community college teachers of Spanish, French, German, and ESL (with a mean of 11 years of experience) in strategies-based instruction and studied the effect of the training on their teaching. She analyzed their resulting lesson plans for: (1) the incorporation of learning strategy types, (2) a demonstration of how strategies were incorporated, and (3) the explicitness of strategy instruction. She found that about one-third of the teachers, whom she termed the *assimilators*, were able to make the conceptual shift to incorporate learning strategy instruction into their classroom teaching, and were found to model strategies about three times per task. Another third, the *middle-grounders*, almost made the shift, but only implicitly – rather than explicitly – embedded strategies into tasks. The final third, the *resisters*, rarely involved students in any discussion or interactive activities at all.

7. For more information about the videodisc, contact Joan Rubin, 2011 Hermitage Avenue, Wheaton, MD 20902 (jrubin@pen.k12.va.us).

8. For a full description of this program, see Weaver and Cohen's (1997) *Strategies-based instruction: a teacher-training manual.* Copies of the manual can be obtained from the University of Minnesota Bookstore. For details, contact: Center for Advanced Research on Language Acquisition (CARLA), Minneapolis, MN, 55414 (carla@maroon.tc.umn.edu).

9. See Oxford and Burry-Stock (1995) and Oxford (1996a) for a report on the validity and reliability of the *SILL.* See 5.3.2 (under 'Data analysis procedures') and 5.4.2 for concerns raised about the *SILL.*

10. See Larsen-Freeman and Long (1991) and Ellis (1994) for discussions of the relationships among levels and types of motivation, strategy use, and language learning.

11. The class as a whole lists what needs to be accomplished in a given task and then learners are divided into focus groups to arrive at suggested strategies for dealing with the task at hand.

12. This could be done through whole-class sessions, in small groups, in pairs, or even individually. For example, learners could inform the class as a whole through retrospection as to how they accomplished a given task. Small groups of students or students in pairs could share with each other the strategies that they use to deal with a difficult reading passage. In addition, the students could, for example, perform a writing task and keep an introspective and retrospective log as they are writing.

13. Contact carla@maroon.tc.umn.edu for more information.

14. This is a revised version of pp. 184–9 from Cohen (1992).

15. Books are now appearing which focus on the teaching of strategies for vocabulary learning. One recent one by Tréville and Duquette (1996), for example, is directed at teachers of French as a foreign language. It starts with a quiz where the reader is to choose those statements that most closely represent his or her beliefs about vocabulary and ends with another quiz to see how the book has influenced the reader's views. What distinguishes it from numerous other vocabulary texts for teachers is its focus on learner strategies in vocabulary learning and the role of the teacher as a support to the learners in this endeavor.

16. The language that the teacher uses in the classroom to describe these strategies can be more or less technical, depending on the level of the students. So, for example, the teacher may refer to *metacognitive strategies* with one group of learners, while with another a less technical phrase is used, such as 'strategies for supervising strategy use.'
17. Described in Chapter 3 for the purposes of data collection, *dialog journals* also play a role in instruction. Students do their writing assignments on, say, the right-hand page in their notebooks or take reading notes on the right-hand page, and then write down queries about their writing or reading tasks in the target language on the left-hand page. The teachers collect these journals from time to time and respond to the students' queries. Teachers respond to the content of the messages but do not correct them, thus allowing the learners a 'safe space' to express themselves freely without fear of having the form of their message criticized.

5 The impact of strategies-based instruction on speaking a foreign language

Andrew D. Cohen, Susan J. Weaver, and Tao-Yuan Li[1]

5.1 Introduction

This chapter considers the impact of strategies-based instruction on speaking a foreign language, briefly reviews literature relating to this issue, and then focuses on a study conducted at the University of Minnesota. This study set out to examine the contribution that formal strategies-based instruction might offer learners in university-level foreign language classrooms, with a particular focus on speaking.

In the study, 55 intermediate foreign language learners at the University of Minnesota were either participants in a strategies-based instructional treatment or were comparison students receiving the regular ten-week language course. Both groups filled out a pre-treatment questionnaire and then performed a series of three speaking tasks on a pre–post basis, along with filling out the *SILL* and the strategy checklists after performing each of the three tasks. Twenty-one of the experimental and comparison group students also provided verbal report data while they filled out the post-test strategy checklists – indicating their rationale for their responses to certain items, as well as their reactions to the instrument itself. Since the checklists for strategies used before, during, and after each speaking task contained strategies that were, at least to some extent, designed specifically for the given task, the intention was to make a fine-tuned link between strategies and their use on specific language tasks. Such a link had been missing from previous research which reported strategy use in broad terms but not necessarily linked to specific tasks. The data analysis looked for links between an increase in the use of certain strategies included on the strategy checklists and an improvement in rated task performance on a series of scales.

5.2   Review of the literature

5.2.1   Mixed reactions to the language strategies movement in the literature

The field of strategies training has received mixed reactions from professionals in the field, primarily because until recently there were few empirical studies that could be drawn on to demonstrate that, under certain conditions, such training had irrefutable benefits.

The following are two sets of criticism. The first was leveled at training in communication strategies by Kellerman (1991), who maintained that learners need not be taught compensation strategies for dealing with gaps in vocabulary knowledge because they already have these strategies in dealing with gaps in first language vocabulary. Kellerman would explain an apparent inability to use an L2 strategy effectively as resulting from a lack of L2 language proficiency or from the inhibitory atmosphere in the classroom, rather than resulting from a lack of control over the strategy.

The second, more elaborate critique was rendered by Rees-Miller (1993). She made a strong case for how learner training had not been adequately assessed empirically. The studies that Rees-Miller cited lent some support to the conclusion that such training was not so effective. Her challenge to researchers was that they find evidence that using a strategy is better than not using it, and that they determine the factors that make learner training conducive to success. She suggested that the stage the learners are at in the learning process, their language proficiency at that stage, the educational background that they have, their beliefs about language learning and the beliefs of their teachers, their varying cognitive styles, and any cultural differences that exist across learners all complicate the implementation of learner training. She posited that these and other factors may result in differential success according to who the learners are. She also voiced concern about the duration of the effects if there were any. She recommended longitudinal research to determine the relative effects of these variables. Her conclusion was that the teachers need to proceed with caution in the use of strategy training in the classroom until more research was conducted.

In a response to these criticisms, Chamot and Rubin (1994) started by pointing out that it is not a particular strategy that leads to improved performance, but rather the effective management of a repertoire of strategies. They cited studies which supported the claim that strategy use does, in fact, correlate with improved performance. They went on to emphasize that making strategy information teachable means:

(1) discovering and discussing strategies that students already use for specific learning tasks;

(2) presenting new strategies by explicitly naming and describing them;
(3) modeling the strategies;
(4) explaining why and when the strategies can be used; and
(5) providing extensive practice.

They also highlighted factors which have been found to influence the effectiveness of learner training: the length of training, the degree of integration of the training into the regular curriculum and ongoing classroom activities, and the development of expertise among teachers in how to conduct learning strategies instruction.

In a book which extensively reviewed the role of strategies in foreign language learning, McDonough (1995) indicated his willingness to use common sense in the face of 'science', which for example, criticizes verbal reports as unreliable. He reviewed strategies for speaking (strategy use in classrooms, compensatory strategies, strategies in the realization of speech acts), strategies for receiving and understanding language, and strategies involved in the writing process. He divided the research on language learning strategies into *descriptive studies* (McDonough, 1995: 81–4) and *interventionist studies* (96–101). He then further divided the interventionist studies into **general** ones aimed at teaching strategies for overcoming a number of learning problems encountered in several aspects of language learning and **specific** ones attempting to teach particular strategies for, say, reading comprehension or vocabulary learning. As empirical evidence for general interventionist studies, McDonough cited only a study by Wenden (1987b) and then several studies by O'Malley and Chamot and colleagues (described in O'Malley and Chamot, 1990). He found the results to be mixed. In one study, for example, O'Malley and Chamot (1990) compared the improvement on certain language tasks for three groups of learners, and related the learners' performance to the strategy training they had received. On the speaking task, the group given explicit training in metacognitive, cognitive, and social–affective strategies improved significantly more than the control group. In studies of this kind where learners' report of strategy use is not linked to performance on specific proficiency tasks, it is not possible to measure the extent to which the explicit strategy training contributed to gains in performance.

With regard to **specific** interventionist studies, he cited the second language reader training study by Hosenfeld (1984), the Carrell *et al.* 1989 study of metacognitive strategies in reading, and Kern's (1989) strategy training in learning reading vocabulary in context. His general conclusion was that improvements in language proficiency caused by strategy training were relatively weak and only showed up on certain kinds of measures.

In another critical review of empirical research on language learning strategies in the field of SLA, Gu (1996) also pointed out that the literature on the effectiveness of strategy training had not produced definitive results with regard to the relationship between strategy use and actual language performance. He noted the problem of referring only to the **frequency of use** of strategies, without noting the appropriateness of using those strategies in the given contexts. He referred to empirical work in the field as 'largely fragmentary, unsystematic, as well as narrow in scope' (Gu, 1996: 22). He suggested that it was still too early to be making pronouncements about 'what every teacher should know' before the strategy research had been adequately linked to the performance of specific tasks, ideally through longitudinal studies. Finally, Gu made a request that future research document the ways in which learners' strategy inventories have been broadened by learner training.

5.2.2   More recent interventionist strategy research

Not only have more interventionist studies now appeared in the literature since those cited in the McDonough (1995), but also they have tended to be more finely-tuned than the preceding ones. Here we will briefly review two that have dealt with training in listening comprehension and three dealing with training in speaking. The following section (5.2.3) will look in depth at a fourth interventionist study dealing with speaking, the one conducted at the University of Minnesota.

One interventionist study involving listening strategies included this component as part of a listening diary homework program for Japanese junior college students of oral English (Fujiwara, 1990). The strategies were taken from the list developed by Chamot (1987). Of the 45 students in the two second-year oral English classes that participated in the listening diary program, 80 per cent felt that their listening had improved, and of those 36, 16 felt that the listening diary homework was the most helpful component. Through the diary project, students reported that they:

(1) learned new listening strategies and adopted for their own continued use those that they found most helpful;
(2) became aware of what and how to learn;
(3) improved their ability to evaluate their strengths and weaknesses as listeners in the foreign language;
(4) began to set learning goals for themselves; and
(5) developed a (more) positive attitude toward learning through listening.

The second study was an experiment involving 24 college students of intermediate-level (third-year) Russian in the experimental group and 12 in the control group (Thompson and Rubin, 1996). The experimental group was given 15 hours of strategy training in listening comprehension, using 45 videotaped segments. The control group also received the same videotaped stimuli but their strategy training just focused on speaking and writing, not on listening. The findings showed a slight significant difference in favor of the experimental group on a test of video comprehension which was developed by the researchers and which included items representing four different types of TV genres – simulated authentic material, authentic movies, interviews, and news reports. In the absence of more significant findings, the researchers concluded that the treatment was not decisive or long enough.

With regard to interventionist studies involving speaking strategies, one such study was conducted with a sample of 122 first-year and fourth-year students in the Department of English at an Egyptian university, half receiving the treatment and half in the control group (Dadour and Robbins, 1996). The treatment consisted of 15 weekly three-hour sessions which provided the learners with instruction on using strategies to improve their speaking skills. Each session had a warm-up, teachers' presentation and explanation with examples of new strategies, activities for practicing the new strategies and for discussing them, homework assignments for group work, and students' presentations and discussions of the homework. The course gave direct instruction in the speaking skills that the students needed to master and the learning strategies that they were required to practice in order to improve their skills, and provided communication activities as well. The course stressed the idea of giving students more responsibility for their own learning.

Four instruments were used to collect data: an EFL teacher's speaking skills inventory developed for the study, the *CLEAR Oral Proficiency Exam*, the *SILL*, and the *Style Analysis Survey* (see 2.3.5). Covariate analysis found the experimental group students at both the first- and fourth-year levels to outperform the control group in speaking. Specific differences were found in fluency, vocabulary, and grammar, but not in pronunciation. The experimental group was also found to use more strategies of all kinds (memory, cognitive, compensatory, metacognitive, affective, and social) than the control group. The conclusion was that a well-structured strategy instruction course that allowed creativity on the part of both teachers and students could have a positive effect on oral communication and on the use of strategies of all kinds.

A second speaking study was conducted with 60 undergraduates in a compulsory English for Arts Students (EAS) course (Nunan, 1996). There was low motivation to learn English because the students' focus was on Putonghua, which was to be the official language once the Territory went back to China. Strategy training was deemed valuable because there was limited time to study English. Subjects were assigned to four classes, two experimental and two control groups. The experimental groups received key learning and study skills strategies incorporated into their language teaching program. All subjects were administered a pre-course questionnaire to measure their motivation, their knowledge of 15 key strategies, their use of these strategies, and their perception of the value of the strategies. During the course, subgroups of students participated in focused interviews regarding their perceptions and feelings about studying English and especially about this EAS course. Then the motivation and strategy questionnaires were re-administered on a post-test basis.

The study found that motivation improved over the duration of the semester, for significantly more experimental group than control group students (56 per cent versus 26 per cent). Knowledge of strategies was also found to improve for the experimental group. In addition, the experimental group increased in perceived utility of strategies. Yet reported frequency of deployment of these 15 key strategies was low and the difference between the experimental and the control groups was minimal. There were areas in which the experimental group reported using strategies more than the control group: selective listening (because of changed listening demands – different dialects of English), predicting, confirming, cooperating, applying, and classifying. Nunan was surprised that the experimental group was not ahead in reflecting, but he speculated that differences would only show up over time. Finally, students' reported strategy preferences shifted from memorizing, summarizing, and co-operating at the beginning of the semester to inductive learning and selective listening by the end (their first at the university). The conclusion was drawn that training had a significant effect on student motivation. Based on results on a strategy-by-strategy basis, it was concluded that there was some differential impact of training on certain strategies.

While the Nunan study had an elegance of design and neatness in its 15 selected strategies, the study did not provide solid evidence for two types of important connections: (1) a link between statements about strategy 'deployment' (as the study referred to 'strategy use') and some actual specific tasks, nor (2) a link between reported strategy use and performance as judged by outside raters. With regard to the first, it would mean using both the generalized self-report questionnaires of strategy use preferences, as Nunan did on a pre- and post-test basis, as well as lists of strategies linked to specific tasks that the learners performed on a pre- and post-test basis.

In a third interventionist study of speaking, this time just looking at communication strategies, an experimental group of Hungarian high-school students was trained on three communication strategies: *topic avoid-ance* and *replacement, circumlocution,* and using *fillers* and *hesitation devices* (Dörnyei, 1995). For six weeks, they received three lessons (20–40 min-utes each) per week, embedded in their regular English instruction. The teachers modeled the strategies, had learners practice them in their native language, Hungarian, and then gave the students time to prepare for the use of these three strategies in the foreign language, English. One control group received nothing and the other received role play, games, and discussion in pairs and groups (overall N=109). There was a written and an oral pre-test, and an oral post-test. The oral test consisted of the following: topic description (talk about the topic for 3 minutes), cartoon description (cartoon strip of 3–4 pictures), definition formulation (five Hungarian concepts to describe or define in English – including 'child care benefit,' 'school leaving certificate,' and 'specialization course').

Post-testing showed improvement in measures related to both quality and quantity of strategy use; there was improvement in the quality of circumlocutions and in the frequency of fillers and circumlocutions. The effectiveness of the training was found to be unrelated to the learners' competence, which indicated to the investigator that such training could come early on, when learners are still at the beginning levels. In addition, attitudes towards such training were found to be positive. The researcher concluded that it does pay to do direct teaching of communication strat-egies because 'they provide the learners with a sense of security in the foreign language by allowing them room to maneuver in times of diffi-culty. Rather than giving up their message, learners may decide to try and remain in the conversation and achieve their communicative goal' (Dörnyei, 1995: 80). These findings would seem to provide a response to Kellerman's (1991) assertion that learners need not be taught L2 compensation strat-egies because they already have them in their L1. The response is that perhaps some or many of the L1 strategies will eventually transfer on their own, but explicit training may hasten the process along, as well as teaching some communicative behavior that is not learned automatically.

While the Dörnyei study was consistent with our interests in providing instruction in the use of strategies for speaking in a foreign language, it was limited to only three communication strategies. What remained to be done, therefore, was not only to broaden the strategy base to a more normal range of strategies for before, during, and after performing a task, but also to somehow link learners' report of specific strategy use to the rating of their language proficiency on tasks which would call for those specific strategies. The focus of the University of Minnesota study, then, was to explore the full range of possible strategies across skills, with an emphasis on the skill of speaking. Thus, we not only looked at communication and performance (i.e. language use) strategies, but we also emphasized a broad range of learning strategies that would contribute to students' efforts at speaking a foreign language. It was with this broad intention in mind that the study was designed, within the framework of the Second Language Learning Strategies Project of the National Language Resource Center at the University of Minnesota.[2]

5.2.3   The focus of Minnesota's SBI experiment

As detailed in 4.2 above, there are numerous means of providing strategy instruction for learners, such as through general study-skills courses, awareness training by means of lectures and strategy workshops, peer tutoring, the insertion of strategies into language textbooks, videotaped mini-courses, and the integration of strategies directly into the foreign language classroom through strategies-based instruction (see 4.2.3). Since past experience at the University of Minnesota had indicated that various short-term interventions (e.g. periodic workshops for students on strategies for reading, learning vocabulary, speaking, and writing) had only short-term effects at best, it was determined that a more effective program would most likely be one of providing learners with a broad range of strategies as a regular feature of classroom instruction – that is, one that began with intensive teacher development and then relied on the teachers to provide strategies-based instruction (SBI) for their students in the foreign language classroom.

As noted in 4.2.3 above, SBI is a learner-centered approach to teaching that has two major components: (1) students are explicitly taught how, when, and why strategies can be used to facilitate language learning and language use tasks, and (2) strategies are integrated into everyday class materials, and may be explicitly or implicitly embedded into the language tasks. This study, then, set out to examine the contribution that SBI might offer learners in university-level foreign language classrooms, with a particular focus on speaking. The emphasis was on speaking because this area had received limited attention in the research literature on strategy interventionist studies (as noted above), although it is in many cases the most critical language skill of all. The study asked the following three research questions:

1. How does explicit instruction in language learning and language use strategies affect students' speaking proficiency?
2. What is the relationship between reported frequency of strategy use and ratings of task performance on speaking tasks?
3. How do students characterize their reasons for reported strategy use while performing speaking tasks?

5.3   Research design

5.3.1   Sample

The sample consisted of 55 students enrolled in intermediate-level foreign language classes (of their own choosing – not randomly assigned) at the University of Minnesota. Thirty-two students comprised the experimental group and received strategies-based speaking instruction (7 in their sixth academic quarter or 10-week class of French, to be referred to as 'advanced intermediate French,' 11 in their fourth quarter, or 'intermediate French,' and 14 in their fourth quarter of Norwegian, referred to as 'intermediate Norwegian'). Twenty-three students served as a comparison group[3] (7 in advanced intermediate French, 11 in intermediate French, and 5 in intermediate Norwegian). Twenty-one students out of the larger group of 55 were selected on a volunteer basis from the six classrooms to provide additional data in the form of verbal report protocols regarding their strategy use and language learning (see below). These students represented three different levels of speaking ability in their respective classes, as determined by their instructors (8 from advanced intermediate French, 7 from intermediate French, and 6 from intermediate Norwegian).

A background questionnaire was designed to determine how similar the experimental and comparison groups were in the following areas: previous language study, reasons for studying the target language, contact with native speakers (how, where, and why they had had contact), visits to the target culture (e.g. for work or for vacation), current work schedule (part- or full-time), grades in previous courses in the target language, and college grade point average (cumulative and in the major field). Analysis of mean differences between the two groups using t-tests found that the two groups did not differ significantly on any of the background characteristics. None of the experimental or comparison groups had had SBI before.

Six instructors participated in the study as well. The instructor for the advanced intermediate French experimental class had lived in France for six years, had a BS in Education, and was working on a PhD in the College of Education. The instructor for the intermediate French experimental class was a native speaker of French, who was also working on a PhD in the College of Education. The instructor of the advanced intermediate French comparison group had a PhD in French literature from the University of Minnesota, and the instructor of the intermediate French comparison group had lived in France for two years, and was working on a PhD in French medieval studies. The experimental group instructor of Norwegian had lived in Norway for over two years and was studying in a PhD program in applied linguistics at the university. The instructor of the Norwegian comparison group was raised in the US as a bilingual speaker of Norwegian and English, and was working on a PhD in Scandinavian literature.

The three experimental teachers had participated in a 30-hour course designed specifically for providing strategies-based instruction in university-level foreign language classrooms. The goal of this course (entitled 'Learner Training in Foreign Language Learning Strategies') was to prepare a larger group of 14 foreign language instructors (representing a total of nine foreign languages) to provide strategies-based instruction for their students. The course consisted of lectures, readings, small-group and paired activities, and peer micro-teaching sessions. The teachers received practical training in techniques to raise awareness of individual differences and learning style preferences, to introduce systematic strategy use in the classroom, to integrate strategies-based activities into daily lesson plans, and to facilitate discussions of strategy effectiveness.

Whereas the three instructors of the comparison group students had not received any special training in how to conduct strategies-based instruction, the instructor of the intermediate French comparison group indicated working with his students on strategies such as circumlocution, and the Norwegian teacher reported encouraging her students to use the strategy of preparing flash cards to assist in their learning of vocabulary. In fact, all six teachers were committed to a communicative approach to language teaching, and all were aware of the importance of supporting learners in the language classroom.[4]

5.3.2   Instrumentation and data collection procedures

TREATMENT

Both the experimental and the comparison groups followed the syllabi of their respective language departments (French and Norwegian). The students in the experimental group not only followed the syllabus, but received instruction in a strategies-based format throughout the 10-week class. Rather than being presented in a separate lesson, the strategies were incorporated into the regular classroom learning activities. At times, the focus on strategies was explicit in that the instructors provided strategy training, and at other times the strategies were implicitly embedded into the classroom activities. The learners received instruction in a broad range of foreign language learning and foreign language use strategies, but the teachers emphasized those strategies that could be applied to the skill of speaking. The teachers and students together created a list of strategies useful for the preparation, self-monitoring, and self-evaluation of students' speaking task performance (see Appendix 5 at the end of this chapter).

The investigators also collected retrospective accounts from the Experimental teachers as to the structure and content of the treatment classes. Detailed individual and group interview sessions with the three teachers provided valuable insights used in interpreting the correlations between speaking task performance and strategy use.

INSTRUMENTS

The *Strategy Inventory for Language Learning (SILL)*

During the first week of class, all subjects completed the 80-item *Strategy Inventory for Language Learning (SILL)* (Oxford, 1990). This version of the *SILL* (for English speakers learning a new language) represents a set of strategies for language learning across skills. Some of these strategies are more general in nature (e.g. 'I look for similarities and contrasts between the new language and my own') while others are more specific (e.g. 'I try to notice my language errors and find out the reasons for them'). Some strategies on the list have direct relevance to the skill of speaking (e.g. 'I direct the conversation to a topic for which I know the words'), while others do not (e.g. 'I read without looking up every unfamiliar word'). These strategies are not linked to any specific tasks, but rather represent strategies that the learner could use throughout the language learning process. The *SILL* was re-administered to all of the subjects at the end of the term. According to Lybeck's (1996) report, the period between pre- and post-testing was seven weeks. This was because the pre-test was given at the end of the second week (out of ten) and the post-test was given in the ninth week.

Speaking task battery

A Speaking Task Battery was designed and piloted, and consisted of a series of three speaking tasks. All subjects from the experimental and comparison groups were asked to complete the same three tasks on a pre- and post-test basis to determine whether there were gains in speaking ability over the ten-weeks. The prompts were written. The data were collected in a language laboratory in a semi-direct fashion, with the subjects audiotaping their responses to the tasks at their individual consoles, and were collected during non-classroom hours due to constraints on class time. For each of the tasks, students were allowed time to prepare what they would say before they began their individual recordings. Forty-five minutes were allotted for all three tasks, or about 15 minutes per task. The respondents were told in their written instructions that they should 'take a few minutes to prepare for each task.' The following are descriptions of the three speaking tasks in the battery:

1. *Self-description*: This task required students to make use of previously studied material. In this task, the students were prompted by a hypothetical situation where they were asked to pick someone up at the airport (a native speaker of French/Norwegian who did not speak English). The students were asked to describe themselves in the target language in order for the visitor to recognize them. Because this topic was based on content the students had already covered in their classes and it simulated an authentic language exchange, we considered the task to be the most naturalistic. The respondents were not given any vocabulary to assist them on this task – in order to stimulate them to use compensatory strategies when they were unable to produce the necessary vocabulary. This task was the first administered, to help put the students at ease.

2. *Story retelling*: This task called upon the students to learn new material. The students were given a short reading passage (approximately 300 words) adapted from French/Norwegian folklore with some unfamiliar words or phrases. A glossary of these unfamiliar words and phrases was provided on the task sheet in order to ensure that it was more a learning and speaking task than one of reading comprehension. After reading the text, the students were asked to summarize the story orally, referring back as little as possible to the written text.

3. *City description*: This task called for the use of both previously learned and new vocabulary in describing a favorite city. The learners were provided with a list of 30 target language words/phrases and their English equivalents relevant for describing a city in order to stimulate their production. They were asked to give a brief description of their favorite city and to give the reason why they had chosen to describe it. The list of words was provided for this task because it was meant to simulate classroom tasks where language is provided, unlike in the self-description task, which was meant to tap their knowledge base.

The three speaking tasks were expected to elicit a range of learning strategies, including grammar and vocabulary retrieval strategies. For example, some students were more likely to prepare their responses and even write words and phrases down, a strategy that is possible with a semi-direct test such as the one in this study. Across all tasks, it was assumed that if the students did not have the linguistic ability to easily complete a particular task, they might be expected to employ a range of language use strategies.

Strategy checklists

Immediately following the completion of each of the three tasks, the students were asked to complete the corresponding strategy checklists, which varied according to the nature of the particular task. These checklists were designed to elicit data on self-reported frequency of strategy use at three points in time: before the students began the speaking task, during the task itself, and after the completion of the task (including projected strategy use beyond the testing context). The checklists were intended to capture the three-stage process involved in strategy use: (1) preparation before using the language skill, (2) self-monitoring during the use of the skill, and (3) self-reflection afterwards. The subjects were asked to indicate on a five-point scale the extent to which they used each of the strategies on the checklists. Examples of these strategies included: rehearsal, note-taking, prediction of potential difficulties, self-encouragement ('positive self-talk'), word coinage or substitution, attention to grammatical forms, reflection on task performance, and plans for future learning. Specific to the individual tasks were the strategies of visualization, accessing known material, inferencing, memorization or repetition for remembering words/phrases, simplification, as well as others. The strategies on the checklists reflected both those found in the language strategies' literature, as well as those particular to the three tasks in this battery.

The post-test version of the checklists also included four additional questions for self-reflection. Three of these questions dealt with the students' experiences as language learners in completing the three tasks: the extent to which the tasks had elicited their knowledge about the foreign language, whether the tasks had allowed them to demonstrate this knowledge, and how aware they were of their learning patterns and strategy use. The purpose of the fourth question was to determine whether they had become more independent language learners as a result of participating in the ten-week language course.

Since the checklists for strategies used before, during, and after each speaking task contained strategies that were, at least to some extent, designed specifically for the given task, the intention was to make a fine-tuned link between strategies and their use on specific language tasks. As noted above, such a link had been missing from previous research which reported strategy use in broad terms but not necessarily linked to specific tasks.

Verbal report protocols

The post-test data collection also included an extra feature for the subsample of the 21 students from both the experimental and comparison groups (representing high, medium, and low proficiency in speaking, as determined through teacher ratings). These subjects were asked to give their reasons for the frequency-of-use ratings that they had assigned to each strategy on the checklists by providing a verbal report while completing them. This involved removing the audiotape that they had used for the speaking tasks and inserting a different audiotape to record their thoughts while they were filling out each of the three checklists. The subjects were given a demonstration of how to provide verbal report data while performing the checklist tasks. This consisted of a recorded sample of a respondent performing verbal report as she completed the checklists, as well as an opportunity for the subjects to ask questions about the verbal report procedure.

DATA ANALYSIS PROCEDURES

A native speaker and near-native speaker of Norwegian rated the student tapes in Norwegian and two near-native speakers of French rated the tapes in French. The raters did not know whether the responses to the three tasks which comprised each taped sample were from the experimental or comparison groups, nor whether they were from pre- or post-testing.

The interrater reliability coefficients for the two raters of the French speaking tasks and for the two raters of the Norwegian tasks were highly significant (p < .001) using Kendall's tau[5] (r=.63 on the French pre-test and .67 on the post-test; r=.59 on the Norwegian pre-test and .62 on the post-test). Given the similarity of ratings by the two pairs of raters, the average of each set of raters was used as the respondent's score.

The self-description and the city description tasks were rated according to a set of five-point, multi-trait scales especially designed to assess three aspects of the spoken language that the students produced:

(1) demonstrated *self-confidence* in delivery – namely, smoothness and uninterruptedness of speech flow, wherein pauses are clearly in order to find appropriate material rather than signaling a loss for words;

(2) acceptability of *grammar* – namely, subject-verb agreement for person, number, and tense; correct use of negation and articles; and

(3) control over *vocabulary* – namely, variety in word choice, contextual appropriateness, and degree of fine-tuning.

The story retelling task was rated on two scales:

(1) identification of key story *elements* – namely, the 12 elements that native speakers[6] had deemed essential in the Norwegian fable and the eight in the French fable; and

(2) the appropriate *ordering* of these elements (rated on a five-point scale) – namely, the extent to which the order of the identified elements corresponded to the sequence given by native speakers.

Data obtained from the pre- and post-test speaking task battery were used to determine students' improvement in speaking proficiency. The statistical method used for analyzing the data was analysis of covariance using SPSS. Post-test means were compared, adjusting for initial differences on the pre-test means. Before adjusting the post-test scores of the experimental and comparison groups on the basis of the pre-test scores on the three speaking tasks, it was determined that the data met the *homogeneity of slope* requirements for analysis of covariance. That is, the relationship between pre- and post-test scores was found to be similar for both groups.

Reliability was calculated for the instrument as a whole and for the six subscales on the basis of an underlying assumption associated with the *SILL*: more reported use of all of the strategies included in the questionnaire is inherently more beneficial for language learning than less reported use of them. The overall Cronbach alpha reliability for the 80-item questionnaire given as a pre-measure was .94 and .99 on the post-measure. Whereas the reliability was high for three of the subscales (*using mental processes*, n of items=25: .91 pre, .93 post; *organizing and evaluating learning*, n=16: .88 pre, .85 post; *learning with others*, n=9: .87 pre, .84 post), it was lower for a fourth subscale (*remembering more effectively*, n=15: .70 pre, .74 post) and appreciably lower for the remaining two (*compensating for missing knowledge*, n=8: .51 pre, −.14 post; *managing emotions*, n=7: .48 pre, .63 post).

Patterns of strategy use specific to each task were determined through the students' self-ratings of the frequency of use of different strategies, as reported on the strategy checklists following each task. Pre–post gains on the speaking tasks were analyzed in relation to pre–post gains in the reported use of strategies for the given tasks. In other words, the effects of increased frequency of use of a given strategy were calculated by correlating the gains in performance on task subscales (tasks 1 and 3: self-confidence, grammar, vocabulary; task 2: story elements and organization) with an increase in the reported use of the strategy. The analysis involved correlating the gain scores for performance on task subscales with the gain scores for all of the items on the strategy checklists, using the Pearson correlation statistic. A similar analysis was run correlating pre–post gains on the three speaking tasks with pre–post gain scores for the *SILL*.

As indicated above, the verbal report protocols from the subsample of 21 learners also provided information regarding the reasons why students chose a certain frequency rating for each strategy on the checklists. The verbal report data were analyzed separately from the speaking task data, and were categorized into two sets: insights about strategy use and feedback on the strategy checklists. This verbal report feedback on the checklists served as a qualitative means for determining whether the checklists were reliable and valid, and the results are reported in 5.4 below, under 'Feedback on the strategy checklists.'

5.4   Findings

5.4.1   Research question 1: the effects of strategies-based instruction on speaking proficiency

In response to our first research question, regarding the effects of strategies-based instruction on speaking proficiency, the results of analysis of covariance showed that the experimental group outperformed the comparison group on the third of the three speaking tasks, the city description (see Table 5.1). The adjusted mean differences for the first and second tasks, self-description and story retelling, were not significant. Thus, the explicit strategy training seems to have contributed to the students' ability to use both their own vocabulary and words from a list to describe their favorite city. When analyzing task performance by subscales, there was another significant difference, again in favor of the experimental group. They were rated as higher in *grammar* on the post-test city description task, after adjusting for pre-test differences (see

TABLE 5.1   Overall speaking performance by task
Post-test means adjusted by pre-test using ANCOVA

	Task 1 Self-description	Task 2 Story retelling	Task 3 City description
Experimental group (N=32)	3.95	4.24	3.73*
Comparison group (N=23)	3.82	3.69	3.34

* $p < .05$

Table 5.2). It is likely that the guidance the experimental group received about how to plan ahead, monitor their speech, and reflect back on their performance, contributed to more grammatically accurate speech in the perception of the raters.

TABLE 5.2   Speaking task performance by scales
Post-test means adjusted by pre-test using ANCOVA

Key: SC = self-confidence   V = vocabulary   O = organization of elements
      G = grammar   E = elements of story

	Task 1 Self-description			Task 2 Story retelling		Task 3 City description		
	SC	G	V	E	O	SC	G	V
Experimental group (N=32)	4.23	3.94	3.67	4.69	3.79	4.00	3.63**	3.59
Comparison group (N=23)	4.35	3.69	3.43	4.15	3.23	3.66	3.12	3.20

** $p < .01$

Looking just at the learners of French, while there were no significant differences in **overall** mean performance on any of the three tasks (Table 5.3), there was one difference in the French post-test results when looking at task performance by **subscale**. The experimental group students

TABLE 5.3   French overall speaking performance by subscales
Post-test means adjusted by pre-test using ANCOVA

	Task 1 Self-description	Task 2 Story retelling	Task 3 City description
Experimental group (N=18)	4.16	3.59	3.91
Comparison group (N=18)	3.98	3.16	3.47

were rated as higher on the *vocabulary* subscale for the self-description task (Table 5.4 overleaf). This result is consistent with the aims of the treatment since emphasis was placed on strategies for both learning and using vocabulary while speaking. There were no significant differences in overall mean performance on any of the three tasks nor by subscale within each task for the students of Norwegian.

TABLE 5.4   French speaking task performance by scales
Post-test means adjusted by pre-test using ANCOVA

Key: SC = self-confidence   V = vocabulary   O = organization of elements
G = grammar   E = elements of story

	Task 1 Self-description			Task 2 Story retelling		Task 3 City description		
	SC	G	V	E	O	SC	G	V
Experimental group (N=18)	4.40	4.16	3.99*	3.80	3.43	4.16	3.71	3.87
Comparison group (N=18)	4.52	3.84	3.57	3.18	3.10	3.78	3.26	3.33

* $p < .05$

TABLE 5.5   Gain in task performance correlated with change in reported
strategy use (pre–post)
Task 1: self-description for airport meeting

Key: E = Experimental group (N=32)   C = comparison group (N=23)

	Self-confidence	Grammar	Vocabulary
Before			
3. translated specific words from English		E .52*	
9. tried to visualize airport	C –.50*		
10. thought about similar tasks that I had done	E –.40*		
During			
3. paid attention to pronunciation		C .46*	C .46*
5. when couldn't remember word, I substituted it with another word/phrase			C –.44*
7. when couldn't remember word, I just skipped that part of description		C –.42*	C –.47*
9. used notes that I had written before task	C .48*	C .44*	
14. just worked quickly and didn't pay much attention to what I was saying			E –.41*
After			
5. learned something new/useful about target language during task		C .45*	
8. immediately started filling out checklist without giving my own performance much thought	E .43*		

* $p < .05$

TABLE 5.6   Gain in task performance correlated with change in reported
strategy use (pre–post)
Task 2: Story Retelling

Key: E = experimental group (N=32)   C = comparison group (N=23)

	Elements	Organization
Before		
2. drew pictures to help remember story		E .40*
5. tried to translate story to help summarize it		C –.55*
9. practiced pronunciation of specific words before I began recording	E .42*	
During		
4. purposely tried to use new vocabulary words from story.	C –.42*	
After		
1. will discuss task with other participants in project		C .51*
5. before started checklist, I thought about what could do differently next time		C .44*
8. immediately started filling out checklist when I finished speaking		C –.42*

* p < .05

5.4.2   Research question 2: the relationship between reported frequency of strategy use and task performance

In this section we will report results linking speaking performance to task-specific and more general strategy use, collected by means of the strategy checklists and then the *SILL* respectively.

TASK PERFORMANCE AND THE STRATEGY CHECKLISTS

We will now consider those correlations which suggested a significant relationship between task performance and strategy use on the 'before', 'during', and 'after' checklists for each of the three tasks (see Tables 5.5, 5.6, 5.7).[7]

Task 1: self-description

Strategies before task 1

With respect to strategies before performing the self-description task, there was one strategy situation in the experimental group data where an

TABLE 5.7   Gain in task performance correlated with change in reported
strategy use (pre–post)
Task 3: City Description

Key: E = experimental group (N=32)   C = comparison group (N=23)

	Self-Confidence	Grammar	Vocabulary
Before			
3. wrote out what would say in full sentences before began	E .42*		
10. practiced pronunciation of specific words before began recording	E .43*	E .50*	C −.42*
11. thought about similar tasks that had done in class			E .41*
During			
3. tried to encourage self through positive self-talk	C .43*		
4. used information that had learned outside of class		E .49*	
5. used a mental picture of favorite city while speaking			C .46*
6. when couldn't remember word, substituted it with another word	C .62**		C .48*
11. when couldn't remember word, 'made up' word	C .68**	C .59**	C .56**
After			
8. immediately started filling out checklist when finished speaking	C .51*		

* p < .05   ** p < .01

increase in reported use of a strategy from pre- to post-testing was
related to a gain in performance on the task. 'Translating specific words
from English' correlated significantly with increased task performance
on *grammar* (r=.52) (see Table 5.5). Those in the experimental group
who increasingly analyzed material through translation perhaps also took
greater care in selecting their grammatical forms. However, an increase in
the use of this preparation strategy was also correlated with a lower rating
in *self-confidence* (r=−.40). This finding is not consistent with expectations since mental reference to other similar tasks can be viewed as a
confidence-building strategy. It might have been that those who were
thinking more about other tasks that they had done were perhaps distracted from the task at hand. Thus, they were perceived by the raters as
less self-confident on the post-test. Comparison group respondents who
increased their use of 'visualizing the airport' were also rated as having
decreased in *self-confidence* (r=−.50) from pre- to post-test. So perhaps

the act of visualizing on this specific task made the comparison students sound somewhat less fluent, just as 'thinking about other tasks' did for the experimental group.

Strategies during task 1

Those in the comparison group who paid increasing attention to pronunciation were also rated as increasingly more *grammatical* (r=.46) and as improving in their *vocabulary* rating as well (r=.46). A logical interpretation would be that paying greater attention to the pronunciation of specific sounds reflects a form of monitoring that would also extend to the monitoring and selection of appropriate vocabulary items and grammatical forms. In contrast, those experimental students who reported an increase in 'working quickly without paying attention to the task' were also perceived by raters as lower in *vocabulary* (r=−.41). Hence, there seems to be some real benefit in attending to the output, shaping it, and monitoring it.

Comparison students who increased in their 'use of notes written before performing the task' also increased in their *self-confidence* (r=.48) and *grammar* ratings (r=.44). These findings are logical since the use of notes can enhance self-confidence, as well as make speakers sound more grammatical. This finding would seem to suggest that a task performance strategy, namely, referring to notes taken while preparing to perform a language task, can provide positive support to students in a testing situation.

There were also three instances where the comparison group students' increased use of certain communication strategies appeared to be to their detriment. First, an increase in substituting a word they could not remember with another word or phrase correlated with a lower *vocabulary* rating (r=−.44). Likewise, an increase in skipping parts of a description altogether when they could not remember the words correlated significantly with a poorer rating not only in *vocabulary* (r=−.47) but in *grammar* as well (r=−.42). A plausible interpretation would be that since this group was **not** receiving systematic guidance in how to apply communication strategies for gaps in vocabulary or grammar, their performance suffered. The ratings that they received on these task scales would suggest that this was the case.

Strategies after task 1

The experimental students who increased in not giving their performance much thought while filling out the checklists were the ones who were **increasingly** rated as more *self-confident* on the task (r=.43). It would appear that the more self-confident students did not rely on these types of metacognitive strategies, such as reflecting on upcoming language tasks and previous language performance.

The comparison group students who reported having learned more about the target language at the time of the post-testing than they had reported in the pre-test were rated **higher** in *grammar* (r=.45). The difference here could be explained in that those comparison group students who contributed to the significance of this correlation were probably more versed in target language grammar at the end of the class, and thus received higher ratings.

Task 2: story retelling

Strategies before task 2

The experimental group findings on the story retelling task seem to show the positive effects of the treatment in terms of advanced preparation for language tasks. An increase from pre- to post-test in 'drawing pictures to help remember the story' correlated significantly with increased ability to correctly *order* the elements of the story (r=.40) (see Table 5.6). During the treatment, this planning strategy of visualization (in this case, on paper) was reinforced through several different learning activities. Since this strategy can serve as a means to plan and organize one's thoughts before a task, as in the case of retelling a story with a plot, one likely benefit of this form of preparation is being able to better order the elements of a story,

In addition, it was found that those experimental students who reported an increase in 'practicing the pronunciation of specific words' were also found to improve in their *identification of the elements* in the story (r=.42). Once again we see that a heightened degree of preparation (in this case, focusing on the pronunciation of specific words) correlated with increased language performance (in this case, discriminating the key elements of a story).

An increase among the comparison group students in translating the story to help summarize it related significantly to doing a **poorer** job of *ordering* the elements in the story (r=-.55). It appears, therefore, that the use of translation might not have been a productive strategy for retelling a story orally in this context.

Strategies during task 2

For the comparison group students, an increased ability to *identify the key elements* in the story correlated negatively in post-testing with an effort to 'purposely use new vocabulary from the story' (r=-.42) (see Table 5.6). It would appear that the students producing this negative correlation were perhaps focusing on the vocabulary of the story rather than on the key elements. Whether through a lack of training in strategy use or some other reason, these students were less able to use new vocabulary and focus on the key elements at the same time.

Strategies after task 2

The comparison students were seen in post-testing to have greater use of two strategies which related positively to a more successful *ordering of elements* in the story: 'thinking about what they could do differently next time' (r=.44) and the intention to 'discuss the task with fellow classmates' (r=.51). These two metacognitive strategies both deal in some way with organizing the learning effort. The first organizing strategy, thinking about future performance, is individual in nature, while the second, utilizing others as learning resources, is social. Therefore, increased use of both of these organizational strategies might be expected to correlate with an increase in the correct ordering of story elements.

Task 3: city description

Strategies before task 3

Those experimental students who 'thought more about similar tasks they had done in class' were also rated higher in *vocabulary* in describing their favorite city (r=.41) (see Table 5.7). As with Task 1, these students were improving the likelihood of being better prepared for the task by reflecting on similar tasks that they had done.

An increase in 'writing out the description in full sentences ahead of time' correlated with increased *self-confidence* ratings (r=.42) for the experimental students. It would appear that the process of writing down the sentences before recording their speaking gave the respondents an air of confidence. While this strategy proved successful in preparing those learners for the given task, it is usually not practical in many speaking situations to write everything out in advance. However, students can prepare by writing down key words that they might use during a speaking task.

Another additional preparation strategy is to practice the pronunciation of specific words before speaking. Those experimental students who indicated an increase in this strategy before tape-recording their city description were also rated as increasingly *self-confident* (r=.43) and *grammatical* (r=.50). For comparison group students, an increase in such pronunciation practice was related to a **decreased** rating in *vocabulary* (r=−.42). Those comparison students who increasingly focused on the **sounds** of the words may have become distracted from the use of varied and contextually appropriate vocabulary. After all, these students were without the benefit of systematic training and practice in the use of rehearsal strategies.

Strategies during task 3

For experimental students who indicated an increase in 'their use of information learned out of class,' their *grammar* rating on the task also improved (r=.49). This finding points to the notion that use of the language out of class may contribute to grammatical control. In other words, the more language input and opportunities for practice students seek, the better the chance that grammatical forms will be successfully reinforced.

There were also significant correlations for the comparison group on this task. Students who increased their positive self-talk were also rated as more *self-confident* (r=.43). Whereas it is often assumed that one variable influences another, in this case the influence was most likely reciprocal: positive self-talk can enhance self-confidence **and** increased self-confidence may lead to more positive self-talk. In addition, for the comparison group students, an increased use of a mental picture of the favorite city while speaking correlated positively with a higher *vocabulary* rating (r=.46). Thus, using the strategy of visualization here seems to have helped the students focus on the task at hand.

Furthermore, for the comparison group, an increase in 'substituting another word' when not knowing the exact word correlated significantly with an increase in both *self-confidence* (r=.62) and *vocabulary* (r=.48). Likewise, an increase in the strategy of 'making up a word' correlated significantly with higher *self-confidence* (r=.68), *grammar* (r=.59), and *vocabulary* (r=.56) ratings. What these results indicate is that learners who increase their use of communication strategies (such as paraphrase or substitution) can also improve their ratings on task performance. In these instances, we would have expected the experimental students to have had these positive correlations rather than the comparison group since these were strategies that were emphasized in the treatment. These finding would suggest, however, that even without extensive strategy instruction, some resourceful learners can and do utilize strategies effectively – whether as a result of their own insights about language learning, suggestions provided to them by their teachers or peers, or because of insights provided in the textbooks.

Strategies after task 3

There was only one significant correlation for this category: those comparison students who increasingly reported that they started filling out the strategy checklists as soon as they finished speaking were also those perceived as more *self-confident* (r=.51). As with the finding for the experimental students after Task 1, it would appear that the more self-confident comparison students did not tend to reflect back on their language performance in this instance.

TASK PERFORMANCE AND THE *SILL*

While the primary means for assessing pre–post strategy use in this study was through the strategy checklists, we also measured frequency of strategy use by means of the *SILL*. According to Oxford (Personal Communication, May 17, 1995), this is the first time that the *SILL* was linked specifically to a series of tasks on a pre–post-test basis. For the purpose of this discussion, we will focus on those strategies from the *SILL* that seem to be the most relevant to speaking, and compare the results for the experimental group with those for the comparison group (Table 5.8). It is important to point out that the *SILL* was not designed for use as an instrument specifically linked to given tasks. In any event, since it was not administered immediately following the completion of the three tasks, it cannot be expected to have tapped such differences in the way that the strategy checklists did.

There were several significant positive correlations that only appeared in the experimental group data. For instance, an increase in reported use of idioms or other routines (item 21) on the self-description task from pre- to post-testing correlated with an increase in ratings for *vocabulary* (r=.46). If these students truly relied on well-learned language routines, such as appropriate vocabulary phrases for describing oneself, and also prepared themselves for the task by focusing on well-known vocabulary, it seems logical that they would be perceived as having used descriptive vocabulary more appropriately during the task. In addition, a reported increase in 'previewing the language lesson to get a general idea of what it is about, how it is organized, and how it relates to what is already known' (item 49) correlated with increased ratings on the *grammar* scale (r=.44). It would appear that those students whose checklist results indicated an increase in their desire to preview a lesson before getting into it were also those who were increasingly careful about their use of grammar in speaking, most likely increasing their monitoring of grammar on the task as well.

TABLE 5.8   Gain in task performance (pre–post) correlated with reported strategy use on the SILL (pre–post)

Key: S = self-confidence   E = story elements   E = experimental group (N=32)   V = vocabulary
      G = grammar   O = story organization   C = control group (N=23)

Strategy	Task 1 Self-description			Task 2 Story retelling		Task 3 City description		
	S	G	V	E	O	S	G	V
6. I remember [a new] word by making a clear mental image of it or by drawing a picture	E .56** C .59*					C –.42*		
16. I say or write new expressions repeatedly to practice them								
17. I imitate the way native speakers talk		C .48*	E –.44*		E –.46** C –.44	C –.42*		
18. I read a story or dialog several times until I can understand it		E .50** C .50*						
20. I practice the sounds or alphabet of the new language		E .56** C .58**						
21. I use idioms or other routines in the new language			E .46**			C –.42*		
30. I seek specific details in what I hear or read			E –.61** C –.50*					
31. I use reference materials such as glossaries or dictionaries to help me use the new language					E –.47** C –.55**			

Strategy item								
33. I make summaries of new language material			E .49** C .52* E -.42*					
37. I try to understand what I have heard or read without translating it word-for-word into my own language				E -.41		C -.46*	C -.43*	E -.52** C -.48*
46. When I cannot think of the correct expression to say or write, I find a different way to express the idea		E .52** C .58***						E .53*** C .52*
47. I make up new words if I do not know the right ones	E .50** C .53**	E .40* C .48*						
48. I direct the conversation to a topic for which I know the words	E .57** C .60**	E .52** C .56***						
49. I preview the language lesson to get a general idea of what it is about, how it is organized, and how it relates to what I already know		E .44*				E -.43* C -.44*		
51. I decide in advance to pay special attention to specific language aspects – e.g. focusing on the way native speakers pronounce certain sounds		E .52** C .57***				E -.40*		
59. I clearly identify the purpose of the language activity – e.g. in a listening task I might need to listen for the general idea or for specific facts				E .44* C .43*	E -.42*			
62. I try to notice my language errors and find out reasons for them		C .48*						E -.50*** C -.43*

TABLE 5.8 (*cont'd.*)

	Task 1 Self-description			Task 2 Story retelling		Task 3 City description		
	S	G	V	E	O	S	G	V
63. I learn from my mistakes in using the new language					E −.42* C −.56**			
65. I try to relax whenever I feel anxious about using the new language		E .42* C .56**						
67. I actively encourage myself to take wise risks in language learning, such as guessing meanings or trying to speak, even though I might make some mistakes	E .50** C .52*	E .42* C .42*						
68. I give myself a tangible reward when I have done something well in my language learning			E .59** C .62**			E −.44* C .44*		
69. I pay attention to physical signs of stress that might affect my language learning			C .42					
71. I talk to someone I trust about my attitudes and feelings concerning the language learning process				C .45*				
75. I work with other language learners to practice, revise, or share information	E .56** C .56**							

* p < .05   ** p < .01

There was a negative correlation just for the experimental group between a reported increase in attention to the language itself (e.g. how natives pronounce it) (item 51) and a lower rating in *self-confidence* (r=−.40) on the city description post-test. In other words, those who were perceived by the raters as gaining in self-confidence were also those reporting less attention to language on the post-test. Although correlation does not imply causation, it might be conjectured that it was a gain in self-confidence which led to less need to attend to the form of the language. In addition, those experimental students who decreased in their use of the strategy of 'trying to understand without translating word-for-word into the native language' (item 37) improved in their *identification of story elements* (r=−.41) on the story retelling task from pre- to post-testing. Thus, it would appear that some word-for-word translation, in fact, may have facilitated the students' identification of story elements.

While an increase in the reported use of the strategy of 'giving oneself a tangible reward when something is done well' (item 68) among experimental group students was negatively correlated with increased *self-confidence* on the city description (r=−.44), the correlation was positive for the comparison group (r=.44). The results on this item would suggest that for the experimental group the more self-confident the learners, the less likely they would be to seek external rewards.

On the city description task, increased avoidance of the use of translation (item 37) correlated negatively with increased ratings on *vocabulary* for the experimental group and on all three scales for the comparison group (*self-confidence*: r=−.46C; *grammar*: r=−.43C; *vocabulary*: r=−.52E, r=−.48C). In addition, the experimental and comparison groups had negative correlations between an increased *self-confidence* rating on the city description task and an increase in 'making up new words' (item 47) (r=−.43E, r=−.44C). In other words, the more self-confidence, the less need to make up new words. For the comparison group, an increased *self-confidence* rating on the city description task also correlated negatively with 'remembering a new word by making a clear mental image or by drawing a picture' (item 6) (r=−.42) and 'using idioms and other routines in the new language' (item 21) (r=−.42).

With regard to monitoring for grammatical errors, an increase among comparison group students in 'trying to notice language errors and find out reasons for them' (item 62) correlated significantly with a gain on the *grammar* scale for the self-description task (r=.48). This finding would suggest that as learners pay increasing attention to their grammar errors, they may also be perceived as more grammatical by outside raters. On the other hand, increased use of this strategy of noticing errors worked against both groups of students on their *vocabulary* ratings for the city description task (r=−.50E, r=−.43C). Perhaps the monitoring for language errors in this case was conducted at the expense of appropriate vocabulary in their descriptions.

With respect to affective strategies, results for the experimental and comparison groups were largely similar. For example, an increase in 'trying to relax whenever anxious about using the new language' (item 65) correlated significantly with gains on the *grammar* scale for the self-description (r=.42E, r=.56C). As another example, an increase in 'giving yourself a tangible reward when something is done well' (item 68) correlated significantly with a gain on the *grammar* scale for both groups on the self-description task (r=.59E, r=.62C). Further, the strategy 'actively encouraging oneself to take wise risks in language learning' (item 67) showed the two groups improving their performance on both *self-confidence* (r=.50E, r=.52C) and *grammar* (r=.42E, r=.42C). Increases in *self-confidence* and *grammar* ratings also correlated similarly for both groups with item 47 ('making up new words') (r=.50E, r=.53C and r=.40E, r=.48C, respectively) and item 48 ('directing the conversation to a topic for which one knows the words') (r=.57E, r=.60C and r=.52E, r=.56C, respectively). The interpretation for these findings could be that affective strategies (such as trying to relax when performing language tasks, giving oneself tangible rewards, and taking risks), as well as certain communication strategies, do indeed help students to speak more grammatically and increase their self-confidence when speaking.

5.4.3   Research question 3: students' reasons for strategy use

Verbal report collected from the subsample of students as they filled out the strategy checklists on the post-test was intended to get at the students' reasons for strategy use before, during, and after performing the three tasks. Actually, the verbal report protocols yielded two types of data – namely, insights about students' strategy use and personal reactions, as well as feedback on the checklists as a means of data gathering. The data also yielded a few comments on the four self-reflective questions added to the checklists in the post-testing. Comments on specific items from the strategy checklists (before, during, and after performing the speaking tasks) and on the self-reflective items are presented in Figures 5.1 and 5.2.

INSIGHTS ABOUT STRATEGY USE AND PERSONAL REACTIONS

Experimental group

Before the self-description task, one of the experimental students reported having practiced it a total of three times, including two recordings.

(*continued on p. 141*)

Experimental group

Task 1: self-description

Before
- 'practiced everything before recording'
    "Twice and then I recorded over the first time, so there were three practices."
    "I wrote out what I was going to say and practiced it a couple of times."
- 'tried to use new vocabulary words'
    "I didn't want to use new words that were uncomfortable."

During
- 'when couldn't remember word, substituted another word"
    "Improvised – I couldn't remember how to say 'I wore something,' so I just said 'and tennis shoes.' "

After
- 'learned about my language learning'
    "I can always use more practice."
- 'will discuss task with other participants in project'
    "Look at this as very much an individual effort."

Task 2: story retelling

During
- 'referred back to story'
    "Once because I had a 'mind blank.' "
    "I felt awkward pausing for thoughts so I tried to speak without pauses."

After
- 'learned from task'
    "Able to read and understand from context words that didn't know."
- 'learned about language'
    "It can be more descriptive than English. Norwegian is more precise."
- 'learned about my language learning'
    "Learned I need to relax myself a little more to be able to do the tasks easier with more comprehension."

Task 3: city description

During
- 'paid attention to grammar'
    "If I was in the correct tense."
- 'tried to correct pronunciation'
    "Only if it changed total meaning."

Overall questions
- 'extent that became independent learner'
    "I learned how to learn to speak."

Comparison group

Task 1: self-description

Before
- 'translated all of what would say from English'
    "To get my mind thinking in French."   *continued overleaf*

FIGURE 5.1   Insights about strategy use, based on verbal report data from 21 learners responding to post-test strategy checklists

FIGURE 5.1   *continued*

During
- 'attention to / correcting pronunciation'
    "Find that if I worry too much about it, I won't be able to say anything."

After
- 'learned about my language learning during task'
    "Preparation is good – writing it down helps."

Task 2: story retelling

Before
- 'translating story to summarize it'
    "No. It would have called for two translations: French to English to French."

During
- 'tried to correct grammar as speaking'
    "Attempted to but got confused and didn't."
    "I was unnerved by hearing my own voice. Pronunciation problems resulted in a bad attitude. It altered my story retelling. I spoke with disruption, improper breaks. I altered the way it was read by pronunciation problems."
- 'positive self-talk'
    "Not getting down on myself."

After
- 'learned something useful about the language'
    "My tuition dollars would have been best spent on a semester abroad."
- 'learned something useful about my language learning'
    "How bad my language skills are."
    "I'm trying to show you what comes naturally to me. My point in language learning is to try to get so I can speak it without writing out sentences and things like that, which I think are counter-productive."

Task 3: city description

Before
- 'didn't do any special preparation'
    "I wanted to see how well I could do it without practice – without writing down. Writing seems like cheating – negative skill."

During
- 'paid attention to my pronunciation'
    "Caused me to lose track of what I was doing."
- 'positive self-talk'
    "Encouragement helps to get through it better."

Overall Questions
    "I do feel, now that I've done these three tasks, that I have learned a lot this quarter, though going into the tasks I felt I hadn't progressed at all. I remember this is the same tasks as the beginning of the quarter exactly and they do seem easier at this time."

FIGURE 5.1   Insights about strategy use, based on verbal report data from 21 learners responding to post-test strategy checklists

Experimental group

Task 1: self-description

During
- 'problem with having "working quickly" and "not paying attention to what I was saying" together.'
  "I don't understand *positive self-talk*."
  This respondent indicated that he tried to work quickly but did pay attention. He rated this item a '2' but indicated "not sure what to put."
- 'mental image of self while speaking'
  "Don't know what *mental image* is."

After
- 'before started checklist, reflected on overall performance – thought about what would do differently'
  "As I go through the checklist, I do this – not before."

Task 2: story retelling

Before
- 'thought about similar stories'
  "Not until this question!"
- 'translated parts of the story to help summarize it'
  "I tried to predict some from difficulties last time. For example, I wrote less, talked more."
  "The story was hard to read because it was not factual. It was far-fetched."

During
- 'positive self-talk'
  "Sounds kinda corny."
  "Not real clear on that idea."

Task 3: city description

Before
- 'visualizing favorite city before recording'
  "I did a lot of it last time. I was more confident. I didn't need to prepare as much."
- 'I translated other words I would need from English.'
  "Don't know what this is referring to."

During
- 'making up word'
  "No, I didn't." [Note that he rated his frequency of use of the item with '3' ('part of the time'), which suggests that he and perhaps others were not using the five scale points as intended.]

After
- 'I learned something . . .'
  "The wording on the scale (4 – a lot, 5 – extensively) made it harder to say 'extensively learned a lot.' I prefer a 1 to 3 scale."

Overall questions
  "Not clear what 'independent language learner' meant but the study was good practice. The teacher gave strategies for language learning."
- 'extent to which the three tasks elicit what you know in French'
  "I don't know what *elicit* means here."   *continued overleaf*

FIGURE 5.2   Feedback on the strategy checklist, based on verbal report data from 21 learners responding to post-test strategy checklists

FIGURE 5.2   *continued*

- 'intentionally using what you know about yourself as a language learner'
  "I have difficulty dealing with this question."

Comparison group

Task 1: self-description

Before
- 'didn't do any special preparation'
  "Yes, I did extensively."
- 'thought about similar tasks I have done'
  "I thought about the last time when this was done."

During
- ' "made up" word'
  "For me 'made up' words were those that translated exactly but that might not be a correct meaning of the term."
  "I was unnerved by hearing my own voice."

After
  "Hearing how I sound is not ideal – hearing my own voice is disturbing but insightful."

Comment
  "I wanted a bit more direction as to what the goal was for the task."

Task 2: story retelling

During
- 'I just worked quickly and didn't pay much attention to what I was saying.'
  "I am trying to work quickly and pay attention."

Task 3: city description

Before
- 'translated all of what I would say from English'
  " 'I' – not sure what this means."

During
- 'encourage through positive self-talk'
  "I don't understand the question."

Comments
  "The last task was the most fun. Then the first. It's easier to talk about something you like are familiar with. The story telling task was hard and I didn't like it. Neither did the people I talked to."

Overall questions
- 'extent intentionally used what know about self as a foreign language learner'
  "Weird question – well, I had to know correct pronunciation, vocabulary, grammar."
- 'to what extent used what know about self as language learner'
  "Don't have a clue as to what you mean by this question."

FIGURE 5.2   Feedback on the strategy checklist, based on verbal report data from 21 learners responding to post-test strategy checklists

With regard to trying to use new vocabulary words, another student reported avoiding new words that were 'uncomfortable' for him to use. This is an instance of how learners may pass judgment on the vocabulary that they come into contact with (see Levenston, 1979, for more on learners' accepting and rejecting of vocabulary). The data also included an instance of paraphrase at work. When a student could not remember how to say that she wore tennis shoes, she just said '**and** tennis shoes'. In addition, a student indicated using the strategy of speaking without pauses so as to sound more fluent on the story retelling task.

Students from the experimental group seemed to have some valuable insights about the performance of language tasks, about the target language, and about their language learning. Another made the observation that Norwegian seemed more descriptive and more precise than English. A third student had the insight that by relaxing more, she understood more and the tasks became easier to perform. Finally, a learner shared the a breakthrough for him that thanks to strategies-based instruction, he had learned how to learn to speak.

Comparison group

One student indicated translating all of what he wanted to say to English as a means of getting his mind to think in French. In general, the strategy of making a complete translation as preparation for speaking was seen to be counter-productive, as it was both time-consuming and likely to create unnecessary negative transfer problems. Another student did not translate because it 'would have called for two translations: French to English to French' on the story retelling task. A third student commented that the strategy of writing down what she would say would be a 'negative' strategy since it would be cheating.

Another student shared an experience that the raters engaged in assessing someone's taped speech might be oblivious to, namely, that hearing his accent as he recorded in the language laboratory console unnerved him. According to his account, it altered the way he read the text to himself and affected his attitude towards the task. A second student indicated that the strategy of paying attention to her pronunciation 'caused [her] to lose track of what [she] was doing.' Still another student reacting to the items of paying attention to / correcting pronunciation said, 'I find that if I worry too much about it, I won't be able to say anything.'

After performing the story retelling, one frustrated student exclaimed that the money he spent on tuition would have been better spent on a semester abroad. He came to the conclusion that his language skills were poor and apparently saw the overseas experience as a means of improving them more than in the University of Minnesota language course.

The experimental and comparison group students gave relatively similar feedback regarding the use of the strategy checklists as a means of gathering research data, with one major exception (see Figure 5.2). The four items for self-reflection at the end of the post-test checklists were more comprehensible to those who had been in the treatment since they could better relate to items such as 'To what extent did you intentionally use what you know about yourself as a foreign language learner during the tasks?' and 'To what extent have you become a more independent language learner as a result of your language class this quarter?' These items in particular were addressed to the experimental group whose language learning awareness had been enhanced.

There were, however, other items that were found to be confusing to all respondents. One reason for the confusion was a lack of adequate understanding of the terminology. For example, several respondents did not fully understand what *positive self-talk*, *mental image*, *elicit*, and *made up a word* meant. In the last case, for example, a comparison group student remarked as follows: 'For me "made up" words were those that translated exactly but that might not be a correct meaning of the term.' However, some students may have interpreted this not as making up or changing the meanings of existing words, but actually coining new, non-existent words. As an example of another type of item confusion, the item 'I just worked quickly and didn't pay much attention to what I was saying' was problematic for some. As one respondent commented in his verbal report, 'I am trying to work quickly **and** pay attention.'

The verbal report also brought up the issue of how the process of filling out the instrument can have reactive effects on student performance. On the checklist for strategies before doing the story retelling task, one subject responded that she had not thought about similar stories that she had read until seeing the item on the checklist. This, then, would be evidence of the reactive effect which a research instrument may have – namely, putting thoughts in the respondents' heads.

There were also problems with the scale itself. Sometimes the descriptions at points along the scale did not agree grammatically with the wording of a given strategy item. For example, for those strategy items beginning with 'I learned something . . .' (on the checklist for strategies **after** performing the city description task), an experimental student commented, 'The wording on the scale (4 – a lot, 5 – extensively) made it harder to say 'extensively learned a lot.' I prefer a 1 to 3 scale.' And perhaps a more serious problem was that at times respondents were not necessarily ticking the scale point that best reflected their actual frequency of use of the given strategy. So, for example, in response to the item about making up a word if the necessary word could not be remembered, an experimental student responded, 'No, I didn't.' Yet, he rated his frequency of use of the item with '3' ('part of the time'), which suggests that he and perhaps others were not using the five-points scale as intended. In this instance, he would have had to mark a '1', in order to indicate no use of that strategy.

5.4 Discussion

5.4.1 Recapping the major findings

In this study, 55 intermediate learners of foreign language at the University of Minnesota were either participants in a strategies-based instructional treatment or were comparison students receiving the regular ten-week language course. Both groups filled out a pre-treatment questionnaire and then performed a series of three speaking tasks on a pre–post basis, along with the *SILL* and strategy checklists filled out after performing each of the three tasks. Twenty-one of the experimental and comparison group students also provided verbal report data while they filled out the post-test strategy checklists – indicating their rationale for their responses to certain items, as well as their reactions to the instrument itself. With regard to the question of whether strategies-based instruction makes a difference in speaking performance, the finding was positive: the experimental group outperformed the comparison group on the third task, city description, in the post-test, after adjusting for pre-test differences. In addition, while there were no significant differences in overall mean performance on any of the three tasks for the advanced intermediate and intermediate French students grouped together, there was one difference in looking at the French post-test task performance by scale. The experimental group students were rated as higher on the *vocabulary* scale for the self-description task.

The relationship between reported frequency of strategy use (pre–post) and ratings of task performance (pre–post) was complex. An increase in the use of certain strategies included on the strategy checklists was linked to an improvement in task performance for the experimental group, in other instances only for the comparison group, and in some cases for both groups.

For the experimental group, an increase in certain preparatory strategies (e.g. translating specific words, writing out sentences, drawing a picture, thinking about previous tasks, using information learned out of class, and practicing the pronunciation of words) and monitoring strategies (e.g. monitoring for grammar, paying attention to the pronunciation of words, and analyzing a story for its key elements) related to an increase on one or more of the rating scales – self-confidence, grammar, vocabulary, and identifying and ordering elements in a story. We note that these were primarily language **use** strategies, employed in order to help retrieve language material, to rehearse it, and to use it communicatively. In addition, several of the strategies used increasingly could be seen as language **learning** strategies. Translating specific words and practicing their pronunciation in preparation for speaking were learning strategies if as a result of using them the learners became more cognizant of grammatical relationships, since increases in the use of those two strategies correlated significantly with an increase in grammar ratings.

For the comparison group, an increase in the use of certain strategies during the self-description and city description tasks was positively related to an increase in ratings on task performance. Of the 15 total positive correlations for the comparison group across tasks, 11 of these involved strategies from the 'during' part of the checklists on tasks 1 and 3. While the correlation between creating a mental picture and a higher rating on vocabulary could be viewed as a learning strategy, since mental imagery helps in the storage and retrieval of new lexical items, most of the significant correlations seem to involve language use strategies, such as increased attention to pronunciation and the use of paraphrase being linked to an increased vocabulary rating, and an increase in positive selftalk being significantly correlated with a higher self-confidence rating. All three of these – attention to pronunciation, use of paraphrase, and positive self-talk – could be seen as communication strategies *par excellence*.

Instances such as these, where comparison students had positive correlations and experimental students did not, would seem to run counter to expectation, since the strategies were emphasized in the treatment. A possible interpretation for these findings is that even without extensive strategy instruction, some resourceful learners can and do utilize strategies effectively – whether as a result of their own insights about language learning, as a result of suggestions provided to them by their teachers or peers, or as a result of insights provided in the textbooks.

There were also instances where an increase in use from pre- to post-testing could be seen as detrimental to the students' performance on the given speaking tasks. Most of these negative correlations were found in the comparison group data: an increase in substituting a forgotten word with another word or phrase related significantly with a lower vocabulary rating, an increase in skipping parts of a description calling for forgotten words related to a poorer rating in both vocabulary and grammar, an increase in translating the story to help summarize it related to doing a poorer job of ordering the elements in the story, an increased ability to identify the key elements in the story correlated negatively with an effort to purposely use new vocabulary from the story, and an increase in pronunciation practice was related to a decreased rating in vocabulary. These findings would suggest that students without the benefit of systematic training and practice in strategy use over time were consequently less adept at using certain strategies to their benefit.

We note that the strategy checklists as a means for gathering research data seemed to capture the dynamics of strategy use – namely, that strategies are linked to specific tasks. This point is underscored when a comparison is made between the results from the checklists and from the *SILL*. While the strategy checklists proved themselves effective as a measure in linking task-specific strategies with improved task performance, the *SILL* performed more as a general measure of the patterns of strategy use, in keeping with its intended purpose. Nonetheless, the results of the data analysis suggested certain items on the *SILL* were sensitive enough to correlate significantly with increases on ratings scales for the various tasks. Several of these items, such as attending to language form and avoiding the use of translation, might be seen as primarily language learning strategies, while previewing language lessons, relating the material to previous knowledge, word-for-word translation, remembering words by their image, and using idioms could be viewed as primarily reflecting language use strategies.

With regard to verbal report characterizations of the processes involved in completing the strategy checklists, it was found that at least one experimental subject conducted multiple practices before recording a particular response. In addition, the students reported avoiding new words that they were not yet comfortable with, paraphrasing when they lacked a precise word, and sometimes avoiding pauses so as to sound more fluent. Students also reported having learned certain things about themselves as language learners, such as recognizing the benefits of relaxing more while performing language tasks.

With respect to the comparison group, the use of translation into the native language mostly came up as a counter-productive activity, but one student reported using it as a way to get his mind thinking in the target language. Another student saw it as 'cheating' to write out a response to an oral task ahead of time. Finally, there were students who voiced frustration at their limited language skills, something that did not come up in the experimental group verbal report data.

The verbal report data also provided some useful insights as to weaknesses in the strategy checklists themselves, insights which could be put to good use in follow-up research (see below).

5.4.2   Limitations of the study

As with all studies of this magnitude, there are various limitations. The very fact that the study was intended to be of an applied nature meant that certain controls possible in a laboratory environment were not possible in this case. Yet the factors operating in this study seemed more reflective of genuine classroom situations.

As indicated in 5.3 above (see note 3), the treatment could only be offered by teachers who had been trained to provide strategies-based instruction, and there had to be corresponding classes at the same level for the sake of comparison. This constraint produced the rather modest sample size of 55, with which the numerous statistical analyses were conducted. In addition, the students were not randomly assigned to the experimental or to the comparison group because of scheduling constraints. The small sample size for the Norwegian students helps to explain the non-significant result regarding the effects of the treatment (research question 1).

With regard to the background of the teachers participating in the experimental group in the study, it is not surprising that two of those teachers who had volunteered to participate in the seminar on strategies-based instruction (and were subsequently eligible to teach the experimental group classes) were doing their doctorates in education and in applied linguistics respectively, while one of the teachers of the comparison group had her doctorate in literature and the other two were doing theirs in literature as well. It could be argued that perhaps those who were studying about language learning and teaching processes were also likely to do a better job of supporting their students in their language learning efforts, and in the use of speaking strategies in particular. To counter that claim, it could be pointed out that all foreign language teachers at the University of Minnesota receive rather intensive training and are provided in-service workshops and support in the latest methods of language instruction. Hence, we would like to think that the main difference between groups was the special training that the experimental students received over the ten-week period in how to use speaking strategies to their advantage.

With regard to 'the power of suggestion,' it is possible that filling out the *SILL* as a pre-measure as well as the checklists after each task could have supplied the comparison students with suggestions for use of strategies, therefore affecting the results of the study. In other words, although they did not receive strategies-based instruction, the comparison students may possibly have gleaned some suggestions from the questionnaires alone. Yet experience has shown that the power of suggestion alone is not usually enough to produce strategy use. Rather, there appears to be a need for presentation, explanation, practice, and application to ensure successful strategy use, especially with the more complex strategies.

Also, with regard to the checklists, although they had been piloted and revised, they had not been submitted to rigorous reliability and validity checks. In fact, the verbal report protocols gathered during the use of these checklists even suggested that some of the items were still in need of refinement, such as the one referring to 'positive self-talk.' In addition, questions have been raised concerning the *SILL*, despite the published reports of extremely high reliability and validity coefficients (Oxford and Burry-Stock, 1995; Oxford, 1996a). We note the mixed reliability findings for several of the scales of the *SILL* in this study (see section 5.3.2 above, under 'Data analysis procedures') in contrast to the published findings. Furthermore, a study with 28 EFL graduate students by LoCastro (1994) found discrepancies between responses on the *SILL* as compared with responses in group interviews. She also questioned the *SILL*'s placing of memorization outside of cognitive strategies.

A study by Gu, Wen and Wu (1995) may provide an explanation for the inconsistencies in the LoCastro study. Twenty of the *SILL* (Oxford, 1990) items were given in four parallel questionnaires to 120 college students in Hong Kong who were non-English majors. The first version did not specify any dimensions of reference, the second instructed them to compare themselves with their classmates, the third asked them to compare their present behavior with their past experience in secondary school (e.g. 'I often do this now but not in the past'), and the fourth asked them to rate the truthfulness of the given statement for them as compared with their behavior in other language areas (e.g. 'I always look for opportunities to listen to English but I don't find opportunities to practice the other three skills as much'). They found that the results for 13 of the 20 items differed across the questionnaires. They attributed these differences to the differing reference systems: when clear references were provided, responses to the same questions were mostly different from those elicited through the non-referenced questionnaire. The study called into question the ambiguities of the Likert-type five-point scale in learning strategy elicitation, and the recommendation was made to use more specific indices of oftenness – e.g. 'about two hours a day every day' v. 'about half the time.'

With regard to the distinctions made in Chapter 2 between language learning and language use strategies, although some effort was made to distinguish the two in this study – especially in the choice of strategies by task for the strategies checklists, it was still not necessarily clear from the findings whether the learners were using strategies for one of the purposes or both. It would have been necessary at the verbal report phase to have them indicate whether they viewed the use of a given strategy for the purpose of learning or for that of using the language – whether through retrieval, rehearsal, communication, or cover strategies. Actually, given that the tasks were designed to have them display what they had already learned, we would perhaps expect to find more language use than language learning strategies, as appeared to be the case. All the same, it is possible to use language learning strategies on tasks, especially on a task such as the story retelling where the learners had new vocabulary with glosses provided.

Another limitation of the study was its emphasis on the **frequency** of use of a strategy rather than on **successful** use. The concern is that repeated use of a strategy may just be a sign that the learner is continuing to use a given strategy unsuccessfully, as was pointed out in Chapter 2. On the other hand, it may mean that the learner has genuinely found the strategy useful. This study did not have a direct measure of how successfully the learners used the strategies, but an indirect measure was the correlation between an increase in the frequency of use of a strategy and an increase in task performance. What enhanced this link was the fact that the three strategy checklists were constructed with those three specific tasks in mind. Since students use strategies but often use them inconsistently or in an uninformed way, one goal of the treatment was to help the students use the strategies more systematically and purposefully. It was not possible to say in this study at just what point in the task the respondents used a particular strategy. The data do not allow such a pinpointing effort. A doctoral study currently in progress at the University of Melbourne (Gruba, forthcoming) is including this feature. The study investigates listening comprehension strategies in Japanese as a foreign language, using videotaped news, and the researcher has been able to localize the strategy use to a given moment in the task. It should also be pointed out that in listening tasks it is possible to be more intrusive than in speaking tasks.

In addition, it should be noted that the speaking tasks in this study were non-participatory ones. Hence, they were not necessarily capturing the same form of discourse as they would have had they been conducted with an interlocutor. They did not reflect 'normal' conversation – in fact, they did not constitute a conversation at all. But then again, testing tasks are not 'normal' conversation even if they are participatory. Also, in semi-direct tasks, learners can write down parts of the response, which would be difficult to do in participatory speaking tasks. So, there are significant differences in the discourse produced in semi-direct speaking tasks such as in this study in comparison with direct speaking tasks. Shohamy (1994) found the semi-direct, tape-based version to be tapping a more literate kind of language than the version with an interlocutor. O'Loughlin (1995) found the same to be true in a study that he conducted, but he determined that it was the degree of interactiveness rather than the test format (direct v. indirect) which made the difference. He found that the higher the level of interaction, the lower the degree of lexical density in the output, and so he recommended making semi-direct tests more interactive. In the case of the Cohen, Weaver, and Li study, this would perhaps have meant allowing less time for preparation and adding certain kinds of rejoinders to the tape-recorded prompts, in order to simulate more the situation where there is a live interviewer.

Furthermore, it could be argued that an increased rating on the speaking tasks might have been due in part to test-taking ability (see Chapter 7 for more on this phenomenon) as well as reflecting actual gain in speaking, since semi-direct tasks do not make the same demands on the speaker that direct tasks do. In fact, it could be argued that those who were better at taking speaking tests altogether – and especially those who could do well on such semi-direct tasks – may have had an advantage. The concern would be that the tasks were favoring learners who needed some time to collect their thoughts and perhaps jot down some words and phrases, but who would not necessarily do so well in authentic speaking situations.

With regard to the statistical findings, and especially those involving correlations between gains in task performance and changes in frequency of use of given strategies, we need to remember that correlation does not imply causality. Rather, such correlations simply indicate that increased strategy use was **related to** gains in task performance. All the same, the statistical findings are suggestive of possible trends in the data.

Another artifact of correlating strategy use with task performance on a pre–post basis was the focus it put on only those students for whom there was some significant change in frequency of strategy use or performance. Therefore, those students whose task ratings remained constant from pre to post (i.e. at the top or bottom of the scales) were not well represented in the statistical analyses. Their performance would limit the distribution of scores and thus depress the correlations coefficients. It could also be considered a limitation of this study that no report was given for those students going through SBI who did not show any link between increased use of strategies and increases in rated performance (Jim Lantolf, Personal Communication, March 24, 1996). Another issue could be that the seven-week span for the treatment between pre- and post-testing was not really long enough for there to emerge truly substantive results. The results that were obtained would speak against that concern. But another concern might be whether such a short period would suggest that the respondents might have been using the strategies just in this time frame but not after the termination of the SBI experience. This would call for follow-up research to determine the extent to which the experiment students continued to use their insights from SBI.

5.4.3   Suggestions for further research

The somewhat limited sample size in this study meant that certain kinds of investigation were impossible. One was that of determining whether the increase of strategy use was related to a similar increase in task performance for **both** the more and less proficient learners. Unfortunately the sample size was too small to further divide it along the lines of proficiency. So there is a need to conduct a similar but larger study so as to be able to run analyses according to the proficiency level of the students and other factors. It would seem that while many strategies may prove beneficial to **all** learners in some moments in the performance of some tasks, there may be strategies that are better suited for beginners and others for more advanced learners. It would also be possible to compare and contrast language learning strategies with language use strategies, especially in tasks such as the story retelling one, in which some learning was expected to be going on while reading the text and using the glosses that were provided. Would the SBI intervention have a more dramatic impact over time on language learning strategies (e.g. learning vocabulary through the mnemonic keyword device) than on language use strategies? This issue could be investigated.

Another area for investigation would be to document through videotape and other means the nature of the treatment. It would be useful to spell out just what strategies-based instruction looks like in the same classroom over time and in different classrooms throughout a language course. In this study we relied primarily on retrospective reports from the three experimental group teachers, and the one written report (Lybeck, 1996).

Yet another suggestion for further research would be to assess the extent to which the learners transfer their strategy training from this experiment to performance in subsequent language classes. Was the advantage of the experimental group in this study just simply an artifact of the experiment, or was speaking genuinely enhanced by strategies that would be accessible for future language study and for speaking situations beyond the framework of the classroom? Also, it would be good to chart the transfer of strategy training to 'real' speaking situations. Of course, some strategies may become automatic and therefore would not be able to be studied as strategies. In addition to looking at speaking, it would be useful to extend these same lines of investigation to the other skill areas – listening, reading, and writing.

Finally, it would be beneficial to pay greater attention to the wording of entries in checklists such as those used in this study, to make sure that all the terminology is clear to the respondents. In addition, it would be valuable to make sure there are no conflicting elements in the same checklist entry, such as 'working quickly' v. 'paying attention.' Also, there may be value in having respondents do practice exercises in the use of a five-point scale, in order to assure a greater homogeneity of interpretation regarding what a '3' or a '1' means in such a scale.

5.4.4   Pedagogical implications

The study was undertaken to determine whether strategies-based instruction should have a role in the foreign language classroom. It would seem that despite the limitations of the study, the results speak in favor of such a role. If instructors systematically introduce and reinforce strategies that can help students speak the target language more effectively, their students may well improve their performance on language tasks. The findings of the study would also suggest that explicitly describing, discussing, and reinforcing strategies in the classroom can have a direct payoff on student outcomes.

The study also seems to endorse the notion of integrating strategy training directly into the classroom instructional plan and embedding strategies into daily language tasks. In this way, the students get accustomed to having the teacher teach both the language content and the language learning and language use strategies at the same time. Such an approach calls for training the teachers in how to deliver strategies-based instruction so that the strategies become an integral part of the fiber of the course, while preserving the explicit and overt nature of the strategy training. In this manner, the students should be better able to consciously transfer specific strategies to new contexts.

5.5   Conclusions

While there is no doubt about the need to conduct further studies as to the efficacy of strategies-based foreign language instruction, and especially to pursue the empirical study of strategies-based speaking instruction that is focused on improving speaking and other skill areas, this study should already provide suggestions for instructional changes in the classroom. It would appear beneficial to engage learners in discussions of speaking strategies, having them review checklists of possible strategies (such as those appearing in Appendix 5 at the end of the chapter) and practice those strategies in class. The students should be the ones who finalize their own strategy checklists, and they need to make their own choices as to the strategies that they will use in different language learning and language use situations.

This study went beyond studies such as that of Dörnyei (1995), which limited itself to a select few strategies (three in his case) in order to conduct a 'neat' study. It also went beyond the O'Malley and Chamot (1990) study, which lacked the direct link between task performance and reports of specific strategy use on a pre–post-test basis. Applied linguistic research that attempts to reflect and draw upon a more authentic classroom environment must draw on a far larger set of strategies – in fact, all those that may have a role in performing given classroom tasks. In this study, learners were free to choose those strategies that they, along with their teachers, had identified as relevant to speaking in a foreign language. The innovation in this study was to make a direct link between the frequency of use of a given strategy and performance on the speaking task for which that strategy was chosen. In addition, the verbal report data provided insights into both students' strategy use and the design of instruments to use in strategy research. What could also be considered a contribution in this research was the effort to combine experimental or quasi-experimental methods with more descriptive, qualitative approaches. In order to conduct research on strategies, there is an ever-increasing need to use a multi-method approach. Each approach to measurement and description complements the other.

5.6   Discussion questions and activities

1. In the same spirit as the exercises at the end of Chapter 4, you are being requested by your colleagues to justify your school's investment in strategies-based instruction. They are aware of articles such as that by Rees-Miller (1993) which criticize the strategies 'movement' and

would put a damper on any efforts at SBI. Based on your reading of the literature review and of the Cohen, Weaver, and Li study presented in its entirety, you prepare a response to your colleagues in defense of SBI. What are the key points that you make?

2. In what ways might the Cohen, Weaver, and Li study be considered an innovation in research on strategies training? What were the limitations that the authors noted? What other limitations might you add? If you were to design your 'ideal' research study to determine the effects of SBI on the learners, what might your research proposal look like – i.e. research questions, your SBI treatment, sampling procedures, instruments, data collection procedures, data analysis procedures?

Appendix 5   Speaking strategies

(Compiled by S. Weaver along with C. Alcaya, K. Lybeck, and P. Mougel, teachers in the experimental sections of the Speaking Strategies Experiment, NLRC/CARLA, University of Minnesota, November 1994).

1   Before you speak

1.1   LOWER YOUR ANXIETY

- deep breathing
- positive self-talk
- visualizing yourself succeeding
- relaxation techniques
- visualizing yourself as prepared

1.2   PREPARE AND PLAN

- Identify the goal and purpose of the task: what is it you are to learn/ demonstrate in this exercise?
- Ask for clarification of the task if you are unsure of its goal, purpose, or how you are to do it.
- Activate your background knowledge – what you already know about this situation/task.
- Relate the task to a similar situation; make associations.
- Predict what is going to happen.
- Predict the vocabulary you will need; make word maps, groupings.
- Think of how you might circumlocute for vocabulary you do not know; think of synonyms, antonyms, explanations, or non-verbal

communication that can substitute; translate from English to the foreign language any words you predict you will need that you do not already know.

- Predict the structures (grammar) you will need.
- Review similar tasks in your textbook.
- Transfer sounds and structures from previously learned material to the new situation.
- Predict the difficulties you might encounter.
- Plan your responses and contributions.
- Organize your thoughts.
- Prepare a general 'outline' (use notes, keywords, draw pictures).
- Predict what the other party is going to say.
- Rehearse (practice silently, act out in front of a mirror, record yourself and listen).
- Cooperate in all areas if it is a group task.
- Encourage yourself to speak out, even though you might make some mistakes.

2   While you are speaking

2.1   FEELING IN CONTROL

- Take your emotional temperature. If you find you are tense, try to relax, funnel your energy to your brain rather than your body (laugh, breathe deeply).
- Concentrate on the task – do not let what is going on around you distract you.
- Use your prepared materials (when allowed).
- Ask for clarification ('Is this what I am supposed to do?') help (ask someone for a word, let others know when you need help), or verification (ask someone to correct your pronunciation).
- Delay speaking. It's OK to take time to think out your response.
- Don't give up. Don't let your mistakes stop you. If you talk yourself into a corner or become frustrated, back up, ask for time, and start over in another direction.
- Think in the target language.
- Encourage yourself (use positive self-talk).

2.2   BE INVOLVED IN THE CONVERSATION

- Direct your thoughts away from the situation (e.g. test!) and concentrate on the conversation.

- Listen to your conversation partner. Often you will be able to use the structure or vocabulary they use in your own response.
- Cooperate to negotiate meaning and to complete the task.
- Anticipate what the other person is going to say based on what has been said so far.
- Empathize with your partner. Try to be supportive and helpful.
- Take reasonable risks. Don't guess wildly, but use your good judgment to go ahead and speak when it is appropriate, rather than keeping silent for fear of making a mistake.

2.3 MONITOR YOUR PERFORMANCE

- Monitor your speech by paying attention to your vocabulary, grammar, and pronunciation while speaking.
- Self-correct. If you hear yourself making a mistake, back up and fix it.
- Activate your new vocabulary. Try not to rely only on familiar words. Imitate the way native speakers talk.
- Compensate by using strategies such as circumlocution, synonyms, guessing which word to use, getting help, using cognates, making up words, using gestures.
- Adjust or approximate your message. If you can't communicate the complexity of your idea, communicate it simply. Through a progression of questions and answers, you are likely to get your point across, rather than shutting down for a lack of ability to relate the first idea.
- Switch (when possible) to a topic for which you know the words. (Do not do this to avoid practicing new material, however!)

3 After you speak

3.1 EVALUATE YOUR PERFORMANCE

- Reward yourself with positive self-talk for completing the task. Give yourself a personally meaningful reward for a particularly good performance.
- Evaluate how well the activity was accomplished. (Did you complete the task, achieve the purpose, accomplish the goal? If not, what will you do differently next time?)
- Identify the problem areas.
- Share with peers and instructors (ask for and give feedback, share learning strategies).
- Be aware of others' thoughts and feelings.

3.2   PLAN FOR FUTURE TASKS

- Plan for how you will improve for the next time.
- Look up vocabulary and grammar forms you had difficulty remembering.
- Review the strategy checklists to see what you might have forgotten.
- Ask for help or correction.
- Work with proficient users of the target language.
- Keep a learning log (document strategies used and task outcomes, find out what works for you).

Notes

1. Tao-Yuan Li, a doctoral student in Communication Disorders at the University of Minnesota, was responsible for most of the data collection and for the extensive statistical analyses that were conducted. We would like to acknowledge Joel Levin and Micheline Chalhoub-Deville for their helpful comments on earlier drafts of this chapter.
2. The NLRC is housed in the Center for Advanced Research on Language Acquisition and is funded by the Center for International Education, US Department of Education.
3. This group is referred to as a *comparison*, rather than a *control*, group because there was no random assignment of students or of classrooms to the conditions of the study. The treatment could only be offered by teachers who had been trained to provide strategies-based instruction, and there had to be corresponding classes at the same level for the sake of comparison.
4. It must be remembered that all six teachers were responsible for preparing the learners to take the ACTFL-based language proficiency battery, which the students need to pass in order to obtain credit for the equivalent of two years of college language study. Thus, both written and oral skills were emphasized in the classes.
5. Kendall's tau was used to compare ratings across raters because it is better able to handle the problem of tied ranks in rank-order correlation than is Spearman (Hatch and Lazaraton 1991: 453).
6. Two native speakers of each language were selected to perform the story retelling task and their retellings served as the baseline for rating the non-native subjects' performance.
7. Tables 5.5 to 5.7 provide for each of the three tasks respectively all significant correlations of .40 or above between increased reported use of a strategy and the gain in performance as determined by the raters. Statistically significant correlations below .40 were not included because they were deemed low enough to be questionable with regard to their psychological meaningfulness.

6 Strategies for choosing the language of thought

6.1 Introduction

So far in this volume, we have defined strategies and strategy training, and have demonstrated ways of investigating strategy use, focusing as we did on perhaps the most elusive skill, namely, that of speaking. At this point in the volume, we will turn our attention to two more specialized areas of focus with regard to strategy use since they both play significant roles in the success or failure of language learners and they both have received somewhat limited attention in the literature. The first area concerns the language of thought chosen by the multilingual learner. The second concerns those strategies that learners select for coping with language tests, quizzes, and other measures of their language ability. This chapter will consider choice of language for performing cognitive operations. The next will look at test-taking strategies.

It is likely that for some, if not many, the use of one language or another for thinking while performing language tasks is not seen as a matter of strategy selection or of strategizing. Rather, it is seen as a given. The fact is that for bilinguals and multilinguals – especially for those with at least minimal control of a second or third language, there **is** an element of choice involved in arriving at the language(s) used in performing cognitive operations. Furthermore, the very choice of language of thought may have significant implications for ultimate success at learning, using, as well as forgetting a language or languages. Methods of foreign language teaching and learning are often predicated on the principle that learners need to think as much as possible in the language that they wish to learn. In the first part of this chapter we will explore this assumption. But be that as it may, assumptions do not necessary dictate behavior, and, in fact, language learners and users may revert to thinking in their native language or another language at times or even extensively in their efforts to function in the target language.

Section 6.2.1 starts by exploring what it means to think in a target language. Next, those factors which determine both unplanned and planned use of more than one language for thinking are discussed, and empirical data from a mini-survey and from the author's own language learning and language use experiences are presented. Section 6.2 closes by considering the role of target language thinking in improving language ability, drawing on empirical data from both the mini-survey and the author's experiences.

Section 6.3 looks at mental translation in the reading of college students at the intermediate level in French and Spanish. The section starts by considering the often-heard admonition not to translate mentally into the native language while performing second language tasks. This stand against translation has been one of the guiding principles of various foreign language methodologies. This belief that such mental translation is detrimental to target language development is then questioned. Several studies in the area of foreign language writing are cited which demonstrate that texts written in the native language and then translated may be more effective pieces of writing than those written directly in the target language. Two studies of mental translation to the native language during foreign language reading are then described, one from the literature and the other a replication conducted as an MA thesis at the University of Minnesota. Both studies would lead to the conclusion that foreign language readers might be well-advised to use their L1 to chunk material into semantic clusters, to keep their train of thought, to create a network of associations, to clarify grammatical roles, and to make the input more familiar and consequently more user-friendly. The section closes by offering suggestions for further research and pedagogical implications consistent with the view that mental translation can play a legitimate (though perhaps limited) role in the processing of written text.

Finally, in 6.4 the language of thought among 8 to 11 year olds in an elementary-school Spanish immersion program is examined. Although this study diverges from the others in this volume by dealing with elementary-school learners as opposed to adult learners, its focus and research methods would nonetheless seem relevant to expanding our knowledge base regarding adult foreign language learning patterns as well. The study sought to determine the roles of the native and target languages in the processing of oral and written prompts and formulation of oral and written responses by learners immersed in a target language program. The investigation dealt with the extent to which learners use their native language and the foreign language when performing the cognitive operations involved in math problems.

The findings revealed that for the immersion pupils under study, English seemed at times to play a more prominent role in their internal language environment than did Spanish. They read the problem in Spanish but would shift to English immediately or as soon as they had some conceptual difficulty. These findings may help to provide at least one explanation for gaps that have been noted in the spoken and written output of immersion pupils.

Given the responses from the mini-survey of multilinguals, insights from the author's own experiences, and the findings from the mental translation studies and from the elementary-level Spanish full immersion program, some conclusions are drawn as to the relative benefits of thinking through the native language, the target language, or some other language for the purposes of learning and using a target language. It is suggested that further research could help to generate guidelines for learners as to their full range of strategies with regard to the selection of language of thought and as to the effects on learning of selecting those particular strategies.

6.2   The role of language of thought in language learning[1]

Is it beneficial for learners to attempt to think as much as possible in a language that they wish to learn or to improve their mastery of? Might it be detrimental to their learning if they limit their use of that language as a vehicle for thought? This issue has not been expressed as a set of research questions until recently, and the intuitively based assumption has been that the more thinking through the target language, the better. There is evidence from research on foreign language reading and writing, however, that selective translation into the native language may play a **positive** role for some, if not many, language learners in the comprehension, retention, and production of written texts (cf. Kern, 1994; Hawras, 1996, with regard to reading; Jones and Tetroe, 1987; Lay, 1988; Friedlander, 1990; Kobayashi and Rinnert, 1992; Brooks, 1993, with regard to writing). Under what circumstances might the more successful language learners think partially, extensively, or exclusively in the target language that they are using? While multilinguals may actually have differential strengths in their various languages, according to discourse domain (Selinker and Douglas, 1985), the extent to which they use these languages for solving cognitive tasks has remained a relatively unexplored phenomenon.

This section of the chapter will:

(1) explore what it means to think in a target language (L_T);
(2) look at results from a mini-survey and from the author's self-examination regarding unplanned and planned use of more than one language for thinking;

(3) consider the same empirical data regarding the role of L_T thinking in improving language ability; and

(4) examine additional empirical findings regarding multilingual thought patterns and the implications of these findings with regard to foreign language teaching and research.

6.2.1   What it means to think in a target language

Many language educators would maintain that the best way for learners to achieve native-like control of an L_T is to make an effort to think in that language rather than to translate or reprocess the material into their L1 or into some other language which they have learned (the L_O). Is this folk wisdom that we need to liberate ourselves from or is it sound advice? Let us now explore this issue.

First of all, what does it mean to 'think in a target language'? For the purposes of this discussion we will concern ourselves only with **verbalized** thoughts (whether silently, subvocally, or aloud) and not with non-verbal thoughts (images, symbols, and sensorimotor representations). The extent and nature of L_T thinking can vary from minimal, passing thoughts (e.g. just a word or two) to more extensive and 'deeper' (i.e. more cognitively complex) ones, depending both on the nature and quality of the language learning environment (e.g. an L2 v. a foreign language learning situation), and on the degree to which the learner has mastery over the L_T. Since there appears to be relatively little systematic research in this area, we can only speculate as to the extent to which non–natives' thoughts are in the L_T and the effectiveness of 'thinking in the L_T' as opposed to thinking in the L1.[2]

Unless we are thinking out loud, our thoughts reflect *inner speech* – that is, the thinking that we do in our minds that is in the form of words rather than images or symbols. This inner speech could be both *self-directed* or 'private' in the Vygotskian sense (i.e. not intended for others and perhaps difficult to interpret because it is incomplete in grammatical form and vocabulary but adequate for the thinker) as well as *other-directed* or 'public' (i.e. interpretable by others) (Vygotsky, 1961).

In considering the language-of-thought issue, the first question that arises concerns the extent of proficiency or *threshold level* necessary in order to have thoughts in that language. In other words, how well do learners need to function in a language in order to think in it? In order for inner speech to take place in an L_T, learners may need to attain a certain functional level with regard to vocabulary and structure. In addition, some areas of thought may be more demanding than others for given learners. But since thinking in a language involves different levels or depths of meaning, the answer to the question is complex. While greater proficiency in a language is likely to increase the possibility that thinking will occur in that language, we cannot assume this to be the case. It is more than likely that even someone with somewhat limited proficiency in a language could still have thoughts in that language.

Another issue that which might influence the selection of language for verbalized thoughts but even more so the very nature of the thoughts themselves is that of the grammatical structure of the language Slobin (1996: 76), for example, refers to what he calls *thinking for speaking* as a special form of thought that is mobilized for communication and involves picking those characteristics of objects and events that fit some conceptualization of the event and are readily encodable in the language. So, for example, in describing a picture story where a dog is running away from a swarm of bees and at the same time an owl witnesses a boy fall out of a nearby tree, the progressive tense can be used to describe the running in English and Spanish but not in German or Hebrew. In addition, in order to tell the story in Turkish, it would be necessary to make the distinction between whether the boy's fall was witnessed or not. Slobin's point is that when you describe a picture, you take a grammaticized point of view. In other words, the set of grammaticized distinctions in the language guide you to attend to certain features of events while speaking, and that this grammatical organization affects the ways in which you think when you are speaking.

Another approach to the interrelation of imaging and the verbalizations that we use to describe them is that while thoughts as linguistically formulated can influence our imaging processes, so imaging can operate on linguistic descriptions to aid our understanding. As Keller and Keller put it (1996: 126): 'Linguistic forms and images are reciprocally accessible and in interactive functioning can be mutually constitutive' (124). They go on to point out that not only might language structure have an impact on imaging as in the examples from Slobin's work, but that the quality of the imaging may have an impact on the way language is used and may, for instance, block some effort at problem solving. While in both the Slobin and the Keller and Keller work, the assumption is that the thinker is a native of the given language, the relationship between language and thought may also be affected by whether or not the thinker is a nonnative.

It is also reasonable to assume that thinking through the L_T is more likely in a discourse domain over which the learner has greater control. It has been hypothesized in the literature that learners generate their own highly personal discourse domains. These domains are 'internally-created contexts, within which . . . interlanguage structures are created differentially' (Selinker and Douglas, 1985: 190). Selinker and Douglas (1985) gave the example of a discourse domain in civil engineering generated by a native Spanish-speaking graduate student. They demonstrated in their research how non-natives may be more conversant in talking about content in certain discourse domains than in others. There is also research which shows that even non-natives with limited language proficiency may still be more conversant in talking about content within their professional discourse domain than less knowledgeable native speakers (Zuengler, 1993).

Another way to characterize thoughts might be through distinguishing those of an academic nature from those of an interpersonal or social nature, consistent with the distinction between academic and conversational language proficiency made by Cummins (1991). If learners wanted to use the L_T to think through a word problem in math or refine the research questions for a study, then they would need to call on their academic language proficiency in the L_T in order to do so. Likewise, if they wanted to think L_T thoughts of a sociocultural nature, possibly even emotionally charged ones (e.g. planning a complex speech act, such as complaining, apologizing, or making a delicate request; or relating an emotional upset to a close friend), then the learners would need the appropriate conversational language proficiency in the L_T.

In certain language contexts, such as that of the workplace, both non-native learners and bilinguals who have the L_T as one of their languages may only be able to perform work-related cognitive operations in that L_T (e.g. in scrutinizing the language of a legal document or of a patient's medical record, in negotiating an auto repair, or in functioning successfully in an academic discipline such as psycholinguistics). They may not know how to think about work-related issues in their L1 if their only exposure to the material (e.g. through schooling and/or through a work experience) is in the L_T, and if, in addition, they have done little or no reprocessing of this L_T material into the L1 or another language. In other domains, such as that of social interaction, the language of thought may be the L1 or an L_O in which the speaker feels more comfortable. Hence, we could consider this a case of diglossic thinking where the speaker has the capability of thinking in two or more languages and uses these languages for distinctive and largely complementary purposes.[3]

There has been at least one sociolinguistic survey which investigated the *internal functions* of language for 59 bilingual students and teachers (23 Francophone Africans, 12 Finns, and 24 from other language backgrounds; ages 18–35), who all functioned at a high level in two languages (Cook, 1994). The survey was in part prompted by a desire to improve upon definitions of bilingualism which do not typically take into account internal or *private* functions of the two languages, such as self-organization (e.g. making appointments and shopping lists), mental calculations (e.g. counting things and adding up numbers), memory tasks (e.g. remembering phone numbers, travel routes, days of the week, and historical dates), unconscious uses (e.g. talking to oneself and dreaming), praying, and display of emotions (e.g. feeling happy, sad, tired, pained, or frustrated).

The results showed prayer to be the activity that drew the largest concentration of reported L1 use – 60% (with 20% indicating use of both languages and 20% use of just the L2). The next highest reported use of L1, 55%, was for mental arithmetic, while 17% reported using both L1 and L2, and 28% reported using just the L2. Unconscious uses was next with 49% reporting the use of the L1, 38% reporting both L1 and L2, and 13% just the use of the L1. For memory tasks, 48% reported using the L1, 23% reported using both languages, and 29% indicated use of the L2 alone. Finally, 44% of the respondents indicated displaying their emotions primarily in their L1, 39% in both, and 17% in their L1. This study constitutes one of the only attempts to determine the extent to which bilinguals use their two languages for such private functions. It also needs to be pointed out that the results of such a survey will vary according to the demographics of the given sample.

While this survey gives a broad report of the language of thought for selected activities, there is a need for more such surveys along with the details of actual experiences. For example, the survey would suggest that about half of those sampled preferred to think emotionally charged thoughts in their L1. Ten years of participation in a support group in Israel provided me with some insights that would corroborate this finding. The support group averaged ten members, of whom some four were native speakers of Hebrew and six were native speakers of English, although all were fluent in both languages. In situations where there was a need to communicate on highly sensitive, emotional matters, the participants appeared to be thinking about issues primarily in their L1[4] and almost invariably communicated their thoughts in the L1.

Although probably less common, there may also arise instances where non-native speakers wish to distance themselves from their message by thinking and talking about it in the L_T precisely so that it does not have the same emotional impact. A colleague related to me that while a college student of German used English when she thought to herself about her horrible experience of having been a rape victim, she was only willing to share the details of this ordeal with others in the foreign language, German. Presumably, some, if not many, of her thoughts about this traumatic experience were in German, at least at the point when she externalized them for her listeners. Hence, she was distancing herself from the event.

6.2.2   Factors influencing the language of thought

In an effort to explore the factors influencing the language of thought and the role of L_T thinking in improving language ability, two methods of data gathering were employed. First, a short questionnaire was constructed (see Appendix 6 at the end of the chapter) and disseminated in December of 1993 to graduate students in a University of Minnesota L2 teaching methods course and to ESL teachers at the Minnesota English Center. Completed questionnaires were obtained from 17 anonymous respondents, of whom 13 were English native speakers, 2 were native speakers of Japanese, 1 a native Turkish speaker, and 1 a native Hungarian speaker. While 3 of these were bilingual, all the others were multilingual – 8 being trilingual, 4 quadrilingual,[5] 1 quintilingual, and 1 sextilingual.

Second, since it was largely my experiences in studying 12 languages and continuing to use 7 of them that prompted this study, I decided to draw on some of my own multilingual thinking experiences as a source of data. I lived for 16 years in a Hebrew and Arabic speaking community, 2 years in an Aymara-speaking community within the Spanish-speaking world, a year and a half in a Portuguese-speaking country, and four months in a French-speaking environment.

The following discussion of language of thought and the contribution of L_T thinking to language learning will draw on selected responses from the mini-survey and from my own experiences. There would appear to be a number of factors which determine which language(s) people think in at a given moment. Some of these factors trigger the use of a given language in an automatic or unplanned way, while other factors may involve planning. Let us now look at both unplanned uses and planned choices of languages for thought.

UNPLANNED USES OF LANGUAGE(S) FOR THOUGHT

Learners may find themselves thinking in a language and actually be surprised by this realization. Sometimes the switch is triggered by a memory about people or situations, as two respondents indicated:

> English-L1 trilingual: Sometimes when something triggers a memory of being abroad where I spoke an L2 (i.e. Guatemala, Poland, etc.), I think in the language I used at the time, especially if the memory involves conversations or encounters with native speakers in those places.

English–L1 quadrilingual: I think in Hebrew, French, or German when I'm thinking about people who speak those languages or situations in which I used those languages.

Another unintentional switch takes place when speakers want to speak in the third language (L3) but thoughts come to them in their L2, a language in which they are more proficient:

Hungarian–L1 trilingual: It often happens to me when I try to speak in my L3 (German) that I find myself thinking in my L2 (English) – as if my brain knew that it should be a foreign language, but words come to me in the foreign language that I'm more proficient in.

One of the respondents from the survey, an English–L1 trilingual, described a somewhat frustrating but not atypical experience in multilingual thought in a language class he once took:

I studied Spanish in Sweden as an exchange student. A question would be posed in Swedish with the goal of a reply in Spanish, but in my head it went Swedish English Swedish, as if I were speaking 'foreign' – that is, any language other than English was 'foreign.' It was very confusing for the instructor, and I often wouldn't know which language I had produced in.

The above respondent was thus describing a recurring situation in which he was reprocessing the teacher's input that for him was Swedish as an L2 into English as an L1, and then instead of responding in Spanish–L3 as he wished, the thoughts and subsequent utterances would sometimes emerge in Swedish, almost involuntarily. In other words, his mind would go into a 'foreign language' mode and what would appear would be the dominant foreign language rather than the target one.

The English–L1 sextilingual indicated shifts back to the L1 from a second or foreign language because of language inadequacy, as well as noting a fascinating pattern of repeatedly shifting to the L6 in dreams:

I often have thoughts that begin in a second language but end in my L1 because of language inadequacy. I also have thoughts that begin in a second language and switch to L1 when I remember that I can use the L1 for the interaction I am anticipating. I'm used to living in a non-English environment. I have had dreams where I am attempting to talk to someone in my L3 but keep lapsing into my L6.

When my wife, two children (ages 13 and 9), and I lived in São Paulo, Brazil, from 1986 to 1987, English was the language of the family at home, Hebrew the family language on the streets (for security reasons), and Portuguese the language that I used at work in the university. It was not a strictly triglossic situation in that while conducting classes and meeting with students in Portuguese, I continued to use English at work for my own research purposes. Also, we would use Portuguese on the streets with Brazilian friends and sometimes use English as well. Given this multilingual environment, I noticed that I would inadvertently have trilingual thoughts – beginning them, say, in Portuguese, continuing them in Hebrew, and ending them in English. When I would become aware of this, it would usually amuse me. I remember attributing that phenomenon to the fact that I was using all three languages frequently and in highly contiguous situations, but I never analyzed just where the shift took place (i.e. if there was some trigger word or phrase [see Clyne, 1980] that induced it).

PLANNED CHOICE OF LANGUAGE(S) OF THOUGHT

It is true that multilingual language learners often think in a given language without having consciously chosen to do so. Yet there are times when they may purposely use the L_T as the language of thought or when the instructional method encourages them or requires them to do so. While learners may not be able to control the language in which certain thoughts emerge, there are various moments when they do consciously select the language of thought or are instructed to do so. The use of L1 thinking is likely to be comforting at least and at best beneficial in dispelling early on any potential misconceptions about the meaning of what is heard, spoken, written, or read. Let us look at some of these forms of planned choice.

Warm up: 'din in the head'

A language learner may choose to think in an L_T for the purpose of rehearsal – to warm up or to enhance the 'din in the head' (Krashen, 1985) for that language. Here is an example from the mini-survey:

> English-L1 trilingual: Yes – I planned what I would say and prepared for various scenarios ahead of time in a language – thinking of what words I would use and how to express myself in a situation. It was very helpful and after a few months, I gave it up because I no longer needed to rehearse.

Depending on how well the language is known, carrying on an imaginary conversation in the mind or planning for such a conversation may contribute to more successful oral communication. By the same token, reading bits and pieces of a newspaper in the target language or doing a little unmonitored speed writing may constitute useful warm ups to subsequent reading and writing efforts respectively. The amount of time the learners need for a warm up will vary according to their proficiency in that language and the recency of last contact with it.

Formulating thoughts through the L1 or and L_O in learning the L_T

Learners may think in their L1 or an L_O (see the examples from the trilingual and the sextilingual below) in order to learn some formal rule of grammar in the L_T. In fact, they may only attempt to think in the L_T itself when the intent is to use the language in free conversation, and they perform most or all of the metalinguistic tasks in the L1. It is possible that the learners do not think complex (e.g. metalinguistic) thoughts through the L_T at all, but rather make passing reference to the L_T in the form of fleeting or limited thoughts. So, for example, if learners have worksheets to complete where they have to supply the appropriate verb form (tense, number, and so forth) or particle, they may think through the target language briefly while decoding a given sentence (although even there they may just translate it into their L1), and then they revert entirely to the L1 in order to figure out how to supply the missing element in the given blank. For this reason, the question has arisen as to whether the L_T actually serves as a language of thought or as a language of reference (Personal Communication, Richard Kern, January 12, 1994). This brings us back to the question raised at the outset concerning what constitutes 'thinking in the L_T.'

The extent to which learners' metalinguistic thoughts would be through the L_T may depend in part on the learners' motivation to submerge themselves in the language (and culture). It also depends, perhaps to a large extent, on the instructional method and on the type of task. If, for example, the method is one of grammar translation, where much of the formal learning of the language takes place in the native language of the learners, many of the learners' thoughts during language use could well be through their L1. Having recently gone through a four-month accelerated course in first-year college Japanese (two semesters in one), I am acutely aware of how easy it is to revert to a grammar translation mode and to perform the metalinguistic tasks exclusively in the L1. In fact, the method and textbook used in the course promoted a rote mastery approach with the focus on structure, with at least half or more of the classroom discussion being in English. Some of the speaking tasks and many of the writing tasks were elicited by means of L1 prompts, and most of the reading tasks called for translation into the L1 as a means of checking for comprehension (Cohen, in press (a)).

Multilingual learners may also consciously draw material from several L_Os while learning an L_T. For example, in devising mnemonic devices for remembering L_T words, learners may choose to use words or expressions from an L_O. So, for example, when I was learning Hebrew, I usually generated mnemonic keywords from English but occasionally from Spanish. Thus, when I wanted to remember the Hebrew word *arbolet* 'whirlpool,' I used the Spanish keyword *árbol* 'tree,' and created an image of a dead tree caught in a whirlpool. Likewise, in learning Japanese, I sometimes created mnemonic keywords using Hebrew keywords, such as the keyword *sakanáh* 'danger' to remember the Japanese word *sakana* 'fish' (e.g. 'Some fish are dangerous'). In 4.3.5 above, I gave the example of how I learned *shukudai* 'homework' by means of a Hebrew mnemonic keyword phrase using *shuk* 'market' and *dai* 'enough.' I thought of being assigned enough (= so much) homework that I did not have time to go to the market.

Likewise, multilingual language learners may choose to think at times or even extensively in one of their L_Os while learning the given L_T. This L_O may be closer to the target language in grammatical structure and vocabulary than is the L1. The work by Slobin (1996) would suggest that a desire for similarity in structure might even be motivated by a preference to have verbalized thoughts in a language that describes reality in similar ways. In such cases, the language learner is consciously or unconsciously applying principles of contrastive analysis in the language learning effort (see James, 1991).

Again using myself as an example, as a native speaker of English, I learned L4 (Spanish) by thinking primarily in my L3 (French); I learned my L6 (Aymara), L7 (Portuguese), and L11 (Italian) by thinking extensively in my L4 (Spanish); and I learned my L9 (spoken Arabic) by thinking most of the time in my L8 (Hebrew). When I speak these languages I often still think – at least to some extent – in the language that I used as a language of thought during the learning process.

In learning spoken Arabic, I was in a class with Hebrew speakers and the vocabulary was glossed in Hebrew. The system for writing the spoken Arabic involved the use of a transliteration using Hebrew letters (written from right to left). When I speak Arabic today, I think partly in Hebrew (as Arabic and Hebrew share common words and grammatical structures) and partly in English. Interestingly enough, I call up an English transliteration (from left to right) in my mind even though I learned through Hebrew transliteration. The mnemonics that I used to learn Arabic vocabulary mostly involved both English and Hebrew key words and phrases. An example of an English mnemonic key phrase for the Arabic word *ebtihan* 'exam' was 'empty handed' 'he → went into the exam empty handed.'

With regard to the experiences of the 17 respondents surveyed, none indicated that they used a global strategy of thinking through an L_O, as I had done systematically in the learning of at least five languages. However, several indicated the use of an L_O in the learning of L_T grammatical structures:

> Turkish-L1 trilingual: The grammar of my L3 (English) is more similar to my L2 (German) than my L1 (Turkish). When I was learning English I was comparing it with German rather than with Turkish.

> English-L1 sextilingual: I guess when I learned Spanish I compared verb conjugations with French, which I had studied previously, because person, tense, and gender matched better than comparing with English.

> English-L1 quadrilingual: When I studied Russian and Farsi, I relied on my knowledge of the verb conjugation paradigms from the Romance languages I had studied. I found many phonological similarities which helped me to remember subject pronouns and verb endings. My knowledge of German helped me be more open to the concept of the case systems in Russian.

One respondent did indicate frequent interlingual comparisons for the purpose of practicing the different languages:

> English-L1 quadrilingual: I do this all the time, for the purpose of practicing my other languages. I'll take an English thought, and ask myself, 'How would I say this in Spanish, or Ukrainian?' Then, additionally, I might ask myself, 'Which language seems to express that idea, or that thought, or feeling the best?'

6.2.3 The role of L_T thought formulation in improving language ability

While researchers in the field of language learning have begun to investigate the strategies that learners use to succeed at L_T learning (O'Malley and Chamot, 1990; Cohen, 1990), the issue of the language used in **verbalized** thoughts has not received much attention in the language learning strategy literature. As mentioned at the outset, there is an intuitively based assumption that it is beneficial for foreign language learners to think as much as possible through the language that they are learning. This assumption has been at the core of certain foreign language learning methods that have avoided the use of the learner's L1, at least during the initial phase of instruction – methods such as the Silent Way, the Natural Approach, and Total Physical Response.

With regard to the Silent Way, Gattegno expressed his position as follows:

> Throughout our oral work with the rods and the visual dictation on the charts, we have carefully avoided the use of the students' native languages. We have even succeeded in blocking them so that the students relate to the new language directly . . . (Gattegno, 1976: 99)

Krashen and Terrell (1983: 20) stipulated the following with regard to the Natural Approach:

(1) the instructor always uses the target language;
(2) the focus of the communication will be on a topic of interest for the student; and
(3) the instructor will strive at all times to help the student understand.

Asher described his Total Physical Response method as follows:

> Understanding should be developed through movements of the student's body. (1977: 4) . . . When you cast material in the imperative, there is no translation. (20)

In Total Physical Response, not only do learners refrain from speaking in their L1, but they also refrain from speaking the L2 in the early stages as well. The focus is just on aural comprehension.

In methods such as these three, teachers are presumably expected to implicitly or explicitly discourage students from translating, and the learners themselves may come to feel that L1 or L_O thinking could be detrimental to the learning process.[6] The argument is that by formulating their verbalized thoughts in the target language, learners are increasing their chances of becoming idiomatically accurate in that language – that they are more likely to stop and ask themselves, 'Now how would a native say or write that utterance?' The assumption behind the 'don't translate' philosophy is that it will lead to greater success at language learning. Although the aim of this position is laudable, it is also unrealistic to expect learners to abide by it.

The University of Minnesota mini-survey on the language of thought asked students whether they were admonished by their teachers to think through the L_T in their language learning experiences. Fifty percent of the respondents in the mini-survey indicated that they were:

> <u>English-L1 trilingual</u>: I was taught early on to do this – at first it took more conscious effort, but now it sometimes 'just happens.'

English–L1 trilingual: The teachers always encouraged us to stop translating and start thinking in the L2.

Chinese–L1 bilingual: She pushed to think in the L2. I remember feeling saturated by all of the pushing she did in the L2.

Turkish–L1 trilingual: Often. My first German teacher encouraged us to think in German and to avoid translating into our native languages.

Japanese–L1 trilingual: I went to a school of English in Japan, where English was the only means of communication. 'Think in English' was the school's motto or philosophy.

Hungarian–L1 trilingual: I have always been encouraged to try to think in the foreign language I'm learning, but I've found that it's much easier to do at a higher proficiency level than at lower levels.

When asked whether they themselves made an effort to think extensively through the target language, 82% (14) indicated that they did. As to the results it produced, most indicated benefits. The first set of responses referred directly to situations of submersion in a context where the language was spoken natively:

English–L1 trilingual: Living over there (in France) for 4+ years with few 'English' contacts made that quite easy.

English–L1 bilingual: Yes – I consciously pushed myself to think in my L2 while I lived in China. The results were quite good, especially since I did a lot of communicating with other L2 learners in Chinese. The more we practiced the language and thinking in the language, the better our communicative competence and linguistic competence.

English–L1 trilingual: Yes, the results of submersion were pretty successful. After a year of living in Mexico, I seldom had to think of a word in English before putting my thoughts into Spanish.

English–L1 quadrilingual: During a time living in France I took a course in speed-reading. Since what I was reading was French, I eventually got to the point where I really read in French – despite lack of oral practice. I continue to read French fast and always in French.

Japanese–L1 bilingual: I tried to think in English when I was studying the language in Japan. But it just didn't work. (I can do it quite easily now [after coming to the US to study].) I think one needs to immerse in the L_T culture for some time before she becomes able to think in the L_T.

<u>Turkish-L1 trilingual</u> (living in the US for some years): Not as much in German (L2). I seldom think in Turkish now. I am much more at home in English (L3) than I ever was in German.

The next set of responses regarding the extent of L_T thought are of a more general nature, not referring specifically to submersion in the language and culture:

<u>English-L1 trilingual</u>: I find that when I do make the effort to make internal dialog in L2, it makes it easier to speak without as much hesitation.

<u>English-L1 quadrilingual</u>: Always – I am successful. I talk to myself in L_Ts, describing even simple things.

<u>English-L1 quintilingual</u>: It seems to aid reading comprehension and oral communication when I try to think in the L_T system.

<u>English-L1 quadrilingual</u>: The first year I studied Spanish, I practiced translating my thoughts from English to Spanish all the time – at work, play, walking around, etc. I believe it served to ingrain my knowledge immensely. I considered it 'studying any time, any place, without even sitting down and opening my book.'

<u>English-L1 sextilingual</u>: Yes. My language ability improved. I communicated more and better. I began to automatically think in the second language and to rehearse mentally what to say in various situations I encountered or anticipated.

<u>English-L1 trilingual</u>: Yes, I can exist in Swedish – and I do not know many telephone numbers of my Swedish friends in English. I have to write them out and translate if I give them, for example, to an international operator.

<u>English-L1 trilingual</u>: If you can do it, it always pays off.

Only two of the respondents had a somewhat negative response to the question about whether they used L_T thought extensively:

<u>Japanese-L1 trilingual</u>: Yes, but I guess that I tended to get exhausted at a particular point in the process of thinking. Also I seemed to be thinking more slowly. (Thus, I was more frustrated.)

<u>English-L1 bilingual</u>: Not usually, unless I'm also speaking or reading in German.

So, the conclusion that one might reach after reviewing the responses from the mini-survey and from my own examples is that there are definite benefits from making an effort to think in the L_T. The issue at hand is what such 'thinking in the L_T' really means and how to do it most effectively. Just as Kern questioned the extent to which the L_T is actually a language of thought as opposed to a language of reference, so Lantolf (Personal Communication, May 13, 1994) has contended that when non-natives plan and rehearse what they want to say subvocally in an L_T (as some of the respondents reported doing above), this does not really constitute thinking in the L_T; likewise, Lantolf sees this activity more as thinking about the L_T. In other words, the fact that the speakers have to engage in such activity might suggest that they cannot think in the L_T. Of course, if they are rehearsing the L_T material and also thinking about it in the L_T at the same time, then perhaps this would more directly constitute thinking in the L_T.

Once we have all of these various distinctions sorted out and arrive at a good working definition of what we mean by thinking through the L_T, then it will be beneficial to conduct a series of studies assessing the effects of both qualitative and quantitative differences in the amount of L_T thought on outcomes at various stages in the learning process. At present, we are still in search of the best terminology for describing the choice of language for cognitive operations. The above discussion was intended to begin the effort of describing the phenomena. The interim conclusion is probably that it pays to do some or even extensive systematic thinking through the L_T, but not to be hesitant about thinking in the L1 when it is comforting and perhaps necessary to do so. Is L1 thought a trap? Perhaps if practiced in the extreme – at the expense of L_T – it is.

6.3 Studies on mental translation into the first language during foreign language writing and reading tasks

6.3.1 The admonition to think directly through the target language while learning/using it

'Actually [thinking in Spanish] is something that I've been working on, um . . . cause my Spanish teacher in high school said "You're not gonna get anywhere if you keep translating in your head." ' This quote is from an advanced learner of Spanish at the university level (Hawras, 1996: 55). The student is simply echoing the oft-heard taboo against mental translation. In situations where the objective is to become fluent in a foreign language, both in the receptive and productive skills, learners such as the one cited above have often been encouraged to think through the target language as much as possible during the language learning and language use process. Learners may come to believe that it is detrimental for them to rely on their L1 habits rather than making the effort to comprehend the target language on its own terms.

Whereas a fair amount of research has now been conducted to evaluate the benefits of explicitly teaching learners how to apply foreign language strategies in their language learning and language use (see Cohen, 1990; Cohen *et al.*, 1995; Dörnyei, 1995; McDonough, 1995; Mendelsohn, 1994; O'Malley and Chamot, 1990), the issue of the language of **thought** has not received much attention in the language learning strategy literature. As illustrated above, there is an intuitively based assumption that it is beneficial for foreign language learners to think as much as possible through the language that they are learning. This assumption has been at the core of certain foreign language learning methods that have avoided the use of the learner's L1, at least during the initial phase of instruction – methods such as the Silent Way, Total Physical Response, and the Natural Approach (as reflected in the above quotes).

In methods such as these three, teachers implicitly or explicitly discourage students from translating, and the learners themselves may come to feel that L1 or other-language thinking could be detrimental to the learning process. The argument is that by thinking in the target language, learners are increasing their chances of becoming idiomatically accurate in that language. This maxim has been applied to the more visible forms of language – namely, speaking and writing – because they are so external and visible. With respect to the speech of non-native interlocutors, for example, natives of a target language notice errors which they might ascribe to the influence of the native language. For example, a native Hebrew speaker may say, 'The policeman didn't give me to enter here,' a direct translation from the L1. Teachers might suggest that such errors would disappear if the speakers were to think more through the target language while they are speaking.

As for writing, there has also been a focus on those errors which appear to be a result of negative transfer from the native language while trying to write in the target language. Again, the assumption would be that thinking through the target language while writing would decrease the number of such errors. Yet there have been a series of studies which have looked at the influence of thinking through the L1 while writing in the L2, and the results tend to go against the maxim. While Chelala (1982) found that the use of Spanish L1 to compose in the L2 was more detrimental than it was helpful, Lay (1988) found in a case study of four native Chinese-speaking ESL students at the intermediate level, there were a number of benefits from thinking through the L1:

(1) greater ease at brainstorming about topics and finding points to make about them;
(2) increased facility at raising questions;
(3) increased likelihood of being able to work through complicated ideas;
(4) ease at recalling past experiences;
(5) greater facility at evaluating the organization of the essay;
(6) the enhancement of their self-expression;
(7) the availability of greater lexical variety; and
(8) greater propensity to display cultural sensitivity.

In a study of 28 Chinese-speaking college students, Friedlander (1990) found that the students who initially used the L1 to describe a Chinese festival could more richly describe their experience in the L2, and that thinking and writing a rough draft in the L1 had a positive impact on their final product in the L2. Jones and Tetroe (1987) also reported some benefits of thinking in Spanish when composing text in English L2.

While this section will focus on mental translation for the purpose of comprehending text during reading, let us briefly look at several studies that have considered the effects of translation from first language on the production of foreign language writing.

6.3.2   Studies of foreign language writing by means of translation

A study by Paivio and Lambert (1981), for example, found that the translation of individual words called for deeper language processing than simply copying down the foreign language synonymous word or phrase, and that this act of translation helped to fix the words more solidly in long-term memory.

At the text level, a study of EFL composition writing was conducted with 48 Japanese university students who were at the low-intermediate to low-advanced levels and who had all had four years of university (Kobayashi and Rinnert, 1992). Choosing from among four topics, one group wrote their first essay in Japanese L1 and then translated it into the foreign language, English, while a second group wrote directly in English first. The next day the groups reversed tasks and wrote their second essay on another topic.

The results showed that the translations were rated higher (in content and style) than were the essays written directly in English, the foreign language. In terms of content, organization, and style, lower-level writers benefited from translation whereas higher-level writers did not. Syntactic complexity was found to be greater in the translations. When the students were asked for their writing preference, 77% reported preferring direct composition to translation. They based their view on the difficulty of conveying subtle nuances of meaning when translating, and on the tendency to use familiar words and structures and simpler ideas when writing directly. In addition, several indicated preferring the direct approach because they wanted to think in English. As for the advantages of translating, the students felt that the ideas were easier to develop, thoughts and opinions could be expressed more clearly, and words could be more easily found through the use of a dictionary. The students reported being able to think more deeply in their native language and better express their thoughts and opinions. Translating was also viewed by some as helping in vocabulary acquisition.

The investigators asked for retrospective self-report from the students as to 'how much Japanese they thought they were using in their minds while they were writing directly in English.' Since 55% of the higher-proficiency students and 87% of the lower-proficiency students reported using Japanese half the time or more when supposedly writing directly in English, the *direct writing* treatment was actually somewhat less direct than the label would imply.

Another study of foreign language writing through translation was conducted by Brooks (1993). She compared two methods of producing French compositions among intermediate college French students: writing and revising a draft in English and then translating the finished version into French as opposed to conducting the entire process in French. She found that out of 31 students, 17 were rated better on their translated essay than on the one that they wrote directly in French. Twelve students received a higher rating for the essay that they wrote directly in French, and 2 had identical scores. In this study, the students were not asked to report on the extent to which they thought in the L1 while composing directly in the foreign language, French.

Studies such as these two, by Kobayashi and Rinnert (1992) and by Brooks (1993), would lead to speculation that for a percentage of intermediate non-native writers, trying to think directly in the L_T while writing may actually result in a lowered standard of writing than that which can be produced by writing first in the native language and then translating. Contrary to popular belief, the attempt to think directly through the L_T may in fact detract from the production of good writing. If so, this would be an indication of a way in which thinking in the L1 can actually support the production of foreign language despite the admonition that such cognitive behavior encourages negative transfer and is thus counterproductive. Of course, any such conclusions need to be tempered by considering the two languages involved and the learners' control of each, the learners' motivation, and other variables as well.

6.3.3   Mental translation into the first language during foreign language reading
Andrew Cohen and Steve Hawras[7]

While there has been some research done on the impact of first-language thought on L2 writing, few studies have considered the impact of L1 on L2 reading. Part of the problem is that much of reading has generally been considered a far more internal and unobservable process. Fortunately, verbal report methodology is improving (see Pressley and Afflerbach, 1995; Smagorinsky, 1994; Cohen, 1995) and so now there are more finely tuned means available for studying what has until now gone largely unresearched.

Where studies of L1 impact on L2 reading have appeared, their primary emphasis has tended to be on transfer from L1 to L2 reading – especially on negative transfer. While translation of L2 text into the L1 is a widespread occurrence, it is usually viewed as a crutch to be avoided if possible. The position taken by many language educators has been that translation into the L1 may have negative consequences on L2 reading.

A STUDY OF MENTAL TRANSLATION TO THE NATIVE LANGUAGE WHILE
READING IN FRENCH AS A FOREIGN LANGUAGE

A recent study by Kern with native English-speaking readers of French (Kern, 1994) would suggest that there are positive consequences of mental translation into the first language while reading in a foreign language just as there are negative ones. The researcher explored the actual uses for translation into the first language in the language learning and language using process. He had 51 college students of French as a foreign language at the intermediate level (in high, medium, and low reading ability groups) participate in verbal report interviews while reading French texts at the beginning and the end of a 15-week semester. Kern used a pre-test–post-test research design in order to determine if propensity to translate changed over the semester. The subjects were presented with a French text one sentence at a time, which they were to read silently, and then were to report what they were thinking as they read each new sentence. They were asked the following:

(1) what they understood;
(2) what they did not understand;
(3) how they went about making sense of what they read;
(4) whether they made any predictions or inferences; and
(5) whether they translated into English.

Subjects were free to return to earlier sections of the text as needed for clarification.

An analysis of the verbal report data found considerable mental translation and the investigator offered a series of reasons why the learners of French as a foreign language chose to perform mental translation into their L1 or some other language instead. The following is a list of some of the potentially **positive** consequences according to Kern:

1. L1 processing facilitates semantic processing. Storing words as discrete units is more of a burden on memory and it is easier to chunk lexical items into semantic clusters in the L1.
2. The use of mental translation helps to keep the train of thought when chunks are long or syntactically complex. Mental translation allows the reader to represent portions of the text in a familiar, memory-efficient form long enough for meaning to be integrated and assimilated.
3. The reader's network of associations is richer in the L1, so the concepts come alive. The semantic potency of words is greater in the L1 than in the L2.
4. The input is converted into more familiar, user-friendly terms, enhancing the readers' confidence in their ability to comprehend it – thus producing an affective boost and reducing feelings of insecurity.
5. Mental translation may help in clarifying syntactic roles, verifying a verb tense, or checking for comprehension.

The following are what Kern saw as the **disadvantages** of mental translation:

1. Attempts at mental translation may be inaccurate, leading to miscomprehension.
2. Micro-level (e.g. word-by-word) translations may not lead to integration of meaning. They may produce a bottom-up sense of how portions of text and isolated items function and what they mean, without a top-down sense of what the material is all about. Some or much of the thought during mental translation may be of a technical or perfunctory nature – e.g. searching for literal equivalents of L2 forms, rather than determining the general coherence of the text.
3. There is a risk of attending to L2 forms only briefly, with the bulk of meaning processing reserved for L1 mental representation. It is possible that during much of the meaning-integration process, learners focus primarily on transformed L1 representations rather than on the original L2 forms, diminishing possibilities of L2 acquisition.

In some ways the analysis of data for this study was problematic in that what the investigator called *reports of translation* reflected differing kinds of translation behavior. For one thing, the subject was sometimes reporting the translation of a single word, in other cases a phrase or whole sentence. So there was variation in the amount of material being translated. Perhaps the traditional linguistic elements framework is inappropriate for this kind of analysis since the translation of isolated words may constitute radically different types of translation phenomena. The translation of one word may be to check on its grammatical form whereas that of another word is just to help store the meaning in a memory buffer. Thus, there is most likely both a grammatical reality of mental translation and a separate psycholinguistic reality.

The Kern study certainly raises the issue of just how much translation goes on while the reader is grappling with text, how such translation is used and why, and what the results are in terms of comprehension of text. What role does translation play in the reader's effort to determine the meaning of the text?

A STUDY OF MENTAL TRANSLATION TO THE NATIVE LANGUAGE WHILE READING IN SPANISH AS A FOREIGN LANGUAGE

In a replication of the Kern (1994) study, Hawras (1996) started from the same premise, namely, that reading research had not fully addressed one of the fundamental differences between first language and foreign language comprehension: that foreign language readers have **two** languages at their disposal rather than one. Hawras perceived this bilinguality as frequently posing what for many is a dilemma: just what is the proper place of the first language in the learning of a foreign language? He asked the following research questions:

1. To what extent do beginning, intermediate, and advanced-level Spanish students translate mentally as they read Spanish texts?
2. To what extent does mental translation into the L1 actually facilitate foreign language reading comprehension?

The subjects were 27 University of Minnesota students from eight different sections of Spanish language classes, representing three different proficiency levels. So whereas Kern had worked only with intermediate learners and studied them at the beginning and end of a term, Hawras looked cross-sectionally at three levels at the same point in time. The subjects were informed that this was to be an exploration of how foreign language learners mentally process a reading task. They were given a reading task consisting of the first two paragraphs of an essay on European culture (about 220 words). The essay was presented using a technique from Fillmore and Kay's (1983) text interview procedure. The text was printed on ten separate sheets of paper: the first sheet had the first sentence only, the second sheet had the first two sentences, the third sheet the first three, so that the respondents were presented with only one new sentence at a time, but each new sheet included all the preceding sentences. The first two sentences (out of ten) served as the 'warm up,' to get the students acclimatized to the task, and were therefore not counted in the data. The students could read the sentences either silently or aloud. If they did not do so on their own, they were always asked to provide verbal report data as they read each sentence. The verbal report consisted primarily of introspective and retrospective self-observation as to **whether** and **how** they understood each sentence, before going on to the next one. The interviews took from 12 to 30 minutes each and were tape-recorded.

A quantitative analysis of the instances where the respondents actually described their language processing yielded some suggestive results. The beginning and intermediate students reported translating portions of the text mentally into English about as often as they got the meaning directly from Spanish. The advanced group used mental translation into English only about one quarter of the time. This finding that advanced students translated the least would be expected, in that the more proficient one becomes in a foreign language, the less there is a need to rely on the L1.

It also appeared that the more advanced a learner was in the foreign language, the more likely it was that the act of translating actually facilitated comprehension. However, for the beginning group, comprehension was achieved in only about half of all the instances of reported mental translation. For this group mental translation into English either did **not** help them understand some linguistic unit or caused them to misunderstand it as often as it facilitated comprehension. The intermediate and advanced groups were found to be similar with respect to what they comprehended. When they **did** avail themselves of mental translation, these two groups had a similar success rate in terms of the proportion of accurate comprehension of all reported instances of mental translation: 62% for the intermediate group to 68% for the advanced group. This finding might suggest that as learners are more proficient in a foreign language, they acquire a sense of when mental translation into English is likely to yield better results.

With regard to the qualitative portion of the study, Hawras noted that there were perhaps two general strategies or guiding principles employed by the respondents. For some of the beginners, it was to translate word for word. For most students the guiding principle was to read directly in the foreign language, Spanish, and to translate only when necessary. The following is a quote from an advanced respondent who used this principle:

Yeah, the first scan-through I just read it usually without ... thinking, I just read it and I hear the words ... or ... in my head. And then if I don't understand just reading it I have to ... go back ... and I read it slower. Then I stop and think: 'OK, what's that in English?' And then if I **still** don't get it I have to go back and read the whole thing in English, like translate word for word. But I usually don't translate word for word unless I **really** am having trouble understanding it. That's like the last case thing, cause it takes so long. (Hawras, 1996: 54)

The last statement of this respondent calls attention to a potential disadvantage to the use of mental translation, namely, that word-for-word mental translation can be painstakingly slow.

Hawras found that a series of specific translation strategies emerged from the verbal report data. One was for dealing with long sentences, as was evident with several of the subjects in the study. The following is an example of a long sentence and the response from an intermediate-level student:

Con la progresiva industrialización y urbanización y los muchos contactos internacionales que esto implica, y también la continua emigración entre países, todas las naciones avanzadas empiezan a parecerse más. (With the progressive industrialization, urbanization, and the many international contacts that this implies, and also with the continued emigration between countries, all advanced nations are beginning to resemble each other more and more.)

Student: I don't know, 'Advanced nations are starting to ...' um, kind of come up more with 'industrialization,' and 'urbanization ...' I'm not really sure what this sentence ... is getting at.

Interviewer: This is kind of a longer sentence.

Student: Mm-hm.

Interviewer: Are you just trying to get the whole meaning of the whole sentence all at a time?

Student: Yeah. Um, well, actually I'm reading, ... no, I'm reading, um, I take kind of bits and pieces of it, like I took *con la progresiva industrialización y urbanización* and then, but then I look down at *todas las naciones avanzadas empiezan a parecerse más* (all the advanced nations are starting to resemble each other more). Um, so I kind of divided it by the commas, almost, and trying to tell what that little fragment meant, and then, put it together with ... but, I still don't know what it means, so ...

Interviewer: You're getting the meaning of the individual words directly through Spanish?

Student: Mm-hm. (Hawras, 1996: 56)

Here the student explicitly said that she was **not** mentally translating the words of the text. However, she **did** seem to be chunking together words comprehended directly through Spanish into English language semantic clusters (i.e. 'Advanced nations are starting to . . .') in order to get the meaning of the individual clauses of the sentence. Then, she tried to integrate the meanings of the clauses to understand the entire sentence.

There were also examples of short sentences that were still demanding because they contained few contextual clues, syntactic markers, or guiding punctuational features. As one intermediate-level student commented, '. . . I think shorter ones are harder to understand. They're so short, I mean, the other ones I think you can take more context clues' (Hawras, 1996: 58). The following is one example with a beginning student's response to it:

> *Es que las diferencias culturales dependen hasta cierto punto del aislamiento.*
> (That is to say that cultural differences depend to a certain point on isolation.)
> Student: Instead of seeing chunks, I see a long list of words I need to go through. . . . Maybe, maybe it's saying something like, 'Cultures are gonna be different until there's no more isolation.' (ha ha ha) or something like that. It doesn't sound like a very logical thought, but . . . (Hawras, 1996: 58)

The sentence does not lend itself to division into more manageable chunks. The learner ended up resorting to translation, and got the general idea, but did not get it exactly, nor was she very confident of having gotten the right meaning. In this case, the physical size of the linguistic unit would seem to have little direct bearing on the complexity of the psycholinguistic processing being required.

Hawras also found translation to make the material more user-friendly and to remove affective barriers, as had Kern (1994) in his study. One strategic use of mental translation was in order to shift into L1 syntax. The following is an explanation of this strategy by an intermediate respondent:

> I guess what I try, what I do, cause I know all these words in here, but the order in which they are don't often, don't always, make the proper sentence in mind. So then I have to, . . . I guess I kind of translated it a little bit . . . Cause often you know Spanish sentence structures aren't always the same as English, so I put them in, sometimes in English structure, but still using these words. (Hawras, 1996: 59)

Another strategic use for mental translation was to verify that a segment of text was accurately comprehended. The advanced learner in the following example reported striving to read and get the meaning of the text directly in Spanish initially, and only going back and translating when necessary. However, at one point she remarked:

> OK, this one I pretty much got the first time through, but then I went back to make sure, . . . and, um, . . . you know, I went back and kind of translated it as I went along to make sure that I had it. I don't think I did that the first time. (Hawras, 1996: 60)

Even though she did understand the meaning of the sentence 'the first time through,' she translated it anyway. Thus, translating the sentence for verification may serve to reduce a lingering insecurity that even advanced students may feel when reading in a foreign language.

6.3.4   Limitations with the mental translation studies

There are limitations with the Hawras study, just as with the previous Kern study. One limitation is that the genre of the text can have an effect on the extent to which mental translation is used and the benefits that might accrue. In both studies, the texts were in the humanities and were of an academic nature. Perhaps other kinds of texts would prompt other types of behaviors with regard to mental translation. Another limitation was that the procedure allowed for no pre-reading of the text. Readers were allowed to perform backwards reading, each time adding a new sentence, so it meant that they needed to read a certain amount of the text before they could get a sense of the global meaning of the text. Once they reached the final sentence, they could then read the full text. It could be argued that this procedure might have generated more mental translation than would have occurred had the entire text been available at the outset.

Another limitation is that in neither of the studies was there any investigation of how well the respondents read in their native language, English. It could be argued that those who have greater difficulty keeping the main idea in their minds as they read along in native language text would be those who need to resort more to mental translation when reading in a foreign language.

6.3.5   Suggestions for further research

With regard to future studies, it would seem worthwhile to include a measure of native language reading ability, especially using texts that place demands on the reader both in terms of vocabulary and syntax. It might also be beneficial to determine how skillful the readers are at translating text from the target language to their native language. Students could be asked to provide an oral translation of the entire text and then to explain their translation. In other words, the purpose would be to see how capable they are at providing a functional translation that captures both the essence and the particulars of the text. Another purpose for such research could be to see which strategies the readers use for producing their oral translations and how they use them. This information might provide added insights into the nature of *mental* translation in foreign language reading. It may be that the extent and types of mental translation used by readers of a foreign language may be determined to some extent by the strategies for translating from the foreign to the native language that the readers possess.

It may also be valuable to investigate the role that the educational system might play in the development of translation skills. In the North American context, for instance, middle-school and secondary-school students are discouraged from systematic use of translation in their foreign language reading, whereas in, say, Japanese junior and senior high schools, learners may be explicitly trained to read English by translating. Is it the case that those who are systematically trained in translating would develop a more refined set of strategies for performing mental translation than those who are not?

Another issue to investigate would be that of the distance between the L1 and the L2. How would mental translation from Spanish or French L2 into English L1 (as in the studies cited in this section) compare with mental translation from Japanese L2, for example? What might be the relationship between the extent of mental translation and the similarity between the languages in question?

In addition, it may be valuable to look at the extent to which individual readers' use of mental translation differs significantly according to their language learning and language use strategy preferences. Even within the same educational system, individual readers may be more likely to employ mental translation than others.

Finally, an analysis could be made of the time needed to perform mental translation. The Hawras study found that mental translation had the potential of slowing the reader down. Where time is a factor in performance (e.g. on reading comprehension tests), the use of extra time for translation may be a major concern. In other circumstances, extra time in reading may enhance comprehension. In still other cases, **the use of mental translation may move the reading process along more rapidly.**

6.3.6   Pedagogical implications

If teachers choose to look upon mental translation as an unnecessary and perhaps unfortunate crutch, they might request that students make every effort to process written text directly through the foreign language when they read. Teachers could warn learners about doing more translation than they need to, with the assumption that such translations may inhibit the development of an independently functioning L2 system. The challenge is to distinguish a genuine need for translation from a perceived need. For example, a reader may feel a need to employ a heavy dose or even overdose of mental translation in order to comprehend a given text successfully, but, as indicated above, without necessarily learning much of the L2 in the process. They may actually improve their reading ability in that language more by resisting translation and by making an effort to generate the meaning of the text directly through the L2 instead.

The Kern and Hawras studies, however, do provide some evidence that non-native readers systematically (and not so systematically) use mental translation to successfully store and understand text. On the strength of these findings, language teachers might be encouraged to view mental translation as offering at least an interim set of reading strategies while reading proficiency is developing. The assumption here would be that if mental translation has genuine benefits, then teachers should stress those beneficial areas or strategies to all foreign language readers so that they might choose from among mental translation strategies when and if deemed necessary. For example, learners may be advised to use their L1 for the following strategic purposes:

(1) to chunk material into semantic clusters;
(2) to keep their train of thought;
(3) to create a network of associations;
(4) to clarify grammatical roles; and
(5) to make the input more familiar and consequently more user-friendly.

Even though mental translation is not visible, it would still make intuitive sense to suggest to students that they avoid the possible pitfall of being too literal since a straight relexification of the LT text might cause negative transfer from that language. Thus, teachers could model *free* or semantic approaches to translation, with an emphasis on the transfering of whole blocks of meaning and not word-for-word segments (Carl James, personal communication, May 23, 1997).

Undoubtedly, some mental translation activities are unconscious and therefore would fall outside the realm of strategies that are consciously selected. The strategies research cited at the beginning of chapter 5 would indicate that there is some advantage to making language users more conscious of the processes that they use, so that they may take more responsibility for their own language learning and language use. Teachers may help to raise to a level of conscious awareness those unconscious mental translation processes that learners may be engaging in while reading.

Teachers might also suggest mental translation more for some students than others – according to their cognitive styles and language learning and language use strategies. The above studies would suggest that the less advanced students of language indulge more in mental translation than the more advanced ones. Perhaps teachers could alert learners at these levels to the fact that they will translate while reading and even contemplate the various roles that such translation can play.

Let us return to the foreign language learning principle presented at the outset of this section, namely that learners should avoid thinking in their L1 when learning and using an L2. Given the issues raised here and the empirical evidence provided with regard to reading research, there appear to be grounds for language educators to suggest the systematic use of mental translation despite pronouncements against it.

Now let us shift to elementary-school pupils and consider their use of the native language in performing cognitive operations in a language immersion context.

6.4   The language used by full immersion pupils to perform cognitive operations

Because of their focus on immersing youngsters in a target language, early full immersion programs may provide a rich context for SLA research on the extent of target language use in performing cognitive operations. Such language immersion programs, which have been in existence in Canada and the United States for about thirty years, are predicated on the assumption that second language acquisition occurs most easily and rapidly in the target language environment and culture. In fact, immersion schooling was heralded as a means for producing school children who could almost effortlessly gain near-native-like control of a foreign language just by virtue of being immersed from kindergarten in a classroom where the teacher spoke only that language with them. Immersion programs have been designed to simulate to some extent native-like learning conditions by maximizing the time that learners are exposed to the target language and by exposing the learners to the target language culture or cultures as well.

Findings from research on L2 immersion programs have shown that pupils who become bilinguals through such programs make normal or better than normal progress in content subjects which are taught primarily through the L2 (Cohen and Swain, 1979; Genesee, 1987). There is also evidence that pupils who belong to the majority group in Society and consequently develop their bilingual skills in an *additive* or supportive or bilingual education environment, have their general non-verbal abilities enhanced (Bamford and Mizokawa, 1991), as well as their problem-solving abilities in science (Kessler and Quinn, 1982; Rosebery *et al.*, 1992).

The successful results from immersion research have led to claims that immersion pupils gain an ability 'to think in the foreign language.' The implication has been that the more adept they are at thinking in that language, the quicker they will be able to process input and output and consequently enhance their acquisition of that language all the more. In recent years, however, educators have noticed that while there are enormous advantages to this method over others if the aim is to produce a high level of communicative ability among the pupils, there are method effects resulting from the immersion approach. One of these effects is that pupils seem to develop a set of strategies for thinking through their L1 at times when L_T thought may be more conducive to genuine language learning.

In addition, there also appear to be gaps in foreign language proficiency, especially in speaking and writing skills. There are signs that pupils sometimes use English language structures to construct their utterances but substitute foreign language words, a process referred to as *relexification*. Pupils also insert native language words into their utterances, especially adverbs and interjections – a sign that they may be thinking in English and performing on-line translation. Finally, the language produced in immersion programs is seen to have reduced vocabulary and structure (e.g. little or no use of certain complex verb tenses such as the conditional or the subjunctive), similar to the situation with various pidgin and creole varieties of language.

French immersion research, for example, has shown that in spite of having had a number of years of comprehensible input in French, the students' spoken and written French contains numerous morphological, syntactic, and lexical deviations from native speaker norms (Lapkin *et al.*, 1990; Genesee, 1987). In addition, observations of immersion classrooms have indicated that students may have relatively little opportunity for the use of extended discourse in that setting. One study of more than ten 6th-grade (11 year old) French immersion classes found that in only 14% of teacher-fronted activities where students spoke were their utterances longer than a clause in length (Swain, 1988; Harley, Allen et al., 1990).[8]

For these reasons, Canadian immersion education experts began a research effort to explore the different options for increasing conscious attention to output and for pushing the learners to make their output more grammatically correct (Swain, 1992). Without such measures, the immersion pupils tend to fossilize their language ability at a level which is adequate for the immersion classroom but not native-like. In effect, the pupils form a pidgin variety of the language which works for them. They understand each other and so there is no great pressure for them to speak or write any differently. In fact, they are probably reinforcing each others' non–native-like forms since, in that environment, their language output is the norm.

Although in full language immersion programs in the United States the rule has been for pupils to speak only in the L2 in the classroom once they are capable of this, second-grade children in the first US immersion program in Culver City still reported using English in the classroom about half the time (Cohen and Lebach, 1974). Further, this was in a program where the teachers scrupulously adhered to their target language guise and had other teachers provide English language arts in the middle grades. So the fact that the pupils spoke and still speak a considerable amount of English during immersion language classes could contribute to limitations in the productive skills of immersion pupils.

Yet another potential source for gaps between comprehension and production may be a systematic reluctance or inability of the immersion pupils to perform cognitive operations in the target language, both in and out of the classroom. In essence, the pupils may not be as immersed in the target language as teachers and administrators think they are. Nonetheless, it would appear that this phenomenon has not been paid much attention in the research literature on immersion programs. It might be assumed that a program which is conducted primarily in a language other than that of the community is stimulating the performance of cognitive operations largely or exclusively through that language both during the processing of academic tasks (*academic language proficiency*) and during social interactions (*conversational language proficiency*) (Cummins, 1991). The reality may be somewhat at odds with the assumption.

While certain cognitive operations that pupils perform are non-verbal, involving symbols and relationships, many of them are verbalized, whether in the form of inner or private speech or in the form of other-directed or public speech – terms which were discussed earlier in this chapter. Inner speech is abrupt, governed by predicates, often unintelligible because referents are unclear – 'speech almost without words' (Vygotsky, 1961:

529). 'One word in inner speech is saturated with sense to such an extent that it would require many words in external speech to explain it' (Vygotsky, 1961: 531).[9] The more external or public private speech becomes, the more fully structured it is.

The final portion of this chapter will provide an in-depth look at a study of first language use in a Spanish full immersion program in order to examine the phenomenon of strategies for choosing the language of thought in the immersion program context. Before doing that, however, let us consider an anecdote regarding a pupil from the first class of one of the first full immersion programs in the US, since this anecdote also has a bearing on the issue of thought – in this case, deep processing.

6.4.1 An anecdote from a Culver City Spanish Immersion Program graduate

The Culver City Spanish Immersion Program represented, at least in its early years, one of the most conscientious efforts to stick strictly to the target language for academic subjects and for social interaction over the early grades. During the first decade or two of the program, the teachers made a point of sticking to their foreign language guise and never speaking English. They even pretended not to be able to, although they made it clear that they understood all that was said by pupils in English. If the principal or a parent spoke to them in the presence of the pupils, the teachers would only respond in Spanish.

A few years ago I had an opportunity to spend time with one of the star pupils in the first class to go through the Culver City Spanish Immersion Program (starting kindergarten in 1971), and to speak Spanish with her. She had also been one of the subjects in the language attrition studies based on data from Culver City (Cohen 1974, 1975). She had just returned to the US after several years of living and working in France, and was pursuing a graduate degree in business administration at the time. The information that she shared with me and actual insights from her efforts at using Spanish during that meeting underscored for me the need to conduct systematic research regarding the language of thought in such programs. After several years in France and no continued use of Spanish, the former immersion student's Spanish was 'rusty.' She understood most everything but spoke it only haltingly. What was interesting was that she spoke it with a near-native accent and that she reported thinking directly in Spanish when she spoke it.

When she wanted to order a turkey sandwich in Spanish at a fast-food restaurant (the attendant was Mexican-American), she could not remember *pavo* 'turkey,' but instead of thinking, 'How do you say "turkey" in

Spanish?' she thought, *'No es "pollo." ¿Cómo se dice?'* (It's not 'chicken.' How do you say it?) In other words, her thoughts were in a Spanish inner speech. She reported that when she spoke in French after having lived in France for several years, she would often think in English first. As she put it, ' "Glass" is *verre*, while in Spanish the word *vaso* just comes right out directly.'

While the former immersion student was confident that her early start with Spanish made it easier for her to learn French and to learn it well, in some ways she did not and perhaps could not learn French as 'deeply' as she had learned Spanish. Thus, it appears that Spanish had special status in her mind, although considerable language attrition had taken place. Cognitive psychologists have long maintained that the durability of memory traces depends on the depth of processing, or the degree of analysis afforded the material in question during the various moments or stages in the input process (Craik and Lockhart, 1972; Craik, 1977). It would seem that getting an early start on language acquisition through early full immersion and participating in such a program that is rich in repeated exposures to the language would help to enhance or deepen the learning.

It may be of benefit to follow up on this anecdote by determining whether this 'deep processing' phenomenon is shared by other immersion pupils who later became fluent in another language. If so, then perhaps it says something about the quality of the language learning experience in early immersion.

Now let us consider a longitudinal study that was aimed at collecting descriptive data on language of thought in immersion classrooms.

6.4.2 The language used to perform cognitive operations during full immersion math tasks[10]

The following study was designed to examine the nature of the internal language environment that emerges in learners as a result of the specific external language environment established in immersion classrooms. Using the learner as the locus of reference, the *external language environment* was defined as all language-related elements that influenced the learner from without, namely, curriculum goals, classroom policies and procedures, classroom materials and activities, and communicative exchanges between pupils, teachers, and administrators. The *internal language environment* was the term used to describe how learners processed language in their minds – that is, their L1 and L2 systems and the role played by each in performing the cognitive tasks for which the L2 is the primary vehicle used by the teachers and the instructional materials.

The study looked at the processing of numerical and word problems in math, and used these tasks as a means for demonstrating the use of strategies for selecting the language of thought. Dealing with math problems was selected as the area of focus because studies of native English-speaking elementary-school pupils had found that difficulty with word problems was largely because of difficulty comprehending abstract or ambiguous language (Cummins *et al.*, 1988). Thus, it was expected that having to solve such problems in another language would compound the difficulty. Mestre (1988) noted the challenges that pupils face in attempting to solve math word problems in a second language:

(1) they need to understand the written text in order to understand the problem;
(2) they may need proficiency in the technical language of the domain;
(3) they have to distinguish when a word is being used mathematically and when not; and
(4) they need a certain proficiency within the symbolic language of the domain.[11]

The following are the specific research questions that were asked in this study:

1. To what extent do learners use their native language and the foreign language when performing the cognitive operations involved in math problems?
2. When might a language switch take place, if at all?

DESIGN OF THE STUDY

Sample

Thirty-two pupils from the full Spanish language immersion school in St Paul, Minnesota, at the Adams School (six 8-year-olds, seven 9-year-olds, nine 10-year-olds and ten 11-year-olds), participated in the overall study. The sampling started at the grade 3 level because it was found in previous research that by this grade level, children were able to provide verbal reports of their language use strategies (Garner, 1987; Cohen, 1987a, 1991). The pupils were selected by their respective teachers from the four participating classrooms.

The pupils that the teachers selected were intended to represent learners at three levels (high, medium, and low) of Spanish language proficiency and academic skills, and their participation was voluntary.[12] The Spanish language proficiency ratings were based on *La prueba Riverside de realización en español* (Riverside Publishing Company, 1964)[13] and on the teacher's rating. The academic skills rating was based on the SRA *Survey of Basic Skills* (Science Research Associates, 1985)[14] and also on the teacher's rating. The pupils for whom data were available on the processing of math problems included 15 of the 32 subjects – all 10 of the sixth graders and 5 of the fifth graders – and so these fifth and sixth graders constituted the sample for the current report on the study. Their fifth- and sixth-grade teachers were both native English speakers fluent in Spanish. The fifth-grade teacher had lived in Spain as a teenager and the sixth-grade teacher had majored in Spanish and in education in college and had spent summers in Mexico.

In this full immersion program, grades 2–4 had only one hour per day of English instruction, namely, English language arts. In fifth grade slightly more time was devoted to English daily – both to English reading and social studies. In sixth grade, two hours of instruction took place in English, and the time was distributed across all subjects, to help prepare the pupils for junior high school. The instructional approach reflected that of cooperative learning theory, with an emphasis on the whole language approach to reading and language arts in general. While the content textbooks were written in Spanish, they were based on the US curriculum and occasionally read like literal translations of English-language textbooks into Spanish.[15] Furthermore, the texts were what the school principal (who was of Hispanic background) referred to as 'one-dimensional translations', lacking the rich cultural dimensions present in textbooks developed in the Hispanic world proper.

INSTRUMENTATION

Verbal report

As the main purpose of the study was to describe the use of native and foreign language in performing the cognitive operations necessary for solving math problems, the primary means of data collection was that of verbal report, and more precisely: *self-revelation* or *think aloud* (externalizing verbalized thoughts without analyzing what they were doing), *self-observation* (introspecting about current thoughts and/or retrospecting as to something specific that they had just done or had done at some earlier time), and *self-report* (indicating what they tended to do, without referring to any specific cognitive activity) (see Chapter 3).[16]

Questionnaire-based interview

Questions were designed for immersion pupils to answer about their abilities, attitudes, and preferences with regard to thinking in Spanish and with regard to using Spanish as a vehicle for communication with peers and with adults.

Classroom observation

Classroom observation was used to obtain data regarding language use patterns in whole-class, group, and paired interaction – that is, who said what to whom, in what language, and under what circumstances.

Background information

Archival data from the school files were used so as to have Spanish language proficiency scores (*La Prueba Riverside de Realización en Español*) and scores for performance on academic skills (the Science Research Associates' *Survey of Basic Skills*), along with the learners' school grades.

DATA COLLECTION PROCEDURES

A team of five native English-speaking research assistants from the University of Minnesota (four undergraduates and one postgraduate) collected the data over a five-month period from December 1992 to April 1993. This meant that there were repeated interactions with each of the pupils so as to increase the reliability of the findings. The research assistants worked with the same group of pupils (5–10) over the five months. The research assistants reported that their repeated interventions helped them to establish rapport with the pupils.

The fifth- and sixth-grade data to be reported on in this study were collected by the one fluent non-native Spanish speaker and by a limited speaker of Spanish.[17] The pupils were encouraged to provide their verbal reports in whatever language they felt more comfortable in at that moment, as they engaged in solving numerical and verbal math problems (as well as in dealing with social studies, science, and essay-writing tasks, which were not the focus of this study). The investigators tape-recorded the sessions so as to encourage the pupils to do their verbal reporting in Spanish whenever they wanted to, even if the investigator did not understand. On occasion, teacher-fronted classroom sessions were also tape-recorded for later analysis.

For the most part, the pupils were not pulled out of their classrooms nor were they assigned any given tasks in order to participate in the research effort. Consequently, no systematic attempt was made to vary the linguistic complexity of the math word problems about which the pupils provided verbal report. The pupils were studied while doing what they would normally be doing in the classroom with the added feature that the University of Minnesota student had them externalize or think aloud regarding what it was they were doing. At times there was no need to request verbal report because the pupils were naturally talking aloud as they performed their tasks. On a few occasions, the pupil and the researcher would have their interactions in the corridor so as not to disturb the class.

In the interactive sessions, the learners were asked to indicate how they used their languages in dealing with the math problems and to identify areas in which they had difficulty in understanding the teachers' instructions, instructions and content in the textbooks and worksheets. They were also asked to indicate where they got stuck when they were speaking in Spanish. Particular attention was giving to math problems that were part of quizzes or tests, but even those problems appearing on worksheets served as a means of assessing math ability, not just as a means of instruction or practice.

From time to time, the investigators interspersed questions about pupils' ability, attitudes, and preferences into their interactive sessions.

RESULTS

The data from 15 of the pupils gave a relatively clear picture as to the extent to which learners used their respective languages when performing the cognitive operations involved in math problems, and also regarding what triggered language switch. First, we will look at verbal report data concerning the language used when referring to numbers themselves. Then we will consider instances in which Spanish was the primary language for doing math problems. Finally, we will look at the numerous cases in which both Spanish and English were used to do word problems.

In the first reference to subjects, the number will refer to their grade level (fifth or sixth), the first capital letter to their Spanish language proficiency (H = high, M = medium, L = low), and the second letter to their academic skills (also, H = high, M = medium, L = low). So, for example, **Halena (6MH)** means that Halena (a pseudonym) was a sixth grader who had a medium rating in Spanish language proficiency and a high rating in academic skills.

Using language to relate to numbers

While no effort was made to see if any subjects processed numerical problems through symbols alone (i.e. without the use of verbalizing those symbols to themselves), it would appear that most of the pupils probably did not. In other words, when they saw a numerical problem such as $3 \times 8 = 24$, they appeared to think in words, 'Three times eight equals

24.' This process of verbalizing or sub-vocalizing, especially if it were done in the foreign language, could slow them down in their calculations. Yet the remarks from some of the pupils seemed to indicate that they may have been thinking directly in symbols. Hence, this issue is in need of further investigation.

The following are those cases of specific reference to their dealings with numbers:

> Halena (6MH): In math . . . I kind of just think numbers. [Relating to a specific problem] Well, you reduce five and ten, and that would be one and two . . . You have to reduce this majorly. OK, one . . . twenty. Eighty . . . I'm just thinking numbers . . . It's not any language at all . . .
> Researcher: Do you think in Spanish when you do math?
> Peter (5MM): Depends. If the problems are in writing than I think in Spanish. If the problem is in numbers then I think in English. Numbers are just numbers.
> Researcher: Is it hard for you, within the same lesson, to switch back and forth from Spanish to English?
> Mary (5HH): No 'cause it's just the writing that's in Spanish and the numbers are English. There is no numbers in Spanish . . . there's not other numbers; you write them the same.
> Researcher: What about a word problem? Are there a couple of word problems on the page there?
> Sammy (5MM): Ya . . . OK. This says, '*¿Cuánto es* (how much is)[18] nine-hundred and forty five *divido entre* (divided by) seven?' That would be seven divided or nine-hundred and forty five divided by seven.
> R: This is the way you'd normally do it? You kinda translate into English so you understood it better?
> S: Ya.

Although in the case of Peter, it seemed that he was both interpreting what he had to do and solving the problem in Spanish, in another interaction Peter indicated that he tended to switch over to English to solve problems (see below). What makes the interaction with Sammy especially interesting is that the subject even used English words to say the numbers in a numerical problem that was written out in Spanish.

Doing word problems in Spanish

After six and one-half years of full language immersion instruction in Spanish, to what extent are the learners working their math problems through primarily in Spanish? Out of the 15 pupils for whom data were available, only 3 – Henry (6HH), Sandra (6HM), and Carl (6MH) – reported working problems through entirely in Spanish. They were all sixth graders, and were generally both high in Spanish language proficiency and in academic skills as well.

The following is an instance of Henry dealing for the first time in an on-line fashion with a word problem which was written on the chalkboard:

Ema, Marcos, José, y María tienen 9, 10, 11, y 13 años. José es mayor que María y menor que Ema. Marcos es menor que José y mayor que María. ¿Qué edad tiene cada uno? (Ema, Marcos, José, and María are 9, 10, 11, and 13 years old. José is older than María and younger than Ema. Marcos is younger than José and older than María. How old is each one?)

Researcher: Are you using a language to solve this problem?

Henry: *Sí, español.* (Yes, Spanish.)

R: *Dígame, por favor.* (Say it for me, please.)

H: OK. *Primero, tengo que dibujar los personas.* (He makes a sketch.) *Eso es Ema, y Marcos, y José, y María. Y José is mayor que María y menor que Ema. Marcos es menor que José y mayor que María. Entonces, creo que María es el más chico, con 9 años, y después, después, Marcos, con 10 años.* (First, I have to draw the people. This is Ema, and Marcos and José, and María. And José is older than María and younger than Ema. Marcos is younger than José and older than María. So, I believe that María is the youngest, being 9, and then, then, Marcos, who is 10.)

R: *¿Por qué?* (Why?)

H: *Porque Marco es menor que José y mayor que María. Y si María es el más chiquito, Marco tiene que ser segundo y José tercero. Y Ema está el más mayor que todos los otros.* (Because Marco is younger than José and older than María. And if María is the youngest, Marco has to be second and José third. And Ema is the oldest of all of them.)

R: *¡Gracias!* (Thanks!)

In the case of Sandra (6HM), it is important to know that she attended a bilingual preschool and kindergarten in Milwaukee, in which Spanish was used exclusively on alternate days. So, unlike her peers, she had an earlier exposure to Spanish. As Sandra put it, 'I really learned Spanish because they'll show you, like, *perro* (dog) and all that. Then you'll understand. That's how I really learned Spanish.' The researcher asked Sandra if she was performing the calculations using Spanish or English. Sandra replied that she had been using Spanish, and proceeded to complete the remaining problems while speaking out loud in Spanish.

33.   4/5
    + 3/10

Sandra: *Cuatro quintos más 3, 10, y algo, 5 va en 10, dos veces. Cinco va en diez dos veces. Multiplicas 8, 2 por 4 va a ser 8, y 3 multiplicado por 1 es 3. Vas a sumar eso . . .* so *este va a ser once, y va a ser un fracción mixta,* so, *tengo que ponérlo como así, y esto en forma simple, un quinto.* (Four-fifths plus 3, 10, and something, 5 goes into – 2, 2 times. Five goes into 10 two times. You multiply 8, 2 by four will be 8, and 3 multiplied by 1 is 3. You will add this . . . so this will be 11, and it will be a mixed fraction, so, I have to have to write it this way, and this in a simple form, a fifth.)
(This answer is incorrect.)

34.   1 1/4
    + 2 1/3

S: OK. *Estos dos números tienen 12 en común,* so, *voy multiplicas esos por 4 y esos por 3, . . . 10, 11, 12, es un fracción mixta,* so *va ser un-4, 5, 12, algo,* is *12 por 3 cuartavos,* uhm, *9 y 3 cuartos, . . .* uhm, *3, . . .* I think. OK, so, *quintos,* uhm, so *después, no está un fracción mixta,* so *entonces esto va a ser dos por 5, 16 por 4, . . . tienen 12 en común.* I gotta go ask a question.
(OK. This two numbers have 12 in common, so, I will multiply these by 4 and these by 3, . . . 10, 11, 12, this is a mixed fraction, so it will be 1 – 4, 5, 12, something, is 12 by three-fourths, uhm, 9 and three-fourths, . . . uhm, 3, . . . I think. OK, so, fifths, uhm, so then, it is not a mixed fraction, so then this will be 2 by 5, 16 by 4, . . . they have 12 in common.)

The researcher reported being clear that Sandra had command of the Spanish forms required to perform those operations in Spanish. Her math aptitude, however, was lacking. She would often concentrate on simplifying the fractions only to neglect the integer portion of the problem in making the final calculations. In the problem set that the researcher observed, she made numerous such errors, and did not check her work. Finishing was apparently her only objective.

We note that Sandra used English extensively for her metacomments above ('so,' 'OK,' and 'I think'). These forms may indicate a planning and evaluative function, typical of higher forms of cognition. That these emerged in English, not in Spanish, may suggest that her cognitive problem solving was actually being done in English and then reported on in Spanish. No effort was made to see if Sandra could have solved this problem if she had worked on it entirely in English, although this might be a direction for future research. The research assistants did not tell the learners what language to use for performing tasks.

Finally, here is an example of Carl providing a largely English-language description of how he worked through a word problem:

> Researcher: How did you figure this word problem out?
> Carl: It says two kids were playing a game, and at the finish of each game, the loser gave the other person like 10 cents or something, a coin.
> R: You can talk Spanish to me.
> C: OK. I'll just keep . . . And at the end of the hour, Raquel won three games and *Luis tiene tres monedas* (Luis has three coins), and Luis had three coins more than he started with. And then it says, 'How many games did they play?' Well, I thought, he had three left, right? And he had three more than he started, so. If he lost three times, then he had to give him three more coins; so three plus three is six. And then the other guy won three games, so it was three . . . nine games they played.
> R: When you were thinking this, were you doing this in Spanish? Or were you just thinking in English? Or both?
> C: Spanish.
> R: Can you go through the problem like you were thinking it in Spanish? Like, what was happening? Were you saying, '*Tres . . .*' (three)?
> C: Yeah.
> R: Pretend I'm not here. Pretend you're doing the problem the first time.
> C: Like what? I just do it in my mind. I didn't get it at first. And then, I just realized that the loser had to give the other person more money.
> R: Do you think that you can think through that in Spanish? Can you say that, everything that you just told me, only in Spanish?
> C: All right. *Yo pienso que, una per . . . uhm . . . Luis perdió tres pesos y él necesitaba a dar el tres monedas . . . Raquel tiene tres monedas más que empezado. Eso es nueve. Nueve juegos.* (I think that, a per . . . uhm . . . Luis lost three *pesos* and he needed to give the three coins . . . Raquel has three coins more than she started with. This is nine. Nine games.)

In this case, the research assistant was the one with limited Spanish skills, which might help to explain why Carl's Spanish explanation was not as extensive or as detailed as his English one.[19]

While this sample of three is too small to make any generalizations, the results may indicate that the partial or total use of Spanish by non-natives for working through math word problems in immersion classroom is in part linked to higher levels of foreign language proficiency and academic achievement. However, more extensive research would be necessary to make any definitive claims along these lines.

Doing word problems in both Spanish and English

The following are examples of pupils' verbal reports regarding the use of both Spanish and English in solving math problems. An effort is made to let the learners speak for themselves as much as possible rather than simply presenting a summary of language use patterns. While many of the pupils indicated thinking in English in order to make sure that they understood something that was complicated, they produced numerous other reasons for using English.

Ana (6MM): English translation if hard word problem

Researcher: What language do you do math problems in?
Ana: Usually, probably in Spanish. But if it's like a hard word problem, then I have to translate it. . . . Well, I know the words in Spanish. It's just that you want to . . . you sorta like want to go back to the language you know, like, more of . . .

Ana read a math problem in Spanish and solved it in Spanish. In another case, she first read the word problem in Spanish and then translated it into English.

R: Why the translation?
A: Because sometimes English is easier than Spanish.
R: Are there words in the problem you do not understood?
(She indicated *ahorras* ('you save') – a crucial word for understanding and solving the problem.)
A: . . . so you gotta have a dictionary with you when you're doing math sometimes. (But she didn't use it.) Well, I just took out the little clues, and said like, 'How much money would . . .' I was just sort of guessing what it meant . . . if you bought something . . . it's like, you add something together and then you come up with the answer and then you minus what you save, and then you come up with the answer.

Ana then started giving an example of thinking a problem through in Spanish if it was not too hard, but then she switched to English:

A: It's minus. So it's like take away this from this . . .

It appeared not to be a problem of knowing the numbers but of cognitive difficulty – the numbers of operations involved:

A: It's hard for me to remember what number is up here (refers to top integer and fraction in subtraction) and what number is down here (bottom integer and fraction), in Spanish, so I have to translate to English; and then since you can't take away 8 through 9, then I get even more confused . . . It gets really nuts.

Todd (6LM): English if complicated word problem

With Todd, it became clear that work was accomplished against the backdrop of English and that he reverted to English when math problems got complicated for him.

Todd: I usually think in English. It's just . . . it's the language that I know the best . . .
Researcher: Do you get all the ideas in Spanish?
T: Uhm, yeah, I usually do it in Spanish. But if there's something I don't understand – if it's a complicated problem – I'll try to translate it in my mind into English, if I don't understand it in Spanish first.

He then worked through an example which had Spanish and English mixed. The researcher reported observed Todd closely while he worked on a math test, and the words that he mouthed were mouthed in English.

Marina (5HH): Voice in the head switches to English

Marina expressed the same use of languages for processing math problems as did Todd but she spoke about it in terms of the 'voice in her head' switching from Spanish to English when the math problems got harder. The researcher was probing Marina's use of languages in doing division problems. She was taped talking the problem out in Spanish but with pauses and an occasional English word. The researcher replayed the tape for her:

Researcher: You said *ocho* (eight) and then you faded off. What were you doing there?
Marina: Trying to think.
R: What were you thinking?
M: I was thinking, 'Wait a minute!'
R: Did you try to rework the problem?
M: Yes.
R: Were you using language or just numbers?
M: Language.
R: What language?
M: English.

(The researcher played the audiotape of the problem-solving activity one more time.)

R: What happened there?

M: I was thinking again.

R: Were you also using language?

M: Yeah, English.

R: Do you need to translate to solve these problems?

M: Sometimes.

R: If you could describe when the voice in your head changes from Spanish to English, when would that be?

M: When they get harder.

R: The math problems?

M: Yeah.

Peter (5MM): English to understand instructions better

Peter was just finishing a math test when the researcher arrived. On problems 28 and 29, he seemed to think in English, while on 30 he read the problem aloud, thought in Spanish, and later switched to English.

Researcher: When you read these instructions, do you understand right away what it says in Spanish or when you read them do you think words in English?

Peter: I try and get them into English, so I can understand them a little bit better.

30. *Teri usó la computadora 3 veces más minutos que Sue. ¿Cuánto tiempo trabajó Teri con la computadora?* (Teri used the computer three times more minutes than Sue. How long did Teri work with the computer?)

P: OK. Now I think this one might be plus. (He reads the problem aloud in Spanish, then continues.) *Sue está aquí, cinquenta y quatro, 1, 2, 3 . . . 50 . . . OK. ¿Cuánto tiempo . . . ?* (Sue is here, 54, 1, 2, 3 . . . 50 . . . OK. How long?) How many minutes? Three times many minutes than Sue . . . whoa. OK. Fifty-four times three.

He then set up the problem like this:

$$\begin{array}{r} 54 \\ \times\,3 \\ \hline 162 \end{array}$$

R: What were you thinking before you went, 'OK'?

P: I was thinking that Sue, right there, fifty-four; it says three times more . . . than Sue. So, three times four, twelve. Three times five, fifteen six. A hundred and sixty-two.

In this problem, Peter began thinking about how to do the problem in Spanish. He ran into a problem, and then began to think in English.

CYNTHIA (6LL): ENGLISH TO UNDERSTAND INSTRUCTIONS, THEN WORKING
THROUGH PROBLEM IN SPANISH

> Researcher: Do you do math in Spanish or in English?
> Cynthia: Well, actually we do it in both because sometimes we have to translate it because a lot of times we don't understand it. So we usually translate it into English and figure it out and then we do it in Spanish.
> R: When doing a math problem, do you normally think in Spanish or English?
> C: English.
> R: Is it hard to understand the instructions on this or just how to do the math?
> C: When you (know how to) do it, it's easy. . . . But the difference is when you don't know how to do it, when they explain it to you in Spanish.

She said she did not understand math well and what made it more difficult was that the explanations were in Spanish. For example, she did not understand the concept of common denominators. Her language of processing was English and she spoke in English when she asked a peer for help.

Mary (5HH): Learned her numbers in English and found thinking in English quicker

Mary read one word problem out loud in Spanish and gave an answer in Spanish. With another problem, she started in Spanish but changed to English:

> Researcher: When you do math in your head, do you know for sure whether you think in Spanish or English?
> Mary: I think in English. I learned it that way. I learned that two plus two is four and I just do it in my head 'cause it's quicker than *uno por uno es dos* (one times one is two).

Whereas Mary was unable to translate the directions in her math book for how to do division problems with fractions, she indicated that she knew how to do the problems. While the instructions may have been complicated, this inability to produce an English equivalent for technical terms in Spanish is also a consequence of immersion instruction where translations are not, for the most part, provided. The learners need to consult their bilingual dictionaries (which they do only sporadically) or guess at the translation equivalent. The research question is the extent to which the pupils actually understand those words for which they cannot readily produce an English-language equivalent. In the next data set, Karen refers to this problem of not being able to explain to her parents the English equivalent for technical terms from her school work.

Karen (6HH): Vocabulary difficulty, time of day, and peer group language use

Karen was an example of a learner who switched back and forth between Spanish and English freely, but still preferred to use English. In these excerpts she gives various reasons for her switching:

Researcher: Do you do math in Spanish or English?
Karen: The teacher talks to us all the time in Spanish and we have to answer her in Spanish, but usually when I'm just doing it, I'll just speak in English . . . usually. . . . It depends upon the time of day, and what the people around me are thinking, because I have them (words) all memorized in both languages. If, like, the environment around me is speaking Spanish, then it'll just happen in Spanish . . .
K: (Going over a math worksheet) I am doing it in English because the math is kind of hard. . . . Also, I've been speaking English most of the day so it just goes along with that. But when I read the directions, it just came in Spanish. . . . Sometimes I know words about math in Spanish that I don't know in English . . . it feels kind of weird to know a word in Spanish but not in English.

Karen discovered these gaps in her technical English vocabulary when trying to explain something to her parents at home. Again, on a worksheet converting from decimals to fractions, she appeared to be performing the cognitive operations in English. At one point she explained a math problem to a peer in Spanish, but mostly they interacted with each other in English, even regarding task-related activities.

R: What language do you do this word problem in?
K: . . . since it's a word problem in Spanish, I would translate it. And maybe do the numbers in Spanish . . .
(With reference to some math problems from the day before that she thought were kind of hard) Well, this one I do . . . actually I usually do these hard ones in English, because they're really difficult.
(With respect to an easy problem) This one I did in Spanish, because it was really simple, and there was no vocabulary at all, hardly.
R: (With regard to a geometry worksheet) What language do you do this in?

K: Ah, that's hard. I usually go to English. It's not that the vocabulary's hard to understand – but the whole project . . . it's kind of easier to think in English because it comes easier – say, GD (line segment).

Halena (6MH): Peer group language use

Halena also reported doing her math problems in Spanish until she got stuck – a pattern that seemed to be common across pupils. Then, unlike Karen, who reported that in her work groups pupils sometimes did math problems in Spanish and sometimes in English, Halena reported that when she worked with other pupils they tended to talk in English.

Donna (6HH): Uses English because community language

Donna read the word problem in Spanish and then reported thinking through the problem in English, as did other pupils. What she added was a sociolinguistic justification for reverting to English – the fact that English is the language of wider communication in the community at large:

> Researcher: Do you know the words for subtract and divide in Spanish?
> Donna: . . . it's like a whole 'nother language, the math is. I usually use English vocabulary words. Sometimes I'll use Spanish ones. . . . I mean, sure I've been in a Spanish school, and all, but, you just, the environment I live in, it's not like we speak Spanish there. So, I'm adapted to English more, than in Spanish, so it's easier just to switch to English.

Barry (5LM), Alberto (6LL), Sammy (5MM): Using English except for work at the chalkboard

While the majority of the subjects reported using Spanish at least some of the time for doing math problems, there were at least three pupils who reported using English almost all the time in doing math problems – Sammy, Alberto, and Barry. While they include two fifth graders and a sixth grader, note that two of them had low and one had medium Spanish language proficiency, and that their academic skills level was either medium or low as well:

> Researcher: Do you do math problems in Spanish?
> Barry: No, not a lotta times unless I'm doing it on the chalkboard. (The teacher) will ask me to use the Spanish numerals and say it out loud. So I will.
> R: OK, You wanna try a word problem?
> B: Uh hum. (He reads the problem softly in Spanish.) . . . sixteen.

R: So that was the word problem? You did it in English? Mostly?
B: Ya.

Researcher: Normally do you think you would be thinking aloud in English like you just did?
Sammy: Ya.

(The researcher asked Alberto what languages he uses for solving math problems.)
Alberto: All I do is like, um, I just read it in Spanish first, and then I just translate in English and see what it means, and then just try to figure out the problem.

Barry's comments above probably sum up the classroom reality for many of the learners: Spanish was externalized if the teacher asked the pupils to say things aloud, since it was the official language for such large-group communications.

DISCUSSION

Although somewhat impressionist in nature, the findings from this study seem to indicate that the full immersion pupils were, in fact, using their native language more for solving math problems, especially numerical problems, than they were using the foreign language. Both according to their self-reports and as observed through their introspective and retro-spective verbal reports, the subjects usually started processing a word problem in Spanish by reading it to themselves or out loud, and then either (1) performed on-line translation to English before solving the math problem, or (2) continued in Spanish until or unless they encoun-tered a conceptual problem. Whereas it would seem obvious that the learners had to read the problem in Spanish in order to gain access to the task, there were other ways that they could perform the task, such as through asking the teacher or another student for an explanation, and as we have seen, in the latter case this could be in English.

The results from this study, then, seem to lend some support to the popular belief that people think in their native language when they do math, regardless of the language they are speaking at the time. Yet the study also illustrates that this popular belief is at best simplistic when dealing with non-native subjects who are nonetheless taught math in the foreign language from an early age. For example, Peter's remark that 'numbers are just numbers' is perhaps elucidated somewhat by research with bilingual university students which found that number words were identified more rapidly than ordinary words (Frenck-Mestre and Vaid, 1992). The explanation given was that number words are limited in quantity, lack ambiguity, and are governed in use by straightforward syntax. The researchers suggested that number words may be organized in a lexicon specific to numerical symbols, where language is not as important a factor. Peter may have been referring to this special kind of lexicon without having a label for it.

It would appear that for the most part, the pupils needed to read the Spanish text of word problems in order to gain access to the task. Perhaps in some cases (especially with multiple-choice items), it is obvious from the context how the numbers in a word problem are to be manipulated, but such instances of taking shortcuts did not reveal themselves in these data.[20] Thus, the subjects needed to have fairly good Spanish reading skills. Clearly, one of the major advantages of a full immersion program is that the students are adept enough at translating from one language to another that they are capable of rapid, on-line translation so that they can think through in English a word problem written in Spanish. As can be seen from the above data, this pattern of translation appeared to be quite common. One of the reasons why partial immersion pupils have been found to be less successful at math than full immersion pupils (see Swain, 1984: 91) may be that they are not as successful at on-line translation of math concepts into the native language.

Studies in natural translation (i.e. translation by naïve child translators – bilingual children without any special training in translation) have produced some indications as to what may make a 10- or 11-year-old bilingual youngster a good translator (Malakoff, 1992). Malakoff purposely assigned the pupils translation tasks involving ambiguity and word/ sentence segmentation where the native and foreign language patterns were at odds. The main factor contributing to successful translation appeared to be that of metalinguistic awareness – the ability to step back from the comprehension or production of an utterance in order to consider the linguistic form and structure underlying the meaning of the utterance. It stands to reason that the less facility a young bilingual has with the target language, the more unnatural their translating will be.

In addition to comparing full immersion with partial immersion results, one might ask how the language processing of these St Paul immersion pupils compares with that of balanced bilingual children. There is at least one study which looked at L1 and L2 processing of tasks by subjects who were not native speakers of the dominant language of the society. A study by Saville-Troike (1988) focused on nine non-native English-speaking children during their first six months in the US. She reported that a native Chinese-speaking eight-year-old used English in doing her English language workbook tasks, but when she worked in her mathematics workbook, her private speech was not in English at all, but in Chinese (Saville-Troike, 1988: 586).[21] Without having extensive data on balanced bilinguals, it is difficult to know how typical or atypical these results with immersion pupils really are. Perhaps it is an unfair assumption to make that more extensive thinking in the target language is expected or desirable.

Perhaps some comments need to be made about the research methodology in this study. The main source of information was from verbal report protocols. Since the research assistants for this study were all native English speakers, it was seen as beneficial to collect similar data using native Spanish speakers or a combination of native English and native Spanish speakers. In this way, it would be possible to determine the effect of the researchers on the data regarding extent of cognitive processing in Spanish. Fortunately, data for two doctoral dissertations have been collected by native Spanish-speaking investigators in a Spanish full immersion program in Golden Valley, Minnesota. It would appear that, although the researchers were not focusing on this issue *per se* and did not collect verbal report data, their observations regarding the use of Spanish and English for performing academic tasks corroborates the findings of a non-native Spanish-speaking team of research assistants (Maggie Broner, Personal Communication, February, 1997).

Also with regard to cognitive processing, an assumption being made throughout this report was that if a pupil used Spanish or English in think-aloud or introspective data, this was an indication that cognitive operations were also going on in that language. Lantolf (Personal Communication) points out that this may not be the case. In other words, although the verbal report may be in Spanish, it is possible that the cognitive operation is actually being performed in English. In all cases in this study, the subjects were given the option of reporting in Spanish and one of the two researchers involved spoke competent Spanish. Nonetheless, there may on occasion have been mismatches between what respondents said they were doing and what they were actually doing.

On the other hand, some of the most convincing data in the study seemed to be the self-report data regarding what the respondents 'tended to do.' In case after case, they reported tending to use English on a variety of school tasks, and especially for performing cognitive operations pertaining to math. If this was in fact the case, it may help to explain why full immersion pupils in Minneapolis and St Paul, Minnesota (and elsewhere) continue to have gaps in their oral and written production in the foreign language, even after being immersed for almost seven years. The language outcomes are in part a consequence of the extent to which the pupils are choosing to think through the target language. These results link up with the reports offered above by adult multilinguals regarding their efforts to think through a given foreign language, and their sense that the efforts they make to do this (e.g. warming up, rehearsing, and also just having conversations with themselves in the target language) would enhance their speaking ability.

The reality may be that the internal language environment of the pupils is not as intensively foreign language oriented as the outside observer might think. After all, conclusions derived from observations are based largely on investigation of the external language environment, which seems impressively filled with the foreign language: the teachers speak exclusively in that language and when pupils are called on by the teachers, they also speak in that foreign language. Yet the true picture may be more consistent with the findings from this study – that there is an underground of English language use, out of earshot of the teacher, in pupil working groups, and, most importantly, in the pupils' minds, where teachers and course materials do not tread. As one fourth-grade student, Bill (4HH), put it:

> You usually think that in an immersion school, it's totally in Spanish. If you get caught speaking English, you'll like be in trouble, but that's not really what it is. I mean, you're always thinking in English. I mean they can't really stop you from thinking in English. You can think Spanish, you can act Spanish, you can doing everything in Spanish, but you're really not a Mexican.

This resisting being **too** immersed in Spanish may be a sociolinguistic inevitability, especially for immersion programs which take place in areas of the US where possibilities for contact with native speakers of the immersion language are somewhat limited. However, there may be ways in which the use of the foreign language in the internal language environment of the pupils may be enhanced. For example, it may be possible for the teachers to do more thinking out loud as they do math problems, and to make an effort to think out loud as if they were fifth or sixth graders (10–11 year olds), rather than the speedy adults that they are. It may be that the pupils need to hear and internalize more of the carrier language of cognitive processing in the foreign language. With regard to the solving of math word problems in the native language, for example, Wheatley (1991) makes the point that learners need to learn how to carry on a scientific discussion. He views class discussion as important for initiating conversations which pupils then learn to carry on within themselves: 'It is through class discussions that pupils learn to conduct this internal **dialogue. By continuing the conversation within ourselves we begin to act mathematically'** (Wheatley, 1991: 19). **The same principle could apply to** solving math problems in a second or foreign language. Just as a profile of problem areas in the specialized register of mathematics (at the lexical, structural, and discourse levels) has been developed for ESL pupils (Spanos *et al.*, 1988), so it would be possible to do the same for Spanish and for other languages.

It may also be necessary to identify ways of putting more of a premium on thinking in the foreign language by restructuring the immersion program somewhat. At present, for example, the same teachers who teach in the foreign language must drop that guise and teach English and other subjects in English as of grade two in Minneapolis and St Paul (and other) immersion programs. A structural change would be to have different teachers teaching the English and Spanish portions of the curriculum. One of the important purposes of conducting the kind of research that was conducted in St Paul was to provide insights that could be channeled back into coaching the learners, coaching the teachers, and providing insights for administrators concerned about the smooth working of the program.

This study was motivated by the presupposition that what is desired are more bilingual-like language production skills, for speaking and writing in the foreign language. One argument for this would be that these skills would help to enhance the language ability of the learners when they reach the job market. Another perspective to take, however, is that the most crucial concern is for a smooth transition to the study of content subjects in the native language, and therefore the children need to develop and maintain their ability to function in native language skills. Hence, a robust amount of cognitive processing in the L1 could be viewed as a good thing. The present study may actually help to suggest why it is that immersion children do not seem to fall behind children in the regular school curriculum. As Lambert and Tucker posited many years ago in an effort to interpret why French immersion pupils did so well in and through English language skills:

(the) children may never have been on 'vacation' in English at all. Instead, they may have transferred basic skills of reading, concept development, word manipulation, and verbal creativity through French to English by reprocessing in English all the information they received through French, or by simultaneously processing in French and English. The possibility we see in these results (which is only an idea to be tested with further experimentation) is that children of normal intelligence, trained through a second language, process new information encountered in class both in the second language – thereby developing skill with that language – as well as in the native language. (Lambert and Tucker, 1972: 82)

This phenomenon of *reprocessing* is most likely what we uncovered in the current study, where the reprocessing in English was of much, but not all, of the information received through Spanish. It is not so surprising that the pupils in this study switched to English to think through their word problems. After six or seven years of immersion schooling, the learners were behaving externally or socially in Spanish, but not psychologically or cognitively. The development of this other self who can and does perform cognitive operations in the target language may prove to be more the exception than the rule, but more extensive research will be necessary to determine this. This study simply constitutes one initial effort along the lines of the experimentation that Lambert and Tucker had suggested needed to be conducted so many years ago.

6.5   Conclusions

This chapter, then, has looked at a more specialized area of focus with regard to srategy use, the element of choice involved in arriving at the language(s) used in performing cognitive operations. We have seen that learners have a fair amount of control over the language that they select for performing a series of language-based tasks. The intention of the chapter was to underscore the potentially significant role that choice of language of thought might have for ultimate success at learning, using, as well as forgetting a language or languages.

What implications for educational policy and planning at the program and the classroom levels might there be from this line of inquiry? It would appear that educators need to start by acknowledging the role of native language in target language learning and use. Once this acknowledgement has been made, what follows is to determine the strategies for employing the L1 – those that support the learning and use of the target language and those that are detrimental to L2 learning and use. The result can be a list of potentially beneficial strategies for making use of the L1 or another language in learning and using the target language. An example of this would be Kern's (1994) list of instances where mental translation into the L1 may support reading in a target language – for chunking material into semantic clusters, for keeping the train of thought going, for creating a network of associations, for clarifying grammatical roles, and for making the input more familiar and consequently more user-friendly. It would be possible to generate similar strategy checklists for the benefits of using L1 when writing in the target language, since research has indicated that the product of such an approach may outclass that of trying to think exclusively through the target language when composing text. Similarly, we could envision such checklists for listening and speaking in the target language as well.

Unquestionably, there is a need to consider the proficiency level of the learners, since the more proficient have been seen to be less dependent on the L1 for their functioning in the target language. Beyond proficiency level, one must consider the specific task at hand, as well as numerous other factors. The important thing is to explore in more systematic ways just how multilinguals apply their knowledge of their various languages in target language activities, an area that up until now has been under-explored.

6.6 Discussion questions and activities

1. You teach in a college-level foreign language program which makes extensive use of translation in the instructional portion of the course. The rationale is as follows:

   (a) having cues for tasks (i.e. the instructions and the prompts) entirely in the foreign language would be too difficult for the students and would take them too much time;
   (b) having learners provide native language responses to reading passages helps to determine if the learners accurately understand the sentence structure, and such understanding is deemed essential in successful incremental learning; and
   (c) using translation helps to see if the learners really understood the meaning of the material since they cannot simply lift material directly from the prompt or from the text in composing their response.

   Half your colleagues favor the extensive use of translation in the instructional program, while the other half have the uneasy feeling that it may not only inhibit communication, but may ultimately reduce the amount of language learning that goes on. After reviewing the issues, you take a stand somewhere in the middle. Express what that view would be.

2. You have read the research results regarding mental translation in reading and written translation in writing. You are of the opinion that learners need to be aware of the strategies that they could draw on systematically in order to improve their reading of foreign language texts and their writing of expository essays in the language. Prepare a list of strategies for mental translation in reading and for written

translation as well. Compare your list with that of others in your group or class who perform the same task.

3. After reading the research report on the St Paul Spanish Immersion Program and learning about the pupils' tendency to perform their cognitive operations in English, you come to the conclusion that something must be done to reverse this trend. Working in small groups or pairs, devise a plan for how the immersion teachers might organize the instructional program so as to maximize the amount of time that the learners actually function through the foreign language rather than relying largely on their native one. Think in terms of ways in which the teachers might have to revise their instructional style. If the pupils needed some coaching in how to use the immersion language more effectively as a vehicle for thought, what might that coaching consist of?

Appendix 6   Questionnaire: In which language do/should multilinguals think?

1. (a) Did you ever find yourself thinking in some language without intending to? Describe the situation.
   (b) Do you then purposely switch your thoughts to another language? If so, why?
2. Have you ever had multilingual thoughts – i.e. thoughts that begin in one language, continue in another, and possibly end in a third? Describe.
3. (a) Have you ever chosen to think through a second language for the purposes of learning a third language (because the L2 was closer to the target language than your native language, such as in learning Portuguese through Spanish rather than through English)? Please describe the situation.
   (b) If the answer is 'yes,' to what extent do you continue to think through that L2 when you use your L3 today? Please explain.
4. (a) During your L2 learning experiences, have you ever been admonished by your teacher to think through that target language? Describe.
   (b) Have you made an effort to think extensively through the target language? If so, with what results?
5. (a) When you are reading in an L2, to what extent do you find L1 or L3 glosses/translations for words you don't know? Explain.
   (b) To what extent do you gloss words by means of an L2–L2 dictionary?

(c) Think of an L2 you have contact with at present. To what extent do you just read without going to a dictionary? Explain.

(d) How well does this work?

Notes

1. This is a revised version of Cohen (1995). Thanks to Carl James for helpful comments on this section and other sections of the chapter as well.

2. The possibility is raised that so-called L_T thinking may actually consist of little more than 'relexified' L1 – that is, with L_T words replacing L1 words in L1 structures (Jim Lantolf, Personal Communication, May 13, 1994). This is an extreme position. In actuality, the interlanguage reflected by a non-native's L_T thoughts is mediated by experiences, by ethnolinguistic background, by gender, and by the discourse domain. Given that most non-native users of a language lack full mastery in their productive skills (speaking and writing), it is likely that their L_T thoughts will be transmitted through an interlanguage as well. An empirical question would be whether the fact that the L_T thoughts are conveyed through an interlanguage might have a deleterious effect on the thoughts themselves.

3. The phrase *diglossic thinking* is derived from the notion of diglossia wherein there are two co-existing languages or language varieties in a community, each with its own purposes (Ferguson, 1959).

4. This observation was not empirically verified however, such as through retrospective verbal report. The support group, by the way, is still meeting and when back in Israel for visits, I participate in it. The sharing is still in the native language of the participant.

5. One of whom had studied four other languages as well but could not claim any control over them at the time of the survey.

6. The reason why we need to say 'presumably' is that teachers do not necessarily follow to the letter the instructional approach they are using, but rather may diverge from that approach according to their own beliefs or pragmatic urges. Thus, the classrooms of two teachers presumably using the same instructional approach may, in reality, look quite different. (See Woods, 1993, for an example of this phenomenon as witnessed in a comparison of two ESL classrooms where the teachers' own personal teaching style prevailed over the prescribed instructional approach.)

7. This is a revised version of Cohen and Hawras (1996). We gratefully acknowledge input from Peter Gu, Elaine Tarone, and Maria Brisk on earlier drafts.

8. Furthermore, feedback to learners in the form of implicit or explicit correction of their deviant utterances was observed to be inconsistent and infrequent (Swain and Carroll, 1987; Swain, 1988).

9. Actually, the verbal component of thinking can be either silent, subvocal, or aloud, both with regard to inner or social speech. Although inner speech does not tend to be externalized, it may sometimes be prompted. In other words, when asked to think aloud, learners may have inner speech as part of their data – i.e. verbalized thoughts not intended for others.

10. This section is based on Cohen (1994c). Let me acknowledge the then principal of the Adams School in St Paul, Minnesota, Dr Luz María Serrano, for graciously consenting to have us conduct the study at her school. The original article also acknowledged the teachers, Jane Berg, Lori Dragert, Rafael Manrique, Elizabeth Tabbot, and Concha Fernández, and the pupils for their extensive cooperation over the five months of the study, as well as the research assistants for this study – Jim Parker, Shirley Heitzman, Karen Moline, Amy Fjerstad, and Lisa Babbs. Without their tireless efforts and insights,

this study would have been impossible. The verbal report protocols collected by Parker and Heitzman formed the database for this paper, and for these protocols I am most grateful. Finally, let me thank those colleagues whose constructive comments contributed greatly to the original published paper – Jim Lantolf, Elaine Tarone, Dick Tucker, and Merrill Swain.

11. Mestre notes that the target language proficiency may mediate the learning not just of the technical language but also of the symbolic language (e.g. knowing that '2 > × > 8' is not grammatical).

12. Both parents and pupils signed consent forms.

13. Its subtests included: reading (reading comprehension, vocabulary, study skills), language (grammar, capitalization, spelling, punctuation), and mathematics (math computation, math problem solving).

14. Its subtests included: vocabulary, reading comprehension, mechanics, usage, spelling, mathematics (computation, concepts, problem solving), reference materials, social studies, and science.

15. For example, the following phrase from math problem 30 (to be referred to on p. 201) is an example of literal translation from English. The sentence, *Teri usó la computadora 3 veces más minutos que Sue*, is a literal translation from English, 'Terry used the computer three times more minutes than Sue.' *En minutos, Teri usó la computadora 3 veces más que Sue* ('In minutes, Terry used the computer three times more than Sue') would reflect a more Spanish-like phrasing and word order.

16. Note that a usual verbal report contains elements of all three approaches, but that respondents were encouraged to do less self-report and more relating to specific thoughts about tasks currently being executed or just recently executed.

17. She had studied Spanish during her 10th-grade year in high school (at the age of 15).

18. English translations for the Spanish will be provided within round brackets.

19. We notice that while the Spanish that Carl used for problematizing above was quite fluent – as was that of most of the immersion students, it was still an interlanguage characterized by a fair amount of relexification of English.

20. Test-wise respondents on the Scholastic Aptitude Test (SAT) and other standardized tests for older students have indicated that they will avoid reading through all the verbiage in a word problem if they perceive relationships between numbers in the problem that match up with some multiple-choice alternative.

21. Evidence of private speech was determined through the use of videotaping, using a wireless radio microphone system.

7 Strategy use in testing situations

7.1 Introduction

This chapter will now deal with another specific area in which language use strategies play a significant role, namely that of strategy use in testing situations. The insights gained from looking at the test-taking strategies used by L2 learners can help both to improve the assessment instruments themselves and to improve the success that learners have in responding to these instruments.

The chapter opens with a definition of test-taking strategies and then presents selected findings from the test-taking strategy research. Next, a research study aimed at describing how respondents arrive at their responses on a task measuring oral speech act ability through role play will be described in detail. The focus of the study was on the test-taking process that the respondents were involved in and on the strategies that they used to prepare and deliver their speech act responses. The chapter makes the case for taking a closer look at just what learners are being asked to do and what they actually do in order to produce answers on quizzes and tests. The point is made that, at times, teachers may be deluding themselves into thinking that their tests are assessing language ability in some meaningful way, when in reality they are actually only assessing more limited aspects of language, and in some cases not even that, but rather just the ability to 'psyche out' the test. In other cases, the test or quiz may be assessing exactly what the teachers want to measure. The question is whether any qualitative efforts have been made to vali-date that the test **is** measuring what it purports to measure. It is noted that quantitative measures of test validity can go just so far. By crunching numbers, it is possible to determine whether a given measure is con-sistent with other respected measures of the same phenomenon. What is still lacking from these kinds of analyses is evidence regarding the actual processes that the respondents go through in order to produce the responses that society recognizes as 'answers to a test.'

7.2   Strategies in test taking: definitions and examples from research[1]

This section of the chapter examines the role of test-taking strategy data in validating language tests. It is noted that the use of verbal report measures to identify test-taking strategies represents an approach to research that has been more commonly used in second language acquisition (SLA) research than in language testing research. The concern is to consider the processes in test taking so as to determine the effects of the test input upon the test takers – that is, the processes that the test takers make use of in order to produce acceptable answers to questions and tasks, as well as the perceptions that they have about these questions and tasks before, during, and after responding to them. This information is used for two main purposes: 1) in test development in order to assist the test constructor in improving the actual test, and 2) in interpretation of the test results once the test has been finalized and is being used as a measuring device in order to provide the test taker, the teacher, and administrators with a perspective on what the test may actually be testing.

Traditionally, the difference has been relatively clear-cut between language tasks intended for SLA research purposes and language tests constructed for assessing language achievement. An SLA measure (e.g. a communication task such as relaying directions from a map) is not intended for gate-keeping purposes – that is, in order to restrict access to certain programs or positions in society. In fact, such tasks may purposely encourage risk-taking by putting the respondents in a situation where they do not have the vocabulary or other language forms they need to complete the task, in order to determine the strategies that they use. The respondents are usually in a low-anxiety situation because their performance would not normally have any repercussions for their present or future lives. In a traditional achievement testing situation, the testers have usually been checking for control of language that the respondents have been taught. The respondents know that there is a premium put on better performance. While in SLA research tasks the respondents could get points for communication even if they are inaccurate and usually do not have their performance affect their grade in any language course, in instructional achievement testing the respondents are held accountable for their responses, often under time constraints where accuracy counts as well.

In recent years, the distinction between assessment for the purposes of SLA research v. assessment for instructional purposes has lessened somewhat. More and more tasks and tests are being used interchangeably. As language tests become more a part of SLA research, there has been a growing concern about the reliability and validity of such measures. While there is nothing new in pointing out that certain instruments used in SLA research are lacking in validity, it is a relatively new undertaking to use data on test-taking strategies in order to validate such tests. It is being increasingly recommended that not only language testing researchers but SLA researchers as well consider validating the testing measures that they use through triangulation, or multiple approaches. These approaches would include not only the traditional validity measures, but also the collection of test-taking strategy data on subsamples of respondents.

7.2.1   A process approach to test taking

One of earliest calls to testers to pay more attention to the processes of respondents in answering language tests was issued by Bormuth (1970: 72):

> There are no studies, known to the author, which have attempted to analyze the strategies students use to derive correct answers to a class of items. The custom has been to accept the test author's claims about what underlying processes were tested by an item. And, since there were no operational methods for defining classes of items, it was not scientifically very useful to present empirical challenges to the test author's claims.

Bormuth outlined the objectives and major components of a theory for writing items for achievement tests, drawing on structural linguistics, semantics, and logic. Subsequently, studies began to appear that entailed the observation and description of how learners at different age levels actually accomplish L1 testing tasks. For example, with respect to a teacher's oral questioning of young children, it was suggested that in reality 'the interrogator and respondent work together to jointly compose the "social fact" we call an answer-to-a-question' (Mehan, 1974: 44). Mehan's implication was that the interrogator is not a neutral party but rather in a way 'conspiring' to ensure that the responses in the interview be acceptable. Another outcome of his research efforts was to describe the reasoning that went into the production of responses. Mehan indicated that it may be misguided to conclude 'that a wrong answer is due to a lack of understanding, for the answer may come from an **alternative**, equally valid interpretation.'

Since the late 1970s, interest has slowly begun to grow in approaching L2 testing from the point of view of the strategies used by respondents going through the process of taking the test (e.g. Cohen and Aphek, 1979; Homburg and Spaan, 1981; Cohen, 1984; MacLean and d'Anglejan, 1986;

Gordon, 1987; Anderson, 1989; Nevo, 1989; Brown, 1993; Hill, 1994; Abraham and Vann, 1996; Warren, 1996). As of the 1990s, L2 testing textbooks have acknowledged this concern as a possible source of insights concerning test reliability and validity (Bachman, 1990; Bachman and Palmer, 1996; Cohen, 1994a).

Tests that are relied upon to indicate the comprehension level of non-native readers, for example, may produce misleading results because of numerous test-wise techniques that readers have developed for obtaining correct answers on such tests without fully or even partially understanding the text. As Fransson (1984) put it, respondents may not proceed via the text but rather around it. So, on the one hand we have presumptions held by test constructors and administrators as to what is being tested, and on the other we have the actual processes that test takers go through to produce answers to questions and tasks. The two may not necessarily be one and the same. Students may get an item wrong using sound reasoning or get it right using poor reasoning. Discovering that a respondent used faulty reasoning in attempting to answer a reading comprehension item may be of little interest to the test constructors if the problem resides solely with the respondent. However, if the faulty reasoning was precipitated by an overly ambiguous passage excerpt or by an ambiguous question, then the test constructor may wish to edit the text or revise the question.

Even if the problem resides exclusively with the test taker, a concerned test developer and test administrator may wish to have more information about the items that elicit such illogical responses or about the nature of those test-taking strategies that result in incorrect answers. Respondents may be consistently using strategies that are detrimental to their performance on certain types of items or on an entire test. For example, some respondents may plod laboriously through a reading text only to find that once they reach the multiple-choice questions, they have forgotten most of what they read, or perhaps they have failed to focus adequately on those elements being tested. In such a case (especially in a timed test), the strategy of studying the questions carefully before reading the text may be crucial for those particular respondents, especially the ones who do not have good retentive memory when they read in that language (or altogether).

7.2.2   What is meant by test-taking strategies?

While a part of language test performance is dependent on the knowledge that the learners have about the given language and on their ability to use that language knowledge, another part is dependent on their test wiseness, independent of their language knowledge and language use skills. *Test-taking strategies* consist of both language use strategies and test-wiseness strategies. As noted in 2.2 above, *language use strategies* are steps or actions that learners consciously select in order to accomplish language tasks, and include *retrieval strategies, rehearsal strategies, cover strategies,* and *communication strategies.* All four types of strategies are used in test taking, since respondents need to retrieve material for use on the test, may need to rehearse it before using it (such as in speaking or writing tasks), are likely to use some cover strategies in order to look good, and may well need to engage in genuine communication if the tests or quizzes call for it. These various language use strategies constitute *test-taking strategies* when they are used to help produce responses to testing tasks.

Test-wiseness strategies are not necessarily determined by proficiency in the language being assessed, but rather may be dependent on the respondent's knowledge of how to take tests. One such test-wiseness strategy consists of opting out of the language task at hand (e.g. through a surface matching of some information in the passage with the identical information in one of the response choices). A second strategy would be to make use of material from a previous item when it 'gives away' the answer to a subsequent one. This is also a form of matching, but across items rather than within them, and, as in the previous case, the respondent may make the match without understanding the material very well or at all. Another test-wiseness strategy consists of taking shortcuts to arrive at answers (e.g. not reading the text as instructed but simply looking immediately for the answers to the given reading comprehension questions). In addition, a test-wise respondent may choose a multiple-response alternative because it is: (a) the only grammatical one, (b) the longest one, or (c) the first or the last response (when either of these has not been the 'correct' response over a string of items). In such cases, the respondents may be using test wiseness to circumvent the need to rely on their actual language knowledge or lack of it, consistent with Fransson's (1984) assertion that respondents may not proceed via the text but rather around it. It is possible that some learners enhance their grades in foreign language courses not due so much to their actual ability in the language but rather due to their cleverness at using the above and other test-wiseness strategies.

In some cases, test wiseness may be a misnomer for the strategies which respondents use that are less related to how much language they know and more linked to their hunches, beliefs, or attitudes about what the best way to produce results might be. For example, in a study of test-taking strategies in Israel, one college student respondent was seen to produce a written translation of an entire Hebrew foreign language text before he was willing to respond to questions dealing with that text (Cohen and Aphek, 1979). As it turned out, this strategy was counter-productive since it took up precious time which then could not be used elsewhere, and so not so surprisingly the respondent ran out of time to complete the test. Other not-so-wise strategies may be to continue plodding through material that is causing problems rather than jumping to other material that is easy to complete quickly and then returning to the problematic material if time permits. Ironically, sometimes there are language clues in the easier material as to how to complete the more difficult sections.

7.2.3 Frequency of test-taking strategies and their 'compensatory' nature

As was discussed in 2.2, the frequency of strategy use is not necessarily an indicator of success, nor is success at using a given strategy in a given context a guarantee that the next use of that strategy will also be success-ful. The sheer number of strategies utilized to obtain a response to a test item may be no indication of how strategically versatile the respondent is. At times, the use of a limited number of strategies in a response to an item may indicate genuine control over the item, assuming that those strategies are well-chosen and are used effectively. At other times, true control requires the use of a host of strategies.

It is also best not to assume that any test-taking strategy is a good or a poor choice for a given task. It depends on how given test takers – with their particular cognitive style profile and degree of cognitive flexibility, their language knowledge, and their repertoire of test-taking strategies – employ these strategies at a given moment on a given task. Some respondents may get by with the use of a limited number of strategies that they use well for the most part. Others may be aware of an extensive number of strategies but may use few, if any of them, effectively. So, for example, while a particular skimming strategy (such as paying atten-tion to subheadings) may provide adequate preparation for a given test taker on a recall task, the same strategy may **not** work well for the same respondent on **another** text or another portion of the same text which lacks reader-friendly subheadings. The same skimming strategy may also not work well under any circumstances for some other respondent.

The ability of learners to use language strategies has been referred to as their *strategic competence* – a component of communicative language use (Canale and Swain, 1980). Whereas this model puts the emphasis on *compensatory strategies* (i.e. strategies used to compensate for a lack in some language area), a broader theoretical model for viewing strategic competence has been proposed (Bachman, 1990; Bachman and Palmer, 1996).[2] As indicated in 2.3.4 above, this broader framework includes a *goal-setting component* (wherein the respondents identify the tasks and decide what they are going to do), an *assessment component* (whereby the respondents assess what is needed, what they have to work with, and how well they have done), and a *planning component* (whereby the respondents decide how to use the topic knowledge and language knowledge that they have). Thus, when respondents are given a situation in which to perform an oral role play, they may do all the following:

(1) identify the tasks;
(2) decide what they are going to do;
(3) determine what grammatical, discourse, and sociocultural features are needed for the role play and what they have to work with;
(4) figure out how to use their topic and language knowledge most effectively;
(5) evaluate how well they have done on the task (both during the role play and afterwards).

As is the case with any theoretical model, test takers may make differential use of the components of this model when performing specific testing tasks. Hence, there are respondents who might not assess the situation before starting the role play. This approach may work fine or it may lead to the violation of certain sociocultural conventions. For example, a respondent in a Japanese foreign language role play may neglect to take into account the older age and higher status of the interlocutor, and may select language forms that are not adequately respectful. In addition, there are respondents who may set general goals for an utterance or string of utterances in the Japanese foreign language role play without making a detailed plan of their utterances before producing them. Again, this may work out well or it may lead to ineffective utterances that lack grammatical fine-tuning.

By the same token, role-play respondents may also plan specifics without having general goals in mind. In such cases, the respondents may produce one or more Japanese utterances that have been carefully monitored for grammatical accuracy but which do not fit into the overall discourse and, hence, come across as incoherent. There may be still other respondents who just start talking on an on-line basis, without determining either general goals or a detailed plan. Indeed, the same respondent may assume one or another of these response patterns at different moments during a given test-taking situation and/or in different test-taking situations.

Recent research involving the use of verbal report directly after the performance of oral role-play interaction is just beginning to obtain empirical data regarding the extent of assessment and planning that actually takes place before the delivery of speech acts such as apologies, complaints, and requests. In that study, which is described in full in 7.3 below, it was found that half of the time the non-native adult speakers conducted only a general assessment of the utterances called for in the situation without planning specific vocabulary and grammatical structures. Clearly, more such work is needed in order to understand how respondents arrive at utterances in complex speech situations.

Now that we have considered issues of terminology and of theoretical distinctions, let us look at test-taking strategies as they have been seen to appear in tests of reading and writing.

7.2.4   Strategies for taking tests of reading and writing

We will first consider two more indirect testing formats, multiple-choice and cloze, and will then consider strategies for three more direct formats, namely, summarization tasks, open-ended questions, and compositions. We will end with several suggestions which may lead to more effective test taking. Note that when strategy use data are reported, they represent strategies used on tasks and tests which contributed to the students' course grades in language classes unless it is specified that the data were part of a research task.[3]

INDIRECT TESTING FORMATS

Indirect formats for testing – in other words, those formats which do not reflect real-world tasks – may prompt the use of strategies solely for the purpose of coping with the test format. Let us look at two such formats, multiple-choice and cloze, and at some of the research findings regarding strategies used in taking such tests both in L1 and L2 contexts.

Multiple-choice

Investigating a standardized test of English L1 reading (the Cooperative Primary Test, Form 12 A) by sitting down with individual first-grade (6 year old) learners and going over each item separately after the testing session, MacKay (1974) found that learners did not necessarily link the stem and the answer in the way that the test constructor assumed was correct. MacKay determined that the test had a somewhat arbitrary frame of reference. He found that information as to the reasoning used by the children in producing their responses was irretrievable from the test. He

FIGURE 7.1   Three pictured response alternatives for an L1 reading item

noted, for example, that pictures were sometimes ambiguous. In an item requiring the student to link the expression, 'The bird built his own house' to a picture, MacKay illustrated how a student chose the right picture, but for the **wrong** reason. This student chose a nest of twigs with eggs in the middle over a wooden bird house because he claimed that some big birds could not fit in the hole of the bird house. The student missed the element that people, not birds, are responsible for carpentered wooden bird houses with perches.

A test constructor receiving such feedback might wish to alter the item a bit, requiring, for example, that the respondents give their rationale for choosing one alternative over another. Naturally, there would be constraints on such an approach, such as the natural constraints of group testing, the age of the respondents and their ability to provide this extra information, and so on. It might also be valuable to the test constructors (and possibly to administrators and teachers as well) to know if this 'bird house' example is just one isolated case or whether the faulty logic used by this respondent was shared by other respondents as well.

MacKay also gave an example of an item that the young respondent missed because his reasoning was plausible but faulty. The statement, 'The cat has been out in the rain again' had to be linked to one of three pictures (see Figure 7.1). The problem with the third drawing was that the walls adjacent to the door had large spotted wallpaper, and the student perceived this to be snow and so decided that this picture was of the **exterior** of the house. Thus, he marked the dripping raincoat as referring to the cat having come in from the rain. Once the child perceived the wallpaper as snow and thus eliminated the third picture, his selection of the first picture, the dripping raincoat, rather than the third, was perfectly reasonable – since cats could wear raincoats in cartoons. Again the test constructor would want to determine whether this use of logic was an isolated case or shared by numerous respondents. If so, it might suggest the need to improve the pictures somewhat in order to eliminate any ambiguities in them.

Haney and Scott (1987) found patterns similar to those reported by MacKay with regard to the sometimes dubious fit between elementary-school children getting language arts items in L1 right or wrong and their verbal report as to whether they had applied the skill meant to be tested. The investigators found unusual and perceptive interpretations of questions such as a child's interpretation resulting in the wrong answer in the item: 'Which needs least water?' (followed by pictures of a cactus, a potted plant, and a cabbage). His clever logic produced the **wrong** response, 'cabbage,' namely, that the cabbage had been picked and therefore needed no water at all, while the expected correct answer was 'cactus.' An erroneous interpretation resulted in the **right** answer in an item asking why Eva liked to watch TV. The respondent reported personalizing the item and responding according to why he liked to watch TV, in this case producing the correct answer without relating to Eva at all.

With respect to older respondents, the patterns are relatively similar, as in a study of 40 college English as a second language respondents that used retrospective verbal report to gain insights about test-taking strategies (Larson [1981] in Cohen, 1984). As part of a research study, the students were requested to describe how they arrived at answers to a 10-item multiple-choice test based on a 400-word reading passage. Seventeen students met with the author of the test in groups of two or three within 24 hours after the test, while another 23 students met in groups of five or six some four days after having taken the test. The investigator found that the respondents used the following strategies:

(1) they stopped reading alternatives when they got to the one that seemed correct to them;
(2) they matched material from the passage with material in the item stem and in the alternatives (e.g. when the answer was in the same sentence with the material used to write the stem); and
(3) they preferred a surface-structure reading of the test items to one that called for more in-depth reading and inferencing.

It was found that this superficial matching would sometimes result in the right answer. One example was as follows:

Question: The fact that there is only one university in Filanthropia might be used to show why. . .
(a) education is compulsory through age 13.
(b) many people work in the fishing industry.
(c) 20 per cent of the population is illiterate.
(d) the people are relatively happy and peaceful.

Students were able to identify (c) as the correct answer by noticing that this information appeared in the same sentence in the text as did the information appearing in the item stem:

> Text: . . . The investigating travel agency researchers discovered that the illiteracy rate of the people is 20 per cent, which is perhaps reflective of the fact that there is only one university in Filanthropia, and that education is compulsory, or required, only through age 10.

They assumed that this was the correct answer without understanding the item or the word 'illiterate.' They were right.

In another example, students did not have to look in the text for surface matches. They were able to match directly between the stem and the correct alternative:

> Question: The increased foreign awareness of Filanthropia has . . .
> (a) resulted in its relative poverty.
> (b) led to a tourist bureau investigation.
> (c) created the main population centers.
> (d) caused its extreme isolation.

Students associated 'foreign' in the stem with 'tourist' in option (b), without understanding the test item.

It was also found that more reasoned analysis of the alternatives – e.g. making calculated inferences about vocabulary items – would lead to incorrect answers. The following item provided an example of this:

> Question: The most highly developed industry in Filanthropia is . . .
> (a) oil.
> (b) fishing.
> (c) timber.
> (d) none of the above.

This item referred to the following portion of the text:

> . . . most [dollars] are earned in the fishing industry. . . . In spite of the fact that there are resources other than fish, such as timber in the forest of the foothills, agriculture on the upland plateaus, and, of course, oil, these latter are highly underdeveloped.

One student read the stem phrase 'most highly developed industry' and reasoned that this meant 'technologically developed' and so referred to the 'oil industry.' He was relying on expectations based on general knowledge rather than on a careful reading of the text. The point is that his was a reasoned guess, not that of, say, surface matching, as in the previous example. Once again, it would be necessary to see if this reasoning constitutes an isolated case or whether it is representative of a number of respondents. In the latter case, it may pay to revise the item.

It needs to be stressed that the Larson study was a student course project without outside funding and therefore limited in scope. If the test were to be used widely, then it would be advisable to conduct a series of such investigations to determine both the reliability and validity of the verbal report techniques used to elicit the information, as well as how far the findings could be generalized across a range of different students. (See 3.2 for a series of suggestions as to how to improve the reliability and validity of verbal reports as data.)

In an effort to investigate the extent to which multiple-choice questions are answered on the basis of prior knowledge of the topic and general vocabulary knowledge, 32 intermediate and 25 advanced Israeli EFL students were given as a research task the title and just the first paragraph of a passage appearing on the previous year's exemption examination, and then were asked to answer 12 questions dealing with the portion of text not provided. Two weeks later they were given the text in full along with the questions and once again were asked to respond (Israel [1982] in Cohen, 1984). The rate of success on the multiple-choice items was still surprisingly high on the first run – 49 per cent for the advanced group and 41 per cent for the intermediates. These results were far better than the 25 per cent success rate that would be expected on the basis of chance alone.[4] When the students were given the test with the complete passage and questions two weeks later, the advanced group now scored 77 per cent and the intermediates 62 per cent. The score necessary for exemption from further EFL study was 60 per cent. The fact that the average performance on the test was low even when the passage was provided makes the results without the passage that much more striking.

In a research study with 30 tenth-grade (15-year-olds) EFL students – 15 high-proficiency readers and 15 low-proficiency readers – respondents were asked to verbalize thoughts while finding answers to open-ended and multiple-choice questions (Gordon, 1987). The researcher found that answers to test questions did not necessarily reflect comprehension of the text. Both types of reading comprehension questions were regarded by the respondents as 'mini' reading comprehension tests. With respect to test-taking strategies, the low-proficiency students tended to process information at the local (sentence/word) level, not relating isolated bits of information to the whole text. They used individual word-centered strategies such as matching words in alternatives to text, copying words out of text, translating word-for-word, or formulating global impressions of text content on the basis of key words or isolated lexical items in the text or in the test questions. The high-proficiency students, on the other hand, were seen to comprehend the text at a global level, predicting information accurately in context and using lexical and structural knowledge to cope with linguistic difficulties.

In an effort to provide immediate verbal report data, Nevo (1989) designed a testing format that would allow for immediate feedback after each item. She developed a response strategy checklist, based on the test-taking strategies that had been described in the literature and on her intuitions as to strategies respondents were likely to select. A pilot study had shown that it was difficult to obtain useful feedback on an item-by-item basis without a checklist to jog the respondents' memory as to possible strategies.

Nevo's checklist included 15 strategies, each appearing with a brief description and a label meant to promote rapid processing of the checklist. As a research task, she administered a multiple-choice reading comprehension test in Hebrew L1 and French as a foreign language to 42 tenth graders (15-year-olds), and requested that they indicate for each of the ten questions on each test the strategy that was most instrumental in their arriving at an answer, as well as that which was the second most instrumental. The responses were kept anonymous so as to encourage the students to report exactly what they did, rather than what they thought they were supposed to report.

It was found that students were able to record the two strategies that were most instrumental in obtaining each answer. The study indicated that respondents transferred test-taking strategies from first language to foreign language. The researcher also identified whether the selected strategies aided in choosing the correct answer. The selection of strategies that did not promote choice of the correct answer was more prevalent in the foreign language test than in the L1 version. The main finding in this study was that it was possible to obtain feedback from respondents on their strategy use after each item on a test if a checklist was provided for quick labeling of the processing strategies utilized. Furthermore, the respondents reported benefiting greatly from the opportunity to become aware of how they took reading tests. They reported having been largely unaware of their strategies prior to this study.

Another study of test-taking strategies among non-natives revealed that respondents used certain test-taking strategies differently, depending on the type of question that was being asked. For example, the strategies of 'trying to match the stem with the text' and 'guessing' were reported more frequently for inference type questions than for the other question types such as direct statement or main idea. The strategy of 'paraphrasing' was reported to occur more in responding to direct statement items than with inference and main idea question types (Anderson *et al.*, 1991).

That study originated as a doctoral dissertation in which 28 native speakers of Spanish studying at an intensive ESL language school in Austin, Texas, took as research tasks three measures of reading comprehension: a reading comprehension subtest from a test of language skills, a measure of ability to read college-level textbook prose (*Textbook Reading Profile*; Segal, 1986), and a second form of the standardized reading comprehension test (Anderson, 1989). After the first two tasks, the participants provided retrospective think-aloud protocols describing the strategies that they had used while reading the textbook material and answering the comprehension questions. The respondents also provided think-aloud protocols along with the final test. The data were categorized into a list of 47 processing strategies.

In the follow-up phase of the research, data from the participants' retrospective think-aloud protocols of their reading and test-taking strategies were combined with data from a content analysis and an item analysis to obtain a truly convergent measure of test validation (Anderson *et al.*, 1991). The content analysis of the reading comprehension passages and questions was comprised of the test constructor's analysis as it appeared in the test manual and an analysis based on an outside taxonomy; the item performance data included item difficulty and discrimination. This study marked perhaps the first time that both think-aloud protocols and more commonly used types of information on test content and test performance were combined in the same study in order to examine the validity of the test in a convergent manner.

Another study also found the respondents to be focusing on finding answers to test questions, only putting the minimum effort necessary into comprehending the text. The English L1 respondents in the study were seen to pay little attention to strategies that provided an overall understanding of the native language passage (Farr *et al.*, 1990: 223). The investigators concluded that a reading comprehension test is a special kind of reading task – one where skilled examinees contemplate answer choices, use background knowledge, weigh choices, skim and reread portions of the reading selections, and hold off making choices until they feel confident about an answer choice. They suggested that the types of questions following the passage will determine whether the reading focuses only on the surface meaning of the text.

In recent years some attention has been focused on explicit training for ESL respondents in test wiseness. For example, Allan (1992) developed a test of test wiseness for ESL students. The test included stem–option cues, in which it was possible to match information from the stem with information in the correct option; grammatical cues, where only one alternative matched the stem grammatically; similar option, where several distractors could be eliminated because they essentially said the same thing; and item giveaway, where another item already gave away the information. In preliminary validation work, Allan had three groups of students (N=51), with one group writing a brief explanation of how they selected their answers. Even though the items were meant to be content free, it turned out that prior knowledge and guessing were still possible. The reliabilities for the stem–option and similar option items were low, suggesting that these cues were only sometimes recognized by respondents or that only some of the items in the subscales were measuring those test-wise phenomena.

Emerging from these various studies on multiple-choice tests of reading comprehension are a series of strategies that respondents may utilize at one point or another in order to arrive at answers to the test questions. Whether these strategies are of benefit depends to a large extent upon when they are used and how effectively they are used. A composite list of some of the more salient strategies for taking multiple-choice reading tests (drawn from the studies mentioned above) can be found in Figure 7.2. It is divided into test-taking strategies which rely primarily on language use strategies and those which rely primarily on test-wiseness strategies.

Cloze

Research regarding strategies for taking cloze tests is of interest in that it has helped to determine whether, in fact, such tests actually measure global reading skills as they are commonly purported to. As more studies have been undertaken on the cloze test, it has become clearer that the instrument elicits more local, word-level reading than it does macro- or discourse-level reading (Alderson, 1983; Klein-Braley, 1981; Lado, 1986), contrary to the claims of its early supporters, who have maintained that cloze assesses global reading (see, for example, Chihara *et al.*, 1977; Chávez-Oller *et al.*, 1985). So, in the following excerpt from a cloze passage (Cohen, 1994: 234), items 1 and 3 can be answered on a micro-level while item 2 would call for macro- or discourse-level comprehension:

> People today are quite astonished by the rapid improvements in medicine. Doctors __(1)__ becoming more specialized, and __(2)__ drugs are appearing on __(3)__ market daily.

That is, the local context provides the answer to 1, 'are.' The answer to 2, 'new,' depends on an understanding of the opening sentence, so this would be a discourse-level response. Then, once item 2 is filled in, item 3 is simply a local response, based on the immediate context of that

A. Test-taking strategies which rely primarily on language use strategies

1. Read the passage first and make a mental note of where different kinds of information are located.
2. Return to the passage to look for or confirm an answer rather than relying solely on memory of what was in the text.
3. Read the questions first so that the reading of the text is directed at finding answers to those questions.
4. Read the questions a second time to make sure that their meaning is clear.
5. Try to produce your own answer to the question before you look at the options that are provided in the test.
6. Make an educated guess – e.g. use background knowledge or extra-textual knowledge in making the guess.
7. Be ready to change the responses to any given item as appropriate – e.g. in the case where new clues are discovered in, say, another item.

B. Test-taking strategies which rely primarily on test-wiseness strategies

1. Look for the portion of the text that the question refers to and then look for clues to the answer there.
2. Look for answers to questions in chronological order in the text.
3. Read the questions first so that the reading of the text is directed at finding answers to those questions. (also a language use strategy)
4. Use the process of elimination – i.e. select a choice not because you are sure that it is the correct answer, but because the other choices don't seem reasonable, because they seem similar or overlapping, or because their meaning is not clear to you.
5. Look for an option that seems to deviate from the others, is special, is different, or conspicuous.
6. Select a choice that is longer/shorter than the others.
7. Take advantage of clues appearing in other items in order to answer the item under consideration.
8. Take into consideration the position of the option among the choices (a, b, c, or d).
9. Select the option because it appears to have a word or phrase from the passage in it – possibly a key word.
10. Select the option because it has a word or phrase that also appears in the question.
11. Postpone dealing with an item or selecting a given option until later.
12. Estimate the time needed for completing the items and don't spend too much time on any given item.

FIGURE 7.2   Strategies for talking a multiple-choice comprehension test

phrase. It has also become evident that more proficient readers are more skilled at correctly completing cloze items such as 2 that **do** assess discourse-level reading, whether reading in the native or in a foreign language.

Studies on strategies for taking cloze tests have shown that perhaps only a quarter of non-native respondents read the entire EFL cloze passage before responding (Cohen, 1984). A case study shed some light on the issue of reading the text before completing an L1 cloze test (Kleiman *et al.*, 1986). Verbal protocol data provided by a 7th-grade (12-year-olds) Brazilian girl filling in two cloze passages – one as a warm up and the other as the exercise in Portuguese L1 – indicated that the respondent was preoccupied with local clues from isolated elements of text. What emerged was that she did not use global clues until she had completed a substantial number of blanks on the cloze. In other words, it was easier for her to read the cloze passage once it had been partially completed and she had some idea of what it is about, much as a child may have an easier time of connecting numbered dots once the picture that the dots are forming becomes clearer. It is likely that the experience of this one 7th grader is representative of numerous respondents on cloze passages in both L1 and L2, but it would be necessary to verify this assumption.

One of the early studies of strategy use in completing a cloze passage involved indirect assessment of the strategies used. The researchers administered a rational deletion cloze with 23 blanks to 39 EFL subjects from three levels (Homburg and Spaan, 1981). One of four strategies was intuited to be necessary in finding a correct word for each of the blanks: recognition of parallelism, sentence-bound reading, forward reading, and backward reading. Success at items calling for *cataphora* or forward reading was significantly associated with success at understanding the main idea. In verbal report studies, it was found that nearly 20% of the respondents did not use the preceding or following sentence for clues to blanks but rather guessed on the basis of the immediate context (Cohen, 1984).

The picture regarding the taking of cloze tests in the native language does not appear to be much different. One study, for example, involved 18 fifth graders (10 year olds) at three levels of reading (high, inter-mediate, low) who were given a rational deletion cloze test in Hebrew L1 and were asked to think aloud as they completed it (Kesar, 1990). An analysis of the verbal report protocols yielded at least 26 different strategies, which were grouped into seven categories: word-level/part of sentence, sentence-level, and five categories at the level of discourse – intersentential, whole-text level, extra-textual level, metacognitive level, and 'other.' The results demonstrated that although the better readers were more likely to use macro-level schemata and strategies in completing the cloze and also did better on the completion task as a whole, all respondents favored micro-level reading at the sentence level.

Thus, the research on strategies in taking cloze tests would suggest that such tests assess local-level reading more than they measure global reading ability. Furthermore such tests are more likely to test for local-level reading when they are in a foreign language (see for example, MacLean and d'Anglejan, 1986). One explanation for the preponderance of local-level reading in completing cloze passages is that of ease. Having to look outside the immediate context is more demanding. It may require a concerted effort to store the meaning of the local text while reading elsewhere. It also demands powers of inference, especially when other blanks abound.

MORE DIRECT FORMATS

Summarization tasks

Summarizing tasks on reading comprehension tests have a natural appeal in this era of communicative testing, given that they attempt to simulate real-world tasks in which non-native readers have to read and write a summary of the main ideas of a text. In order to summarize successfully, respondents need both reading and writing skills. First, they must select and utilize effectively those reading strategies appropriate for summarizing the source text – identifying topical information, distinguishing superordinate from subordinate material, and identifying redundant as well as trivial information. They must then perform the appropriate writing tasks to produce a coherent text summary – selecting topical information or generating it if none appears explicitly in the text, deleting trivial and redundant material, substituting superordinate terms for lists of terms or sequences of events, and finally, reformulating the content so that it sounds coherent and reads smoothly.

Despite the appeal of a summarization task, the testing situation itself imposes constraints on the respondent that would not be found in the real world. In reality, respondents on such measures are more likely than not to read unnaturally and to write summaries that are quite different from what they would normally prepare in the real world. In the real world, people usually prepare *writer-based summaries*, that is, summaries that are intended for their own future use or for the benefit of someone who has **not** read it. In stark contrast, respondents on a test are usually required to furnish a *reader-based summary* (Hidi and Anderson, 1986). In other words, the respondent is summarizing a text for raters who have their own and/or a pre-determined model for what the summary should contain. In reality, raters may not be consistent with one another even if they have a model that they are supposed to follow.

A study was conducted to determine how respondents at different levels of proficiency interacted with source tests in order to produce summary texts of their own, and how raters responded to these summaries (Cohen, 1994b). The respondents were five native Portuguese-speaking students who had recently completed an English for Academic Purposes (EAP) course at a university in Brazil, a course which emphasized reading strategies and training in how to summarize. The two EAP course instructors who regularly rated the EAP exams of summarizing skill (both fluent speakers of Portuguese) participated in the study as raters. A sample test for assessing EFL proficiency was used as the testing instrument, consisting of three short texts and one longer one, three of which had to be summarized in Portuguese. The respondents were requested to provide verbal report data in their native language during the taking of the test. They also filled out a questionnaire indicating whether the EAP course had assisted them in writing the summaries, what they thought about taking tests of summarizing and about responding to the research assistant's queries regarding their test-taking strategies, and whether difficulties in performance on the summary tasks were due to reading problems or writing problems. In addition, the raters were asked to provide verbal report data while assessing the tests. They were to indicate (1) the way they determined what the various texts were about, (2) the steps they were taking in their rating, and (3) their assessment of the respondents' understanding of these texts.

The findings shed some light on strategies used by the takers of tests of summarizing. The respondents on these Portuguese L1 summaries of EFL texts used various shortcut measures. One strategy employed in the case study was to lift material directly from the passage in summarizing, rather than restating it at a higher level of abstraction or generality. The respondents' hope would be that any ambiguity that the rater had over whether they understood the material would be to their favor. Furthermore, when respondents were in doubt about whether material should be included or deleted, they were prone to include it, with the assumption that a summary that ran longer would probably be preferred by the raters to one that was too terse. The case study found that the respondents spent more time on their strategies for reading the texts to be summarized than they did on the production of their summaries, so unsurprisingly the summaries were not so coherent nor polished.

Let us look just at the performance of one student, Ana, who was considered a low-proficiency respondent, who nonetheless was found to perform unexpectedly well. One factor working to her advantage on the test was that it was untimed, and she took the most time of any of the respondents. In addition, Ana was found to use six strategies to her benefit. With respect to reading the source text, she used the following effectively:

(1) technical facilitation strategies – e.g. underlining discourse markers and words to look up, and circling pronominal referents;
(2) clarification and simplification strategies – e.g. using a dictionary; and
(3) coherence detection strategies – e.g. paying special attention to pronouns and conjunctions.

With respect to writing the text summary, she used the following strategies effectively:

(1) technical facilitation strategies – e.g. providing a detailed answer to include the main ideas; and
(2) metacognitive monitoring – e.g. giving a generalization plus the main idea.

Ana's strategy of supplying many details in her (lengthy) summaries with the hope that they would contain the main ideas reflected more of a shot-gun rather than a lazer-beam approach to the task. Since in this case the raters did not penalize for summaries that were longer than the specified length, this strategy of drawing out the summary could be seen as a facilitating one. We might also see it as a test-wise strategy. Ana's strategy of generalizing and then moving to main ideas worked with one rater and not with the other. Her literal interpretation of an idiomatic phrase ('. . . JVC stole the Berlin radio show') did not work, perhaps an indication of why she was assessed as low-proficiency: her control of vocabulary and especially of idiomatic uses may have been limited.

With regard to the raters, it was found that raters were **not** necessarily consistent with one another even though they had model responses that they were supposed to follow. There were marked differences between the two raters as to how they assessed Ana, for example. One saw her misinterpretation of the idiom about 'stealing the show' to be serious and the other essentially ignored it. In addition, the raters seemed to differ somewhat in their basic criteria: while they apparently agreed on what material should be included, one emphasized more than did the other the production of a coherent, readable text. So in this case, the use of verbal report to track the strategies used by raters in producing their ratings also demonstrates how the description of strategies can enhance our picture of what the assessment process entails – this time from the angle of the assessment, after the tests have been taken.

Open-ended questions and compositions

As with summarization tasks, on open-ended tasks respondents may be prone to copy material directly from a text for use in a response, with two possible consequences. First, raters do not necessarily know whether the respondent in fact understands the material. Second, such copying may produce linguistically awkward responses. For example, in a study of 19 college-level learners of Hebrew L2 which involved retrospective verbal report one week after the learners took their final exam, it was found that students lifted material intact from an item stimulus or from a text passage for use in their written responses (Cohen and Aphek, 1979). Results included verb forms incorrectly inflected for person, number, gender, or tense; verbs reflecting the correct root but an incorrect conjugation; and so forth. A variety of strategies were observed for producing a verb form when the rules for production had not been learned. Among other things, respondents reported taking a form from a tense that they knew, taking one inflectional ending and generalizing it across person and gender, and taking an inappropriate tense from the stimulus and simply adding the prefix for person.

Another strategy that the learners in the Cohen and Aphek study (1979) used in their writing was simply to introduce pre-packaged, unanalyzed material and combine it with analyzed forms. For example, given that Hebrew prepositions such as *mi* 'from' can be prefixed to the object of the preposition through elision (*mi + tsad* 'side,' = *mitsad*), one student learned this form as one word and then affixed another preposition to it in an exam, e.g. **bemitsad* 'on from a side' intending 'on a side.'

Respondents' misinterpretation of essay prompts is a problem which is related to inadequate attention to instructions. Usually, an essay topic is presented in the form of a mini-text which the respondent needs to understand and respond to. Ruth and Murphy (1984) note cases where English L1 students misinterpreted words in the prompt, such as interpreting the word 'profit' as 'prophet,' thus shifting the meaning of the topic entirely. Perhaps of greater consequence are the strategies the respondents make use of in sizing up the nature of the task. Ruth and Murphy gave the example of a supposed informal letter to a friend wherein what was actually called for was a response at a higher level of performance than might be reflected in an authentic letter to a friend. The message here for the respondent is to be extra careful in interpreting these mini-texts. The message for raters is to rate the written product consistent with the prompt and not according to unspecified criteria – such as having to write a friendly letter in a more formal style in order to receive a high grade.

7.2.5 Discussion of the process approach to test taking through looking at respondents' strategies

This section of the chapter has looked at the process approach to language testing, which has usually relied on verbal report techniques to better understand the processes and test-taking strategies that respondents use. The use of qualitative methodologies such as verbal report provides a valuable source of information – perhaps the most focused possible – on the strategies respondents use in their responses and why they do so.

Verbal report can help us see what items are actually getting at, in order to make decisions about which items to keep and which to throw out. One could go so far as to say it is now close to essential to have verbal report as part of the piloting phase in test construction.

Let us take, for example, the case of multiple-choice items since it is clear from the research literature that this extremely convenient format may nonetheless pose problems. Hughes (1989: 60–2) includes the following in his list of shortcomings in the use of multiple-choice:

1. Items meant to assess just grammar may also test for lexical knowledge as well.
2. Respondents may eliminate distractors out of hand as being absurd.
3. Correct responses may be common knowledge to the respondents.

It would appear that test-taking strategy research can be utilized to substantiate or refute claims about multiple-choice items, at least with respect to a given test in a given testing situation with given respondents. In other words, criticism of the multiple-choice format are not new and did not originate from qualitative investigations. However, such qualitative investigations can help us to get beyond such pronouncements to determine what is actually going on. So, for example, a study could be designed whereby students need to indicate the extent to which lexical knowledge assisted them in answering grammar items.

The results of test-taking strategy studies on cloze tests would also appear to provide crucial information regarding what those tests actually measure. The various types of cloze tests have been subjected to careful scrutiny in recent years, and, of the studies carried out, those that deal with response strategies are perhaps among some of the most insightful. Thus, while the reliability of a given cloze test may be high because the individual items are interrelated, the validity as a measure of global reading ability could be questioned if the respondents indicate that they answered most of the items by means of local micro-level strategies.

The above presentation of research on test-taking strategies for the more open-ended formats, such as summarization, open-ended responses to questions, and essays, offered some insights as to respondents' strategy use. Since the assessment of summaries and essays depends on judgments made by raters, there is a concomitant need for more research concerning strategies used in doing the ratings, such as the work conducted by Hamp-Lyons (1989), Connor and Carrell (1993), and Vaughan (1991).

While we are still lacking adequate data to make definitive statements about the links between the use of specific test-taking strategies and subsequent success or failure on speaking tasks, studies are beginning to appear which link the selection of given strategies to rated success at performance in a foreign language. The study by Cohen, Weaver and Li with intermediate college learners of French and Norwegian, for example, identified a link between the frequency of use of a given strategy and performance on the speaking task for which that strategy was chosen. As was presented in Chapter 5, an increase in certain preparatory strategies (e.g. translating specific words, writing out sentences, and practicing the pronunciation of words) and monitoring strategies (e.g. monitoring for grammar, paying attention to the pronunciation of words, and analyzing a story for its key elements) related to an increase in ratings by outside raters on one or more of the rating scales – self-confidence, grammar, vocabulary, and identifying and ordering elements in a story.

Ideally, continued qualitative investigation will produce descriptions that when coupled with quantitative results will yield a convincing picture as to what strategies respondents actually use in order to produce responses to a host of test tasks. As we gain this type of knowledge, we will be better able to train learners to perform more successfully on such measures. Or given this knowledge, we may wish to change our measures so that they tap other kinds of strategies than those currently tapped, ideally with more of a focus on language use strategies and less on test-wiseness strategies. Given the results from test-taking strategy research, however embryonic they may be at present, L2 acquisition researchers would probably want to consider validating the testing measures that they use in their research studies through triangulation, which would include the collection of test-taking strategy data on subsamples of respondents as in the Anderson *et al.* (1991) study. It is a promising sign to see that test constructors at the Language Testing Research Centre, University of Melbourne, are including qualitative investigation of test-taking strategies as a regular part of their test development and test validation. For example, both the development of a semi-direct oral/aural proficiency test in Japanese for Tourism and Hospitality (Brown, 1993) and that of a test of oral English proficiency for prospective migrants (Hill, 1994) included feedback from respondents (as well as from interviewers/interlocutors and from raters) on the tests.

The next section will provide a detailed description of a research study which investigated how respondents arrive at their responses on a task measuring oral speech act ability through role play. The focus of the study was on the process involved and on the strategies used to produce speech acts. Unlike in the Cohen, Weaver and Li study described in Chapter 5, in this study the output of the respondents was not submitted to ratings by outside raters since the focus was exclusively on obtaining a better understanding of the psycholinguistic and sociolinguistic demands put on the respondents in their efforts to generate speech acts in role play.

7.3   Strategies in producing oral speech acts[5]
Andrew Cohen and Elite Olshtain

This section reports on a study describing ways in which non-native speakers assessed, planned, and then delivered speech acts. The subjects, 15 advanced English foreign language learners, were given six speech act situations (two apologies, two complaints, and two requests) in which they were to role play along with a native speaker. The interactions were videotaped and after each set of two situations of the same type, the videotape was played back and then the respondents were asked both fixed and probing questions regarding the factors contributing to the production of their responses in those situations. The retrospective verbal report protocols were analyzed with regard to processing strategies in speech act formulation. The study found that in delivering the speech acts, half of the time respondents conducted only a general assessment of the utterances called for in the situation without planning specific vocabulary and grammatical structures, often thought in two languages and sometimes in three languages (if trilingual), utilized a series of different strategies in searching for language forms, and did not attend much to grammar nor to pronunciation. Finally, there were respondents whose speech production styles characterized them as *metacognizers*, *avoiders*, and *pragmatists* respectively.

7.3.1   Review of the literature

During the last two decades, the literature on communication strategies has been growing (Faerch and Kasper, 1983a; Bialystok, 1990; Dörnyei and Scott, 1997) and along with it, an extensive literature on speech act strategies as performed by natives and non-natives alike. At present, the research literature provides relatively detailed descriptions of realization strategies for perhaps eight speech acts in a variety of situations (apologies, requests, complaints, disapproval, refusals, disagreement, gratitude, compliments) (see, for example, Wolfson, 1989; Blum-Kulka *et al.*, 1989; Olshtain and Cohen, 1983, 1989, 1990; Cohen and Olshtain, 1985; Cohen *et al.*, 1986; Hatch, 1992: 121–63; Kasper, 1992, 1995; Kasper and Schmidt, 1996; Gass and Neu, 1996).

Although there is increasing information regarding the extent to which non-natives (at varying proficiency levels) are likely to approximate native norms for some of these speech acts, there are relatively few descriptions of the cognitive strategies that learners actually use in the production of these speech act utterances. The very complexity of speech act sets such as those of 'apologies' and 'complaints' has made it an area of interest in language learning, since this complexity makes special demands of the speaker. The apology speech act set, for example, is potentially complex because it can be comprised of a series of speech acts, such as expressing apology ('I'm sorry'), acknowledging responsibility ('That was dumb of me'), offering repair ('Here, let me pick them up'), and giving an explanation or excuse. In addition, there are various possible modifications for intensifying the sincerity ('I'm really sorry'), mitigating the apology ('Yeah, but you were in my way!'), and so forth. What adds to the complexity of selecting appropriate strategies is that this and other speech acts are conditioned by a host of social, cultural, situational, and personal factors.

If we apply the Bachman and Palmer (1996) model of strategic competence to the study of speech act processes, we might expect there to be learners who only do a minimal assessment of a situation before starting to speak, which could in turn result in violations of certain sociocultural conventions. Likewise, there are learners who prefer to plan their foreign language utterances carefully in terms of vocabulary and structures before producing them. Seliger (1980) classified non-natives as pertaining to one of two general patterns – the *planners* and the *correctors*, with the former planning out their utterances before delivering them while the latter start talking and make on-line corrections. Crookes (1989) found that when intermediate and advanced ESL students were specifically instructed to plan for 10 minutes before performing descriptive tasks, they showed more variety of lexis (e.g. more explicit adjectives) and more complexity of language (e.g. more subordinate clauses) than a control group not given time to plan.

One of the first studies of speech act production strategies using verbal report was conducted in Brazil by Motti (1987). In that study, ten intermediate EFL university students were requested to produce spoken apologies and then to provide retrospective verbal report data. In their verbal reports, the respondents indicated that they had many things on their minds while responding. For example, they reported analyzing the situational variables such as the interlocutor's age and status. They also reported thinking the utterance through quickly in Portuguese, their native language, before producing it in English, the foreign language. Subjects also expressed concern as to whether they were producing their utterances correctly in terms of vocabulary, grammar, and pronunciation.

A more recent study of speech act production using verbal report had 12 female Japanese ESL students complete a discourse questionnaire with six refusal situations to which they were to respond in writing (Robinson, 1991). The respondents were also requested to provide taped think-aloud data as they completed the situations. The investigator then interviewed the respondents regarding the content of their utterances from the think-aloud session. The findings dealt with cultural and personality issues. For example, respondents sometimes accepted the request rather than refusing it as they were instructed to do because their cultural background taught young women in Japan to say 'yes,' or at least not to say 'no.' There were also specific instances in which the respondents indicated in the retrospective interview that they had not had experience with the given situation (Robinson, 1991).

The current study set out to investigate more fully the processes whereby non-native speakers produce speech acts in an elicited role-play situation. The study was designed so as to arrive at a description of the ways in which non-native speakers assess, plan, and deliver such utterances. The decision to investigate thought processes during complex speech acts was based on the above-mentioned assumption that such sociolinguistic tasks were by their very nature particularly demanding speaking tasks and consequently a potentially rich source of data regarding processing strategies.

A second interest was in exploring the sources for positive and negative transfer of forms from native to target language by attempting to describe just when the thinking was taking place in one or the other language. Whereas the literature on language transfer pays a good deal of attention to the transfer of structures (e.g. Gass and Selinker, 1983; Ringbom, 1987; Dechert and Raupach, 1989), little attention has been paid to the shift in language of thought between and among languages (in the case of trilinguals) during the process of assessing, planning, or delivering a given utterance (see 6.2.2 and 6.2.3 above).

Another purpose of the study was to examine ways that verbal report could be used as a research methodology for collecting thought processes during oral elicitation situations. As noted in Chapter 3, verbal reports have their limitations, just as do other research techniques, but their careful use can provide one more source of data, often a source of data unobtainable in any other way (Ericsson and Simon, 1993). With regard to reliability, respondents have been found to provide more reliable retrospective reports on their cognitive processes if the reporting takes place shortly after the mental events themselves. In any case, respondents need to be aware of the strategies that they are using (without necessarily attending to them) or they will not be able to report about them.

Since verbal report techniques are intrusive, it would be unreasonable to ask speakers to provide such data while they are engaged in oral interaction. Yet once the interaction is over, subjects may not be able to retrospect fully as to the strategy selection that they carried out a few minutes prior to the intervention. For this reason, in the study to be described below, subjects were videotaped interacting in two role-play situations at a time and then immediately viewed the videotapes (one or more times) as a means of jogging their memory as to their thought processes during the interactions.

The following are the research questions that were asked:

1. To what extent do respondents assess and plan their utterances and what is the nature of this assessment and planning?
2. What is the language of thought used in assessing, planning, and delivering utterances?
3. What are the processes involved in the search, retrieval, and selection of language forms?
4. What is the extent of attention to grammar and pronunciation in the production of speech act utterances?

7.3.2   The design of the study

The subjects for this small-scale, exploratory study were 15 advanced English foreign language learners, 11 native speakers of Hebrew (Jackie, Sharon, Shalom, Zohara, Hagar, Nogah, Yaakov, Shlomit, Hava, Galit, and Ricki) and 4 near-native speakers, who were native speakers of French (Michel), Portuguese (Lillian), Spanish (Lily), and Arabic (Wassim) respectively. Ten were females, five males, and their average age was 24. They were undergraduates in the humanities or social sciences, and were all taking a course in reading English for academic purposes at the time of the study.

The subjects were asked to fill out a short background questionnaire (*re* the languages used in the home, self-evaluation of English, time in an English-speaking country, and past and current uses for English; see Appendix 7A at the end of this chapter) and then were given six speech act situations (two apologies, two complaints, and two requests) in which they were to role-play along with a native speaker (see Appendix 7B). These situations were written out for the respondents on cards and the native English-speaking interlocutor, Debbie, also read the instructions out loud just before each situation was role-played. The interactions were videotaped, and after each set of two situations of the same type, the tape was played back and the respondents were asked in Hebrew by a native Hebrew-speaking investigator both fixed and probing questions regarding the factors contributing to the production of their response to that situation (see Appendix 7C).

These retrospective verbal report protocols were analyzed with regard to the following aspects: the extent to which utterances were assessed and

TABLE 7.1   Planning of speech act production

	Assessment	Planning	No Assessment or Planning
Situations			
meeting	7	4	4
book	9	3	3
music	7	3	5
notes	8	3	4
lift	6	9	0
token	7	5	3
Total	44 (49%)	27 (30%)	19 (21%)

planned, the selection of language of thought for planning and delivering the utterances, the search/retrieval/selection of language forms, the extent to which grammar and pronunciation were attended to, and the sources for language used in the production of the utterances (see Appendix 7B for the transcript of the interactions between one respondent, Nogah, and the interlocutor). The independent variables in the study were the speech act situation, the speakers' language and that of their parents, speakers' length of stay in English-speaking countries, and the extent of the speakers' English language use.

7.3.3   Results

Let us now report on the findings for the research questions enumerated above.

THE ASSESSMENT AND PLANNING OF UTTERANCES

It was found that in 49% of the speech act situations, respondents reported that they made an assessment of the general direction that the utterance would go in (e.g. expressing the apology and choosing an excuse such as that of the bus being late), but did not plan the specific utterances that they would use (e.g. pre-selecting the vocabulary and structures that they would use). In 30% of the cases they actually planned out a portion of the utterances, perhaps just several words. In the remaining 21% of the situations, they did not plan at all (see Table 7.1). As can be seen in Table 7.1, the situation of asking for a lift prompted by far the most specific planning. Respondents reported perceiving that since they were asking a higher status person for a ride, they needed to think about it more first.

THE LANGUAGE OF THOUGHT

For the purposes of this research question alone, assessment (choosing goals) was subsumed under the category of planning (identifying and retrieving language forms) in the analysis of the verbal report data. It was found that the language of thought for planning and for delivering the utterance turned out to be a complex matter. The three most common patterns were 'planning in English and responding in English' (21 instances across 9 speakers), 'planning in Hebrew and translating from Hebrew to English in the response' (17 instances across 7 speakers), and 'planning in Hebrew with the response in English' (16 instances across 8 speakers). On theoretical grounds, we might expect that planning and delivering utterances exclusively in English would produce the least amount of transfer from the native language, that planning utterances in Hebrew and delivering them in English would produce more transfer, and that planning in Hebrew with delivery consisting of translation of Hebrew to English would produce the most transfer. The other 16 combinations of thought patterns had far fewer instances.

Whereas the French, Portuguese, and Arabic speakers tended to think in Hebrew – the language they used for daily communication – rather than in their native language, they thought in their native language in one or two situations: the French speaker (Michel) for planning and producing his utterance in the 'lift' situation, the Portuguese speaker (Lillian) for planning in the 'book' and 'notes' situations, and the Arabic speaker (Wassim) for planning in the 'notes' situation. In the case of the Spanish speaker, Lily, whose English was weak, the patterns were most complex, involving both planning in Hebrew and then back to Spanish and translating from Spanish to English in producing the utterance for the 'meeting' situation; planning in Spanish and then in Hebrew, with the response translated from Hebrew to English in the 'book' situation; and planning in both Hebrew and Spanish simultaneously, with the response translated both from Hebrew and Spanish to English in the 'music' situation.

Only one speaker (Jackie), a native Hebrew speaker, used the same thought pattern throughout; he planned his utterances in Hebrew and responded by translating from Hebrew to English. Furthermore, in only one situation did a particular thought pattern prevail across different respondents: in the 'music' situation, 6 speakers out of the 15 reported planning their utterance and responding in English. It would appear that this sort of complaint situation encouraged processing of the language directly in English, at least according to the retrospective verbal reports. This finding might have importance for researchers in their selection of situations for role playing.

THE SEARCH, RETRIEVAL, AND SELECTION OF LANGUAGE FORMS

In this section we will take a look at the communication strategies and concerns that one or more speakers reported in searching for, retrieving, or selecting language forms to use in their speech act utterances. These examples represent all the instances that were identified in the analysis of the verbal protocols for these 15 speakers.[6] Eight of the categories reflect areas that have been much discussed in the communication strategy literature: din in the head, monitor, use of formulaic speech, message omission or abandonment, lexical avoidance or simplification, and approximation. The other four categories reflect insights gained from the use of verbal report protocols: self-debate, afterthoughts, partial delivery of a thought, and delivery of a different thought.

Retrieval process – 'din in the head'

Ricki noted after completing the first two situations that she had difficulty in speaking English because of a long period of non-use: 'When I start speaking English after not speaking it for a long time, my vocabulary is weak and it is hard to retrieve words from memory.' A concept appearing originally in the anthropological literature, that of 'din in the head,' is helpful here in interpreting what Ricki was reporting. *Din in the head* refers to the sense of having the language available for use, which may take anywhere from one to two hours of good input and may wear off after a few days (Krashen, 1985: 40–1). In certain oral elicitation tasks, there may be a warm-up period, but often this period is not long enough to activate the din in the head.

Self-debate before selection

In the 'lift' situation, Hava debated between 'to get a ride' and 'to give a lift,' and finally asked whether she 'could get a lift.' Shalom debated among 'drive,' 'come,' and 'go,' and ended up with, 'Can I come with you?' Galit wanted to make a polite request and was uncertain as to whether she could ask, 'Do you have any room in the car?' As she put it: 'It has a lot of meanings and I wasn't sure that it was correct, so I changed my tactic, and decided she would understand better if I said, "I want to drive with you." I thought of "lift," but didn't know how to use it in a sentence so I left it out.' In the same situation, Lily debated among three expressions, 'in the same neighborhood,' 'your same neighborhood,' and 'in your neighborhood.' She was translating from Spanish and felt that the result was not good. Also with regard to the 'lift' situation, Yaakov debated how to address Debbie – 'Debbie,' 'Teacher,' 'Gveret "lady,"' or 'Gveret Teacher.' He decided to address her the way he would in a high-school class in Israel.

Afterthoughts

In the 'meeting' situation, Ricki used 'very' as the intensifier in her expression of apology, 'very sorry,' but reported thinking to herself afterwards that she could have said 'terribly sorry'. She also used 'stopped' in that situation ('I'm very sorry, but I – I met some friends and they stopped me and I couldn't go on . . .') and, as she put it, 'I knew it wasn't the correct word but I was already in the middle of things.' Sometimes the afterthoughts a respondent has during a given speaking task can, in fact, cause later communicative failure in that their mind is still engaged in some previous language form while they are being called upon to perform a new task.

Awareness of monitoring

Four of the respondents referred to their use or non-use of monitoring. With regard to the 'meeting' situation, Lily commented:

> I always think about grammar and so my pace is so slow. I think about how to structure the sentence correctly, verb tenses and other aspects. E.g.: 'I haven't sleep good' → 'I didn't sleep good.' I thought the first form wasn't correct.

In the 'music' situation, Lily erroneously said, 'you have listened to the music very loud last night' and noted:

> With this confusion, I wondered whether to continue with the mistake or correct myself. I decided that it was important to correct myself because if I am aware of an error and it is possible to correct it, I want to do it.

Ricki could also be viewed as a consistent monitor user. With respect to the 'music' situation, she commented:

> I am always thinking about grammar . . . When I have problems like 'not/don't,' I correct them. 'I was yesterday awake –' just came out that way and I noted that it was not correct.

Hagar on the other hand would be viewed as an underuser of the monitor. With regard to the same situation, she remarked:

> I don't effort at grammar. I am aware that it is bad. I focus on the idea, the message. Grammar gets me stuck. I prefer not to know how

grammatical I sound. I depend on the listeners to see if they understand me, using facial expressions and letting them complete my sentences for me.

Wassim only thought about grammar extensively in the 'notes' situation in which it was not spontaneous in that he was translating from Arabic. In the 'meeting' and the 'book' situations, he reported: 'When I first read the situations, I thought that it would be good to think about my grammar, but I then forgot about it because it was more important for me that Debbie understand me.'

Use of formulaic speech

In the 'lift' situation, Nogah used 'I would love to–' in requesting a ride, which sounded peculiar for the requesting party to use (see Appendix 7B, Situation 5). Nogah noted that she had heard this expression a lot and that is why it popped up in her utterance. Although this was the only reported instance of an unanalyzed phrase appearing in the respondent's data, it is likely that such formulaic speech occurs with some regularity in the output of non-natives (Ellis, 1985).

Utterance omission abandonment or modification

There were also examples of respondents not saying what was intended for lack of the appropriate forms or lack of certainty about them, resulting in utterance, omission, abandonment or modification.

Omission

Two cases of omission of an utterance occurred in the data. In the 'meeting' situation, Lily thought of saying that she was late because of a problem at home, but decided that it would be too difficult for her to say it in English. Instead she chose to say that she usually comes late. She also indicated that in general she chooses the easiest utterance – the one for which she knows the verbs and the sentence structure, and can say it directly 'without having to express it in a round-about way.' In the 'lift' situation, Shlomit debated whether she should address her teacher by name, and then chose instead to say, 'Excuse me, are you going home?' because, as she put it, 'it was a bit more formal. In general, when I address a lecturer in Hebrew, I do it this way.'

Abandoning a word or expression

Five instances of breakdown were identified in the data. In the 'meeting' situation, Galit said, 'I really don't have any exc–' and stopped there. She said she got stuck because of the *x*. In the 'book' situation, Shalom asked, 'Anything I can do to comp – something?' He said that he sort of knew the word 'compensate' receptively. In the 'music' situation, Hagar started the utterance, 'Can't you just –' and stopped. She felt that what she was starting to say was inappropriate and did not know how to convey the correct message in English. In the same situation, Lily produced, 'I want you to – that –' and, in explanation, noted, 'I wanted to say that I didn't want that to happen again but stopped in the middle because it was too complicated for me.' In the 'notes' situation, Nogah wanted to indicate that she always (*tamid* in Hebrew) gave her friend class notes if she wanted them, but did not know how to say it: 'I debated between "often" and "always" and I couldn't remember it, so I let it go.' She simply said, 'When you need things I al – I give you' and made no further attempt to supply the adverb.

Partial delivery of a thought

Two instances of partial delivery of an utterance were identified. In the 'notes' situation, Hagar was not sure whether she should just continue requesting the notes or whether she should simply say that she did not need any favors from her friend and thank her anyway. She chose to be angry but commented that 'anger doesn't come out well in English.' As she put it, 'I started and got stuck because of my English and so I chose a compromise.' Her compromise was to be sarcastic: 'Well, you're very kind to me. I mean I gave you in the past things and it's – uhm – alright, no thank you.' In the same situation, Nogah wanted to use strong language but did not know how to say it in English in a way that would not sound too exaggerated, so instead of saying the English equivalent of *tov lada'at* 'it's good to know' or *ani ezkor et ze* 'I'll remember this,' she simply said, 'I need them too.'

Delivery of a different thought

There were two examples in the data where the respondents delivered a different thought from the one they had wanted to express. These were not simply cases of omission because an alternate thought was supplied instead. In the 'meeting' situation, Hava wanted to indicate that the bus did not come, but she reported that she did not find the words in English, so instead she said, 'I missed the bus.' Galit, in looking for a reason that she needed a ride, said, 'My bus is very late,' which she saw right away to be incorrect. As she explained it, 'I meant that it wouldn't be leaving until later in the evening, but grammatically the sentence was OK so I left it. I let it go because it wasn't so bad – she would understand what I meant.'

Lexical avoidance or simplification

There was one identifiable instance of lexical avoidance and one of simplification in the data. In the 'music' situation, Shlomit wanted to say that her neighbor's music was 'too loud' but avoided the equivalent English forms by saying, 'Your music is – uhm – and I can't sleep with your music.' In the 'notes' situation, Yaakov simplified his utterance in order to deliver it, 'I really don't like – this.' He explained as follows: 'I searched for something else like, "the way you act / your behavior," but it didn't come to mind when I was answering. I used the easiest way out at the moment.'

Approximation

In five instances the word search ended in an approximation as the speaker felt or knew the word was incorrect but could not come up with an alternative. In the 'book' situation, Jackie was looking for a word to express a desire to repair the situation but did not find it. He said, 'I'm shocked, I'm sorry,' but he was looking for the English equivalent for *lefatsot* 'to compensate' and, in his words, 'had a blackout.' Also in the 'book' situation, Galit wanted to say the English equivalent of *xomer* 'material', and could not find a word such as 'notebook,' so she said 'stuff': 'I didn't find the – stuff.' In the 'music' situation, she asked the neighbor to 'reduce' the volume. Her retrospective comment was as follows: 'I had my doubts about the word 'reduce'; it seemed like a literary word to me.' When it was noted that the interlocutor (Debbie) had in fact supplied the phrase when she said, 'I would have turned it down,' Galit replied, 'I was more into my own words than into listening to Debbie's.' In the same situation, Jackie wanted to ask that the neighbor 'turn it down,' and instead he got stuck with 'put it lower.' Finally, in the 'token' situation, Ricki said she used 'Listen–' as an opener 'because I didn't have anything else to use.'

ATTENTION TO GRAMMAR AND PRONUNCIATION

Regarding the issue of attention to grammar, respondents indicated that they were thinking about grammar in 41% of the situations, for example, thinking about verb tenses: 'I haven't sleep good' → 'I didn't sleep good.' As can be seen from Table 7.2, the 'lift' situation was slightly more likely than the others to prompt attention to grammar. In contrast, the 'token' situation was far less likely to prompt attention to grammar. In 22% of the situations the subjects did not indicate whether they were paying attention to grammar.

TABLE 7.2   Attention to grammar in speech act production

	Yes	No	Don't say
Situations			
meeting	7	6	2
book	7	6	2
music	6	6	3
notes	6	6	3
lift	8	4	3
token	3	5	7
Total	37 (41%)	33 (37%)	20 (22%)

TABLE 7.3   Attention to pronunciation in speech act production

	Yes	No	Don't say
Situations			
meeting	2	13	0
book	2	13	0
music	5	9	1
notes	3	9	3
lift	5	8	2
token	3	7	5
Total	20 (22%)	59 (66%)	11 (12%)

Regarding attention to pronunciation, in far fewer situations, only 22%, did respondents indicate thinking about pronunciation in the production of their utterances, while in 66% of the situations that they did not (and no indication in 12% of the situations) (see Table 7.3). Whereas for the most part the respondents paid no attention to pronunciation, there were exceptions. For example, in the 'book' situation, Sharon noted that she was aware of her problem of confusing /z/ with /th/. She was also aware in the 'music' situation that 'ask' came out as /athk/, and Shalom was aware of his Israeli /r/. In the 'lift' situation, Lillian, the native Portuguese speaker, reported that the /owel/ sound in her utterance 'I'll be waiting' made her uncomfortable because it did not sound natural to her. Hagar said that she tried to pronounce properly because of the higher status of the interlocutor. She added, 'When I find the appropriate thing to say, my pronunciation is better.'

In the 'token' situation, Shlomit said that she used 'excuse me' because it was easier to pronounce than 'sorry' as an opener to get the attention of her friend. Hava reported that she felt more confident with this situation than with the preceding one, the 'lift.' As she put it, 'Because I was more confident here, so I was more fluent. When I am fluent, it goes smoothly. When not, I get stuck on vowels and consonants and start to worry about how to pronounce them.' In the 'token' situation, however, she had the feeling of having what she termed 'over-*higui*' (over-pronunciation) – too much attention to pronouncing the word 'token'. In that instance, the friend responded 'What?' the first time she asked, so she asked more decidedly a second time.[7]

EMERGENT SPEECH PRODUCTION STYLES

In the data analysis process, some effort was made to characterize speech production styles, by looking at clusters of strategies as preferred by given respondents. Three such styles emerged.

One style, that of the *metacognizers*, was characteristic of those individuals who seemed to have a highly developed metacognitive awareness and who used this awareness to the fullest. There were individuals whose thoughts included a voice in the back of the head which kept informing them of their general deficiencies, kept them monitoring their language output to some extent, and continued to remind them of their possible or actual production errors from prior utterances. While she was aware that she was purposely not monitoring her grammar, Hagar did report monitoring her pronunciation in order to speak properly to her higher-status professor in the 'lift' situation. When unsure of how to say something, she would use the strategy of *partial delivery of the thought*, such as in the 'notes' situation, where she wanted to express full anger but settled for sarcasm instead.

Ricki alluded to her difficulties in trying to retrieve English vocabulary after not speaking it for a long time. That she would have these problems is not in itself noteworthy, but her calling attention to it brings up the issue of the *din-in-the-head* phenomenon mentioned above. Ricki was one of those who had spent time in English-speaking environments where the *din in the head* was intensified (a month in England four years prior to the study and three months in the US one year prior to the study). Perhaps a voice in the back of her head was reminding her that she was not rehearsed enough in her English to have the words appear effortlessly. Ricki was also a frequent monitor user ('I am always thinking about grammar . . . When I have problems like "not/don't" I correct them.'), which would be consistent with the 'thinker' style.

In addition, Ricki indicated various afterthoughts that she had had after producing utterances. One such afterthought was about having said 'very sorry' in the 'meeting' situation but then thinking to herself that she could have said 'terribly sorry.' Another such afterthought was that 'stopped' was not the correct word in the 'meeting' situation ('I met some friends and they stopped me and I couldn't go on') and that she should not change it because she 'was already in the middle of things.' Such lingering thoughts about prior speech production could possibly interfere with the delivery of the utterance at hand.

A second speech production style was that of *avoider*. For example, in the 'lift' situation, Shlomit did not know whether it was appropriate to call her teacher by name, so she left it out. When in the 'music' situation, she was not sure how to say that her neighbor's music was 'too loud', she avoided the adjective altogether by saying, 'I can't sleep with your music.' Perhaps the behavior most indicative of a systematic avoidance strategy was her conscious avoidance of words that were difficult for her to pronounce. So, for example, in the 'token' situation, she reported saying 'excuse me' because it was easier for her to pronounce than 'sorry.'

A third style to emerge could perhaps be termed that of the *pragmatist*, i.e. the individual who gets by in oral production more by means of on-line adjustment tricks than through metacognitive planning. Rather than simply avoiding material altogether, this pattern involves finding altern-ative solutions that approximate what is called for. Galit would be a good example of such a subject. Not only did she switch to 'I want to drive with you' when she was not sure if she could say 'room in the car,' but she also refrained from mentioning a 'lift' because she was not sure how to use it in a sentence. She was also the subject who in looking for a reason that she needed a ride, let her utterance, 'My bus is very late', stand although she knew right away that it was not what she had meant to say. She left the utterance as it was because it was grammatically acceptable and comprehensible. She also was willing to settle for various approximations instead of struggling to find the most appropriate word. So, in the 'book' situation she settled for 'stuff' when she wanted to say 'material.' Then, in the 'music' situation, she asked for the neighbor to 'reduce' the volume when she meant for him to 'turn it down.' She did not notice that the expression appeared in the prompt itself since, as she put it, 'I was more into my own words than into listening to Debbie's.'

DISCUSSION OF THE SPEECH ACTS STUDY

In summarizing the results of the study, the following patterns tended to reflect the delivery of speech acts:

(1) the respondents only planned out the specific vocabulary and gram-matical structures for their utterances in a third of the situations;
(2) they often thought in two and sometimes in three languages (in the case of trilinguals) when planning and delivering speech act utter-ances; and

(3) they used a series of different strategies in searching for language forms, and did not attend much to grammar nor to pronunciation.

The study also found that there were subjects whose speech production styles would characterize them as *metacognizers*, *avoiders*, and *pragmatists*.

ISSUES OF RESEARCH METHODOLOGY

It could be argued that the elicitation of any oral language production would have served the purposes of this study – that there was no need to elicit speech act behavior. Whereas this may be true, as noted at the outset, the current study chose to investigate thought processes during complex speech behavior because such language behavior was considered perhaps more demanding sociolinguistically than other language behavior and thus a richer source of data on test-taking strategies. Several things made the situations even more demanding.

It might be argued that the use of a role-play interview as a simulation of actual or *semi-ethnographic* behavior (Olshtain and Blum-Kulka, 1985) is making unnatural demands of the respondents. For example, the respondents might be asked to take on a role that they might not actually assume in real life. In some instances, respondents remarked that a given situation happened to them all the time. In several cases, the respondents commented that they had performed that speech act the previous day – e.g. requesting a neighbor to turn down loud music late at night. In other cases, respondents made it clear that the situation had never happened to them.

In instances where the respondent had never had to react in such a situation (e.g. apologizing for keeping a classmate's book two weeks beyond the agreed date), it could be argued that the instrument was forcing unnatural behavior and that if the respondents were not good actors, the results might be problematic for them. The issue would be to distinguish respondents' language proficiency from their situational adeptness. In the research study under discussion, the respondents were not given the choice to opt out of the speech act. If they deflected the stimulus, the interlocutor pursued the issue. This is not necessarily the case in the real world, where a person may opt not to apologize, complain, or request something (Bonikowska, 1988).

Furthermore, it was not spelled out for the respondents how co-operative a stance they were to take in a given situation where several responses might have been possible. In the 'notes' situation, for example, Hagar decided that she would get angry and take the stance of not needing any favors from her friend. The lack of specificity as to the behavior the prompt is calling for raises the issue of just how specific the prompt should be. Just how much context should the respondents be given? For example, should the prompt give culturally relevant information if the situation is culturally specific? Should it tell them what stance to take (e.g. recalcitrant or conciliatory, assertive or reticent), what emotion to express (e.g. anger, frustration, sadness, or sarcasm)?

The fact that the prompts described the situation in the target language gave the respondents the opportunity to use the vocabulary of the prompt even when they did not have mastery over these forms in their productive knowledge. This marks a departure from the format of semi-direct tests such as the simulated oral proficiency interview (SOPI), in which the instructions are presented in the language of the respondents and the response is to be in the target language. Thus, if the respondents do not know the vocabulary item in the target language (e.g. the word for 'house slippers' in Portuguese on the Portuguese Semi-Direct Test; see Stansfield *et al.*, 1990), they are most likely going to be in an uncomfortable position throughout that task.

From time to time respondents did lift language forms out of the text which described the situation – language forms that were only partially or not at all in their productive knowledge. For example, in the 'lift' situation, Hava noted that she lifted 'my bus has just left' out of the text. Also, whereas she would simply say 'token,' she requested a 'phone token' in the 'token' situation because that was written in the text. Wassim also indicated taking the expression 'phone token' from the text. In that same situation, Yaakov said he had used the word 'urgent' because the word appeared in the description of the situation – that he would not have used it otherwise. Likewise, Shlomit said she also used 'urgent' because 'it was included in the situation.' Finally, there was an instance of the respondent's combining his own material with that contained in the text. So, in the 'lift' situation, Yaakov described how he arrived at asking Debbie, 'Can I come by your car?':

> First I thought 'with your car, with you' and that I would not mention the car because I didn't know how to indicate *hamixonit shelax* 'your car.' I worried that she would think I wanted to go for a ride with her. 'To get a ride with you' would be an expression I wouldn't know how to use. 'Can I come' are words that I know how to use. After I heard Debbie read 'by car,' I said 'by your car.'

Notwithstanding the above cases, there were many more instances in which respondents did not make use of the cues provided in the prompt. In fact, some respondents were oblivious, being caught up too much in their own words to use the vocabulary of the interlocutor or of the prompt as an aid to production. For example, as mentioned above, Galit commented, 'I was more into my own words than into listening to Debbie's', with regard to not using the phrase 'turn down' in the 'music' situation.

Furthermore, these speech act situations created a form of time pressure not so prevalent in other forms of elicitation, such as with verbal report of reading and writing processes. The interlocutor purposely pursued each issue until some resolution of the situation took place. This procedure meant that in each interaction there was invariably an unplanned portion where the respondent had to react on an on-line basis. Such was not the case in the Robinson (1991) study where there was no rejoinder. In addition, it should be noted that the order of the different speech acts may have had an effect on the response since respondents indicated that the apologies, which came first, were the most difficult in that the respondents had caused the infraction. The more perfunctory speech acts, the requests, came at the end when the respondents may have been getting somewhat fatigued by the research procedures.

The finding that certain situations may be more likely to cause the respondents both to plan their utterances and to produce them directly in the target language, may be of genuine interest to language acquisition researchers. They may wish to choose their situations so as to encourage this form of cognitive behavior. Until now, investigations of speech behavior have not given much attention to the language-of-thought issue with respect to planning of utterances. As a result, elicitation procedures may have unknowingly called for cumbersome mental gymnastics among the respondents, such as in the 'lift' situation in this study.

The findings reported in this study are based on a relatively new form of data with regard to role-playing situations in that they are by and large process and not product data. The research method of having respondents role-play two situations and then view the videotape seemed to produce richer linguistic information than did the method used in the Robinson (1991) study. There were probably several reasons for this. One was that the interactions were more naturalistic in that they were oral and not written. Second, the retrospective verbal reports were conducted in the respondents' native or near-native language. Third, videotape was used to jog the respondents' memory as to the choices made in selecting material for their utterances.

It could be noted that asking subjects after speech act situations whether they were aware of their pronunciation or grammar would have reactive effects on the subsequent speech act situations. Although the situation that prompted the most attention to grammar (eight respondents) as well as the highest level of attention to pronunciation (five respondents) came in the third set of speech acts, it was also a situation involving style shifting (requesting a lift from a higher-status teacher). Thus, it is difficult to say whether the results reflected incrementally more attention to grammar and pronunciation or were an artifact of the situation.

Fortunately, as more work is done in the elicitation of speech act behavior, more attention is also being given to describing possible research methods and to enumerating their strengths and weaknesses (Kasper and Dahl, 1991; Cohen and Olshtain, 1994). Unquestionably this is an area in which further instrumentation development is called for.

PEDAGOGICAL IMPLICATIONS

There are several pedagogical implications that can be drawn from this study. First, learners may have a more difficult time in producing complex speech forms than teachers are aware, whether they be speech acts or other language forms of comparable complexity. The end product – the learner's utterance – may have been the result of extensive thought processes in two or more languages and repeated internal debate as to which lexical word or phrase to choose. To assess merely the product of the speech act task may be doing the learners a disservice. Teachers may wish to devise a means for finding out more about the processes involved in producing the resulting utterances. Just as teachers might ask learners about the strategies they used to arrive at answers to a cloze test, they may wish to ask them how they produced utterances in a speaking exercise, using an audio- or videotape to assist the students in remembering what they said.

Second, some learners may not be adequately aware of what is involved in complex speech behavior. These learners may benefit from a discussion of what *compensatory strategies* are so that they can better understand the strategies that they use and be more systematic in their use of such strategies. For example, there are students who are stopped in their production of utterances each time they cannot come up with the word or phrase they want. Such students may turn to a dictionary, with sometimes dubious results. Lexical avoidance, simplification, or approximation strategies do not necessarily come naturally to such learners, and so formal discussions could be beneficial.

Finally, teachers need to be aware that not all speaking tasks are created equal – that there are tasks which make far greater demands on learners than do others. In this study, the seemingly simple task of requesting a lift home from the teacher was the task which called for the most mental logistics in terms of thought patterns, monitoring for grammar and pronunciation, and so forth. Teachers may wish to consider the language processing demands which are likely to be made by a given classroom exercise or test task because the level of demands may help to explain the learner's degree of success at completing the task.

Then, especially with tasks such as these, the teacher may be advised to indulge in promoting some non-spontaneous, planned language as a means of promoting L2 development in the classroom (Crookes, 1989). Whereas the use of spontaneous, unplanned language is a common characteristic of communicative language teaching, there is evidence both that acquisition of native-like production by non-natives may take many years (Olshtain and Blum-Kulka, 1983) and that formal instruction can be of some benefit in speeding up the process (Olshtain and Cohen, 1990; Billmyer, 1990).

7.4   Discussion and conclusions

As indicated at the outset of the chapter, a major reason for doing research on test-taking strategies is to determine the demands that various items and tasks make of the respondents in order to better understand:

(1) the respondents' proficiency level;
(2) the quality of the items and tasks; and
(3) the relative benefits of including those kinds of items and tasks at a given point in a test or at all.

This chapter has demonstrated how a look at strategies for responding to assessment instruments across all skill areas can provide useful insights with respect to all three of the areas listed above. As has been noted in previous chapters, the choice of strategies in language use varies according to the modality (listening, speaking, reading, or writing) and the nature of the task. The choice of strategies for performing on tests adds other elements such as the constraints of a particular elicitation format and expectations regarding the output (e.g. the desired quantity, the expected level of accuracy, and the time limit). In any given testing situation, the factors that make the task easier or more difficult may have little to do with the modality being tested but rather, say, the level of formality required. Hence, it was seen that a seemingly straightforward situation of having to request a lift home from a teacher required cumbersome mental gymnastics from the respondents in order to respond orally, while giving a brief oral report on a short academic reading text could be an easy task for the same respondent.

Since assessment is an important part of the learning process, it is useful for learners to know how to do a good job on tests, just as they would want to know how to improve their language learning and language use in general. With regard to language learning, an assessment situation may well provide an opportunity for language learning, especially if the learner uses strategies for language learning (e.g. for learning new vocabulary) during the testing session. It would seem beneficial for curriculum planners and teachers to make sure that an instructional program not just indicate to students what will be on a test, but also the kinds of test-taking strategies that may be expected to produce success on given testing formats. Undoubtedly, some such insights still need to be gleaned from research, but many such insights are already available, such as the ones discussed in this chapter. In addition, the above discussion has underscored the need for including test-taking strategy data in the process of test validation. One way to achieve this goal is by using verbal report feedback from respondents for this purpose. Another way is by collecting verbal report protocols from interviewers just after they have completed a set of interviews. A third way is by having raters provide verbal report protocols while they are rating tests that call for rater judgments, such as oral language samples, written summaries, and essays.

7.5   Discussion questions and activities

1. Define for yourself the term *test-taking strategy*. Now compare your definition with the one in this chapter. How do they compare? Give three examples of test-taking strategies that are used as shortcuts or tricks to getting the answer. Then give three examples of test-taking strategies that reflect significant language learning or language using procedures.

2. Choose a partner and together review the list of strategies for dealing with multiple-choice responses (Figure 7.2). Working in pairs, with one partner providing verbal report as he or she reads a short text and answers the multiple-choice items so that the other partner understands why he or she selected a given alternative as the response. At the end of the task, have the investigator summarize the test-taking patterns of the respondent. Next, switch roles and do the activity again using another text and set of multiple-choice questions. Did you gain any insights about your language proficiency and the quality of the task you performed from doing this exercise?

3. Again with a partner, perform the same type of activity as in 2 above, but this time with some other task in the L2, such as reading a short text and summarizing it in writing, watching a portion of a news broadcast and summarizing it, or giving a short talk on a professional topic. Again, see what test-taking strategies you use and see if you can

determine which, if any, may have contributed to language learning and which were language use strategies. Of the language use strategies, could you identify those that were retrieval, rehearsal, cover, or communication strategies? Again, did you gain any insights about your language proficiency and the quality of the task you performed from doing this exercise?

Appendix 7A   Background questionnaire

1. Field of study and level_____
2. Birthplace and date of birth_____
3. Native language_____Father's native language_____
   Mother's native language_____
4. Self-evaluation of proficiency in English as compared with natives:
   speaking: excellent ___ very good ___ fair ___ poor ___
   listening: excellent ___ very good ___ fair ___ poor ___
   reading: excellent ___ very good ___ fair ___ poor ___
   writing: excellent ___ very good ___ fair ___ poor ___
5. Period of time in an English-speaking country:
   Name of country/countries _____ months ____ years ____
                              _____ months ____ years ____
6. Use of English in the past and currently:
   (a) use for speaking English with English speakers.
        In the past: frequently ___ sometimes ___ rarely ___
        Currently: frequently ___ sometimes ___ rarely ___
   (b) reading in English: magazines, literature, academic texts.
        In the past: frequently ___ sometimes ___ rarely ___
        Currently: frequently ___ sometimes ___ rarely ___
   (c) watching films in English without translation.
        In the past: frequently ___ sometimes ___ rarely ___
        Currently: frequently ___ sometimes ___ rarely ___
   Comments: _____

Appendix 7B   Responses in English to different role-play situations

Instructions

You are asked to participate in six role-play situations. The situations will be presented to you two at a time. Try to respond as you would in a real situation. The situations will be explained to you in English by Debbie and call for role-playing with her. Before you respond to each situation, you will be given a minute to think out your response. Pay attention to all aspects of each situation. It is important that you understand the situation fully. If there is something in it you do not understand, ask us and we will explain it to you in English or in Hebrew. The response to each situation will be videotaped. Then you will be shown the videotape and will be asked a series of questions by Yafa regarding your response to the situation, in order to understand how you arrived at your response in the given situation.

Thank you for agreeing to participate in our study!

Situations

(Note: This is the initial stimulus and then the situations are played out to completion.)

1. You arranged to meet a friend in order to study together for an exam. You arrive half an hour late for the meeting.
   Friend (annoyed): I've been waiting at least half an hour for you!
   You: _____

2. You promised to return a textbook to your classmate within a day or two, after xeroxing a chapter. You held onto it for almost two weeks.
   Classmate: I'm really upset about the book because I needed it to prepare for last week's class.
   You: _____

3. This is not the first time that your neighbor has played loud music late at night, and you have to get up early the next morning. You phone her to complain:
   Neighbor: Hello.
   You: _____

4. A friend who studies with you at the university refuses to share important notes she got hold of before the final exam. You are quite upset because you've often helped her in the past.
   Friend: No, I can't give you these notes. I need them!
   You: _____

5. An evening class has just ended. Your bus has just left and the next one will not be along for another hour. Your teacher lives in the same neighborhood and has come by car. You'd like to get a ride with her, so you approach her after the class.
   You: _____

6. You have to make an urgent phone call. You ask your friend for a phone token.
   You: _____

Transcript of interactions between a respondent, Nogah,
and the interlocutor, Debbie

SITUATION 1 – MEETING

Friend: I've been waiting at least half an hour for you!

Nogah: So what! It's only an – a meeting for – to study.

Friend: Well. I mean – I was standing here waiting. I could've been
sitting in the library studying.

Nogah: But you're in your house. You can – you can study if you wish.
You can do whatever you want.

Friend: Still pretty annoying – I mean – try and come on time next time.

Nogah: OK, but don't make such a big deal of it.

Friend: OK.

SITUATION 2 – BOOK

Classmate: I'm really upset about the book, because I needed it to
prepare for last week's class.

Nogah: I really feel sorry. It's too bad that you haven't told me
before. I forgot. I don't know what's to – what – I don't have
what to say – you're right in whatever you – you say.

Classmate: Well, you know – I'll have to really think about it next time
if I lend you a book again because – you know, I needed it
and –

Nogah: You're right. You're totally right.

Classmate: OK.

SITUATION 3 – MUSIC

Neighbor: Hello.

Nogah: This is your neighbor from the – top floor.

Neighbor: Yeah.

Nogah: I'm sorry to talk with you in this hour of the night but – I
really want to go to sleep and I can't because of the music.

Neighbor: Oh, my music. Is it too loud?

Nogah: Yeah.

Neighbor: Oh, sorry.

Nogah: Usually it doesn't disturb me but – I really have to wake up
early.

Neighbor: Oh, fine. I didn't realize that it – bothered you. I'll turn it
down. Sorry, bye.

Nogah: Thank you.

SITUATION 4 − NOTES

Friend: No, I can't give you these notes. I need them!
Nogah: I need them too. When you need things I al–I give you.
Friend: Yeah, I know, but I – this is different. This is really urgent and I have to go home and study right now, and I – I can't – give them to you. Sorry.
Nogah: I only want to xerox them but it's if it is such – such a disturb for you – so – OK, I will manage without it.
Friend: OK, sorry. I mean – Look, normally I would, but I just can't this time. Sorry.
Nogah: OK.

SITUATION 5 − LIFT

Nogah: Excuse me, are you going to Baka?
Teacher: Yes, I am.
Nogah: Really? Can I have a ride with you?
Teacher: Yeah. Sure. Um – listen, I have to meet someone downstairs – um – I'll be leaving in about five minutes. OK?
Nogah: Fine, if it is OK with you. I will – I would love to.
Teacher: Great – OK. I'll see you there.
Nogah: Thank you.
Teacher: You're welcome.

SITUATION 6 − TOKEN

Nogah: Hey, do you have a – a token?
Friend: Sorry, so – excuse me?
Nogah: Do you have one token for me?
Friend: A token? What – what token?
Nogah: For – to make a telephone call.
Friend: Oh, yeah. Here you are.
Nogah: Oh, thank you.
Friend: That's OK.
Nogah: I really need it.
Friend: Good, OK, no problem.

Appendix 7C   Retrospective verbal report interview

(These questions were asked three times – after each set of two situations. The interviewer used these questions as a starter and then added probes according to the role-play data on videotape and according to the responses of the informants.) Now let us look at your response together.

WHY DID YOU CHOOSE THOSE ELEMENTS IN YOUR RESPONSE?

1. The source for vocabulary and phrases
   (a) material learned in courses – which? _____
   (b) material acquired, as from reading literature or newspapers, from conversations, from classroom exercises, etc. _____
2. Did you have a number of alternatives? Why did you choose that response? _____

HOW DID YOU CHOOSE YOUR RESPONSE?

1. Content
   (a) How did you select the vocabulary? (Interviewer: note intensifiers in the responses, for example) _____
   (b) Did you think out your response in Hebrew or in English? (partially or fully) In your opinion, did you try to respond as an English speaker or as a Hebrew speaker? Please explain: _____
   (c) Were you thinking about grammar while you were producing your response? _____
   (d) Did you think about pronunciation while you were responding?
   _____
2. Did you think out your entire response before offering it, or did you start responding and think out the rest of your response as you went along? _____

Notes

1. This is an abridged and modified version of Cohen (in press (b)). I wish to acknowledge Lyle Bachman, Elaine Tarone, and an anonymous reviewer from Cambridge University Press for their helpful comments on an early revision of this section of the chapter. It has been reworked for this volume.
2. Despite the theoretical shift away from a primary focus on compensatory strategies, a fair number of test-taking strategies are, in fact, compensatory. When put on the spot, respondents often omit material because they do not know it, or produce different material from what they would like to with the hope that it will be acceptable in the given context. They may use lexical avoidance, simplification, or approximation when the exact word escapes them under the pressure of the test or because they simply do not know the word well or at all.
3. This point is made because it is possible that respondents in a research task might use different strategies from those used when the results 'counted' towards a grade. In other words, in the research task they may be more willing to take risks and to reveal deficiencies in their language proficiency whereas on tests they would employ more test-wiseness

strategies and language use strategies such as cover strategies, in order to look good and thus improve their grade.

4. These results are also consistent with those for native English readers, where the results were far better than chance (Tuinman, 1973–74; Fowler and Kroll, 1978).

5. This section is a revised version of Cohen and Olshtain (1993).

6. Except for instances appearing in the protocols that were not included in the given categories and also for instances which the respondents may have been aware of but which they did not recount in their verbal reports.

7. In both the 'lift' and the 'token' situations, the interlocutor purposely pretended not to hear the request the first time around in order to prompt a second, and perhaps more careful, request.

8 Discussion and conclusions

This book has viewed *second language learner strategies* as constituting those processes which are consciously selected by learners and which may result in actions taken to enhance the learning or use of a second or foreign language, through the storage, retention, recall, and application of information about that language. These strategies are in turn divided into language learning and language use strategies. *Language learning strategies* were seen to include strategies for identifying the material that needs to be learned, distinguishing it from other material if need be, grouping it for easier learning, repeatedly engaging oneself in contact with the material, and formally committing the material to memory when it does not seem to be acquired naturally.

Language use strategies include four subsets of strategies: *retrieval strategies*, *rehearsal strategies*, *cover strategies*, and *communication strategies*. *Retrieval strategies* are those strategies used to call up language material from storage, through whatever memory searching strategies the learner can muster. *Rehearsal strategies* are strategies for practicing target language structures. *Cover strategies* are those strategies that learners use to create the impression that they have control over material when they do not. *Communication strategies* are approaches to conveying messages that are both meaningful and informative for the listener or reader.

After making the learning v. use distinction with respect to strategies, then we see that *cognitive strategies* encompass the language **learning** strategies of identification, grouping, retention, and storage of language material, as well as the language **use** strategies of retrieval, rehearsal, and comprehension or production of words, phrases, and other elements of the second language. *Metacognitive strategies* deal with pre-assessment and pre-planning, on-line planning and evaluation, and post-evaluation of language learning activities and of language use events. *Affective strategies* serve to regulate emotions, motivation, and attitudes. Finally, *social strategies* include the actions which learners choose to take in order to interact with other learners and with native speakers.

We noted that the effectiveness of a strategy will depend on the characteristics of the given learner, the given language structure(s), the given context, or the interaction of these. Although it has been suggested that we must perform 'high inference' to interpret which strategy is being used when (Ellis, 1994: 539), this volume took a rather optimistic view that we have other, more rigorous, means for describing strategy use. For example, there is now a series of approaches to obtaining data on strategy use. This book provided critical analysis of six of these: learning strategy interviews and written questionnaires, observation, verbal report, diaries and dialog journals, recollective studies, and computer tracking. In truth, the data that some of these data collection methods yield are not necessarily very informative about learners' strategy use. We saw that less conventional methods, such as verbal report, may provide insights about the strategies used before, during, and after performing language learning or language using tasks. If the appropriate type of verbal report is selected, the data are collected with care, and the write up describing what was done is complete, then this research approach can provide adequate rigor so we need not rely only on our own inferences. Rather we are relying on the descriptive abilities of the learner to recount to us the strategic steps they took in the language learning and use process. Ideally, these learners will have been trained in describing the strategies that they use.

This reason why this book has devoted extensive time to the discussion of the research methods is that the data can only be as informative about actual language use behavior as the instruments allow them to be. In fact, vague questionnaire items unsurprisingly often yield vague, not very useful data. Half the challenge is finding an instrument that gets close to collecting the kinds of data of interest. The other half of the challenge is finding the means to make this instrument as reliable and valid as possible under the existing constraints of the situation. With regard to the situation itself, the more authentic it is – i.e. the more it mirrors real world behavior – the more difficult it is to control the situational factors, as one would do in a laboratory experiment. One way to improve the validity of such measures under less than laboratory conditions is to replicate the study enough times so that the true picture emerges, if it did not do so the first time. Also, an effort can be made to fine-tune the instruments, as in the case of fine-tuning of verbal report methods.

The volume also dwelled on the topic of learner training in order to demonstrate that it is far from one single thing, but rather a wide range of activities that will have differential effect on learners depending on which activity is selected and how it is actualized. The position taken here is that strategies-based instruction provides the most efficient way for learner awareness to be heightened. While there is need for more research on SBI, the available research literature, including the study presented in this volume, provides some indications that this approach is empirically sound. The fact that the same person who provides daily instruction also provides strategies-based instruction to students allows for SBI to be an integral part of the foreign language curriculum. This approach is considered by a growing number of experts to be the most natural, most functional, in some ways the least intrusive, and potentially the most supportive means of getting the message to learners that how they mobilize their own strategy repertoire will have significant consequences for their language learning and use.

In such an approach, teachers would be asking learners to diagnose their difficulties in language learning, become more aware of what helps them to learn the language they are studying most efficiently, develop a broad range of problem-solving skills, experiment with both familiar and unfamiliar learning strategies, make decisions about how to approach a language task, monitor and self-evaluate their performance, and transfer successful strategies to new learning contexts. If learners perform all of these activities effectively, then the success rate in foreign language classrooms will soar.

Without question, learners do not come to language learning with an empty slate. They have a full repertoire of cognitive, metacognitive, affective, and social strategies. It just may be that their repertoire is not being utilized to its full potential. That is where SBI comes in – to enhance the repertoire. The teachers then shift to accommodate this new role that the learners take on as active partners in the process of both learning and using a new language. The teachers begin to look somewhat less like the fountain of knowledge and more like diagnostician, learner trainer, coach, and coordinator of student learning. In addition, some teachers may themselves take on the challenge of learning a foreign language, especially one totally unlike their own, so that they may have more empathy with what the learners are going through in the language classroom. In addition, some teachers may wish to become classroom researchers, collecting data on the learners' experiences and perhaps on their own experiences in teaching as well (e.g. in teaching through SBI).

It is easy to make reference in passing to 'learners' selecting the strategies that best suit them.' However, in reality, it may still be somewhat of a trial and error process for the learners. Choosing an effective strategy depends on many factors, including the nature of the language task (its structure, purpose, and demands), individual learner differences (such as age, gender, learning style preferences, language learning aptitude, prior experience in learning other foreign languages, career orientation, and personality characteristics), and the current and intended levels of language proficiency. No single strategy will be appropriate for all learners or for all tasks, and individual learners can and should apply the various strategies in different ways, according to their personal language learning needs. Once learners have been through the steps of determining that a strategy is needed and selecting a strategy that seems appropriate for that situation, they then have to apply the strategy at the right moment and in the appropriate way. In addition, it behooves them to take note of the results obtained, even though a positive or negative result from one instance of use of that one strategy may not be a sufficient indicator of how they will fare in general in using that strategy in other similar situations. Strategy use is not an exact science. On the other hand, a heightened awareness on the part of learners can go a long way to decreasing the amount of time needed for language learning and may well enhance language use significantly.

This book has focused on a technology that is gaining in refinement and fine-tuning, namely, that of enhancing language learners' awareness of how they learn language(s) and how they can learn more effectively. As was noted above, in its most ambitious form, this new technology is intrusive in that it appears interspersed between activities aimed at learning and using language. It introduces 'meta-talk' about the learning and using process. It challenges learners to be more systematic in their use of strategies. It challenges teachers to embrace new roles that ultimately may make their job of teaching more satisfying and productive. Yet the content of the instructional program need not be altered. The current program simply receives this SBI overlay, and ideally it will function more effectively as a result. Undoubtedly, the introduction of SBI in the classroom will be time-consuming but then ideally the learners will move through the curriculum more expediently, so this should make up for the outlay of time in training them.

The book also delved into the issue of multilingualism, including 'the selection of language' as a strategy in and of itself, since there is an element of choice involved in arriving at the language(s) used in performing cognitive operations. The choice of language of thought may have significant implications for ultimate success at learning, using, as well as forgetting a language or languages. While methods of foreign language teaching and learning are often predicated on the principle that learners need to think as much as possible in the language that they wish to learn, the book illustrated how the assumptions do not necessary dictate behavior, and, in fact, language learners and users may revert to thinking in their native language or another language at times or even extensively in their efforts to function in the target language. We saw that strategies for employing the L1, such as in mental translation while reading in the foreign language, may support the learning and use of the target language. Ideally, research on strategies for using the L1 will ultimately result in lists of potentially beneficial strategies for making use of the L1 or another language in learning and using the target language.

Finally, we have seen that the insights gained from looking at the test-taking strategies used by L2 learners can help to improve the success that learners have in responding to these instruments, as well as helping to improve the assessment instruments themselves. In other words, test-taking strategy data are included in the process of test validation. Aside from collecting test-taking strategy data from learners, it is possible to collect verbal report protocols from those who interview the learners, just after they have completed a set of interviews. It is also possible to have raters provide verbal report protocols while they are rating tests that call for rater judgments, such as oral language samples, written summaries, and essays.

Since preparing for tests and taking them can be an important part of the learning process, it is useful for learners to know how to do a good job on tests, just as they would want to know how to improve their language learning and language use in general. A well-designed assessment situation may actually provide an opportunity for language learning, especially if the learner uses strategies for language learning (e.g. for learning new vocabulary) during the testing session. It would seem beneficial for curriculum planners and teachers to make sure that an instructional program not just indicate to students what will be on a test, but also the kinds of test-taking strategies that may be expected to produce success on given testing formats. Undoubtedly, some such insights still need to be gleaned from research, but many such insights are already available. For example, in tests of communicative ability, teachers could demonstrate the use of genuine communication strategies as opposed to cover strategies which are used to look good at the moment, without any lasting benefit. A genuine communication strategy might be the use of a paraphrase when the desired word or phrase is not available. A cover strategy for the same situation of not knowing a word or phrase might be to use in the response some material from the prompt in the hope that it is appropriate, without having any idea what it means.

Let me end by simply underscoring the intended purpose of this volume: to facilitate the learning and use of languages beyond the first one. This facilitation ultimately depends on the learners and their motivation to enhance their awareness of how they currently relate to the target language and how they could possible relate to it more effectively; on the teachers and their willingness to incorporate approaches such as strategies-based instruction into their classrooms; and on researchers and their continuing efforts to gather the kinds of information that will contribute to language mastery both in and out of the classroom.

References

Abraham R and Vann R 1987 Strategies of two language learners: a case study. In Wenden A and Rubin J (eds.) *Learner strategies in language learning*. Prentice-Hall, Englewood Cliffs NJ, pp 85–102

Abraham R G and Vann R J 1996 Using task products to assess second language learning processes. *Applied Language Learning* 7(1–2): 61–89

Afflerbach P and Johnston P 1984 On the use of verbal reports in reading research. *Journal of Reading Behavior* 16: 307–22

Alderson J C 1983 The cloze procedure and proficiency in English as a foreign language. In Oller J W Jr (ed.) *Issues in language testing research*. Newbury House, Rowley MA, pp 205–28

Allan A 1992 Development and validation of a scale to measure test-wiseness in EFL/ESL reading test takers. *Language Testing* 9(2): 101–22

Altman R 1997 Oral production of vocabulary: a case study. In Coady J and Huckin T (eds.) *Second language vocabulary acquisition*. Cambridge University Press, Cambridge, pp 69–97

Anderson N J 1989 *Reading comprehension tests versus academic reading: what are second language readers doing?* Unpublished PhD dissertation, University of Texas at Austin

Anderson N J 1991 Individual differences in strategy use in second language reading and testing. *Modern Language Journal* 75(4): 460–72

Anderson N J, Bachman L, Perkins K and Cohen A D 1991 An exploratory study into the construct validity of a reading comprehension test: triangulation of data sources. *Language Testing* 8(1): 41–66

Anderson N J and Vandergrift L 1996 Increasing metacognitive awareness in the L2 classroom by using think-aloud protocols and other verbal report formats. In Oxford R L (ed.) *Language learning strategies around the world: cross-cultural perspectives* (Technical Report 13). Second Language Teaching & Curriculum Center, University of Hawai'i, Honolulu, pp 3–18

Asher J J 1977 *Learning another language through actions: the complete teacher's guidebook*. Sky Oaks Productions, Los Gatos CA

Bachman L F 1990 *Fundamental considerations in language testing*. Oxford University Press, Oxford

Bachman L F and Palmer A S 1996 *Language testing in practice*. Oxford University Press, Oxford

Bacon S and Finnemann M 1990 A study of the attitudes, motives, and strategies of university foreign language students and their disposition to authentic oral and written input. *Modern Language Journal* 74: 459–73

Bailey K M 1983 Competitiveness and anxiety in adult second language learning: looking at and through the diary studies. In Seliger H W and Long MH (eds.)

Classroom oriented research in second language acquisition. Newbury House, Rowley MA, pp 67–103

Bailey K M 1991 Diary studies of classroom language learning: the doubting game and the believing game. In Sadtono E (ed.) *Language acquisition and the second/foreign language classroom.* SEAMEO Regional Language Center, Singapore, pp 60–102

Bailey K M and Ochsner R 1983 A methodological review of the diary studies: windmill tilting or social science. In Bailey K M *et al.* (eds.) *Second language acquisition studies.* Newbury House, Rowley MA, pp 188–98

Baily C A 1996 Unobtrusive computerized observation of compensation strategies for writing to determine the effectiveness of strategy instruction. In Oxford R L (ed.) *Language learning strategies around the world: cross-cultural perspectives* (Technical Report 13). Second Language Teaching & Curriculum Center, University of Hawai'i, Honolulu, pp 141–50

Bakan D 1954 A reconsideration of the problem of introspection. *Psychological Bulletin* 51: 105–18

Bamford K and Mizokawa D T 1991 Additive-bilingual (immersion) education: cognitive and language development. *Language Learning* 41(3): 413–29

Bedell D A and Oxford R L 1996 Cross-cultural comparisons of language learning strategies in the People's Republic of China and other countries. In Oxford R L (ed.) *Language learning strategies around the world: cross-cultural perspectives* (Technical Report 13). Second Language Teaching & Curriculum Center, University of Hawai'i, Honolulu, pp 47–60

Belmont J M and Butterfield E C 1977 The instructional approach to developmental cognitive research. In Kail R V Jr and Hagen J W *Perspectives on the development of memory and cognition.* Lawrence Erlbaum, Hillsdale NJ, pp 437–81

Berry D C and Broadbent D E 1984 On the relationship between task performance and associated verbalizable knowledge. *Quarterly Journal of Experimental Psychology* 36A: 209–31

Bialystok E 1978 A theoretical model of second language learning. *Language Learning* 28(1): 69–83

Bialystok E 1990 *Communication strategies.* Basil Blackwell, Oxford

Billmyer K 1990 'I really like your lifestyle': ESL learners learning how to compliment. *Penn Working Papers in Educational Linguistics* 6(2): 31–48

Blanche P and Merino B J 1989 Self-assessment of foreign-language skills: implications for teachers and researchers. *Language Learning* 39(3): 313–40

Block E 1986 The comprehension strategies of second language readers. *TESOL Quarterly* 20(3): 463–94

Blum-Kulka S 1982 Learning to say what you mean in a second language: a study of the speech act performance of learners of Hebrew as a second language. *Applied Linguistics* 3(1): 29–59

Blum-Kulka S, House-Edmondson J and Kasper G (eds.) 1989 *Cross-cultural pragmatics: requests and apologies.* Ablex, Norwood NJ

Bonikowska M P 1988 The choice of opting out. *Applied Linguistics* 9(2): 169–81

Boring E G 1953 A history of introspection. *Psychological Bulletin* 50(3): 169–89

Bormuth J R 1970 *On the theory of achievement test items.* University of Chicago Press, Chicago

Borsch S 1986 Introspective methods in research on interlingual and intercultural communication. In House J and Blum-Kulka S (eds.) *Interlingual and intercultural communication*. Gunter Narr, Tübingen, pp 195–209

Brooks A 1993 *Translation as a writing strategy for intermediate-level French composition*. Department of French and Italian, Vanderbilt University, Nashville TN

Brown A 1993 The role of test taker feedback in the test development process: test takers' reactions to a tape-mediated test of proficiency in spoken Japanese. *Language Testing* 10(3): 277–303

Brown A L, Campione J C and Day J D 1980 Learning to learn: on training students to learn from texts. *Educational Researcher* 10: 14–21

Brown A L, Palinscar A S and Armbruster B B 1984 Instructing comprehension-fostering activities in interactive learning situations. In Mandl H *et al.* (eds.) *Learning and comprehension of texts*. Lawrence Erlbaum, Hillsdale NJ, pp 255–86

Brown H D 1989 *A practical guide to language learning: a fifteen-week program of strategies for success*. McGraw-Hill, NY

Brown H D 1991 *Breaking the language barrier*. Intercultural Press, Yarmouth ME

Canale, M 1983 On some dimensions of language proficiency. In Oller J W Jr (ed.) *Issues in language testing research*. Newbury House, Rowley MA, pp 333–42

Canale M and Swain M 1980 Theoretical bases of communicative approaches to second language teaching and testing. *Applied Linguistics* 1(1): 1–47

Cantor D S, Andreassen C and Waters H S 1985 Organization in visual episodic memory: relationships between verbalized knowledge, strategy use, and performance. *Journal of Experimental Child Psychology* 40: 218–32

Carrell P L, Pharis B G and Liberto J C 1989 Metacognitive Strategy training for ESL reading: *TESOL Quarterly* 23(4): 647–78

Carrell P L 1996 *Second language reading strategy training: what is the role of metacognition?* Department of Applied Linguistics and ESL, Georgia State University, Atlanta GA

Cavalcanti M C 1984 Frames and schemes in FL reading. *Anais V ENPULI* 2. Pontificia Universidade Católica de São Paulo, São Paulo, Brazil, pp 486–506

Cavalcanti M C 1987 Investigating FL reading performance through pause protocols. In Faerch C and Kasper G (eds.) *Introspection in second language research*. Multilingual Matters, Clevedon, England, pp 230–50

Chamot A U 1987 The learning strategies of ESL students. In Wenden A and Rubin J (eds.) *Learner strategies in language learning*. Prentice-Hall, Englewood Cliffs NJ, pp 71–84

Chamot A U 1996 Implementing the cognitive academic language learning approach (CALLA). In Oxford R L (ed.) *Language learning strategies around the world: cross-cultural perspectives* (Technical Report 13). Second Language Teaching & Curriculum Center, University of Hawai'i, Honolulu, pp 167–73

Chamot A U, Barnhardt S, El-Dinary P and Robbins J 1996 Methods for teaching learner strategies in the foreign language classroom. In Oxford R L (ed.) *Language learning strategies around the world: cross-cultural perspectives* (Technical Report 13). Second Language Teaching & Curriculum Center, University of Hawai'i, Honolulu, pp 175–87

Chamot A U and El-Dinary P B 1996 *Children's learning strategies in language immersion classrooms.* National Foreign Language Resource Center, Georgetown University / Center for Applied Linguistics, Washington DC

Chamot A U, Keatley C, Barnhardt S, El-Dinary P, Nagano K and Newman C 1996 *Learning strategies in elementary language immersion programs: final report.* Language Research Projects, Georgetown University, Washington DC

Chamot A U and O'Malley J M 1994 *The CALLA handbook: implementing the cognitive academic language learning approach.* Addison-Wesley, Reading MA

Chamot A U, O'Malley J M, Küpper L and Impink-Hernandez M V 1987 *A study of learning strategies in foreign language instruction: first year report.* InterAmerica Research Associates, Washington DC

Chamot A U and Rubin J 1994 Comments on Janie Rees-Miller's 'A critical appraisal of learner training: theoretical bases and teaching implications'. *TESOL Quarterly* 28(4): 771–81

Chapelle C and Mizuno S 1989 Students' strategies with learner–centered CALL *CALICO Journal* 7: 25–47

Chávez-Oller M A, Chihara T, Weaver K A and Oller J W Jr 1985 When are cloze items sensitive to constraints across sentences? *Language Learning* 35(2): 181–206

Chelala S I 1982 *The composing process of two Spanish speakers and the coherence of their texts: a case study.* Unpublished PhD dissertation, New York University

Chen S Q 1990 A study of communication strategies in interlanguage production by Chinese EFL learners. *Language Learning* 40(2): 155–87

Chern C-L 1993 Chinese students' word-solving strategies in reading in English. In Huckin T *et al.* (eds.) *Second language reading and vocabulary learning.* Ablex, Norwood NJ, pp 67–85

Chihara, T, Oller J W Jr, Weaver K and Chávez-Oller M A 1977 Are cloze items sensitive to constraints across sentences? *Language Learning* 27(1): 63–73

Clyne, M G 1980 Triggering and language processing. *Canadian Journal of Psychology* 34(4): 400–6

Cohen A D 1974 The Culver City Spanish Immersion Program: how does summer recess affect Spanish speaking ability? *Language Learning* 24(1): 55–68

Cohen A D 1975 Forgetting a second language. *Language Learning* 25(1): 127–38

Cohen A D 1980 *Testing language ability in the classroom.* Newbury House, Rowley, MA

Cohen A D 1984 On taking language tests: what the students report. *Language Testing* 1(1): 70–81

Cohen A D 1987a Studying language learning strategies: how do we get the information? In Wenden A L and Rubin J (eds.) *Learner strategies in language learning.* Prentice-Hall International, Englewood Cliffs NJ, pp 31–40

Cohen A D 1987b The use of verbal and imagery mnemonics in second-language vocabulary learning. *Studies in Second Language Acquisition* 9(1): 43–62

Cohen A D 1990 *Language learning: insights for learners, teachers, and researchers.* Newbury House / Harper & Row, New York

Cohen A D 1991 Feedback on writing: the use of verbal report. *Studies in Second Language Acquisition* 13(2): 133–59

Cohen A D 1992 The role of learner strategy training in ELT methodology. In Wongsothorn A *et al.* (eds.) *Explorations and innovations in ELT methodology.* Chulalongkorn University Language Institute, Bangkok, Thailand, pp 174–91

Cohen A D 1994a *Assessing language ability in the classroom.* 2nd edn. Newbury House / Heinle & Heinle, Boston

Cohen A D 1994b English for academic purposes in Brazil: the use of summary tasks. In Hill C and Parry K (eds.) *From testing to assessment: English as an international language.* Longman, London, pp 174–204

Cohen A D 1994c The language used to perform cognitive operations during full-immersion maths tasks. *Language Testing* 11(2): 171–195

Cohen A D 1995 The role of language of thought in foreign language learning. *Working Papers in Educational* 11(2): 1–23

Cohen A D 1996 Verbal reports as a source of insights into second language learner strategies. *Applied Language Learning* 7(1–2): 5–24

Cohen A D (in press (a)) Developing pragmatic ability: insights from intensive study of Japanese. In Cook H M *et al. New trends and issues in teaching Japanese language and culture* (Technical Report 15). Honolulu: University of Hawai'i, Second Language Teaching and Curriculum Center, pp. 137–63.

Cohen A D (in press (b)) Strategies and processes in test taking. In Bachman L F and Cohen A D (eds.) *Interfaces between second language acquisition and language testing research.* Cambridge University Press, Cambridge

Cohen A D (forthcoming) Towards enhancing verbal reports as a source of insights on test-taking strategies. In Ekbatani G and Pierson H (eds.) *Research methods in language assessment*

Cohen A D and Aphek E 1979 Easifying second language learning. Report submitted to the Jacob Hiatt Institute. Hebrew University of Jerusalem, School of Education, Jerusalem (ERIC Document Reproduction Service ED 163 753)

Cohen A D and Aphek E 1980 Retention of second-language vocabulary over time: investigating the role of mnemonic associations. *System* 8(3): 221–35

Cohen A D and Aphek E 1981 Easifying second language learning. *Studies in Second Language Acquisition* 3(2): 221–35

Cohen A D and Cavalcanti M C 1987 Giving and getting feedback on compositions: a comparison of teacher and student verbal report. *Evaluation and Research in Education* 1(2): 63–73

Cohen A D and Cavalcanti M C 1990 Feedback on compositions: teacher and student verbal reports. In Kroll B (ed.), *Second language writing: research insights for the classroom.* Cambridge University Press, Cambridge, pp 155–77

Cohen A D and Hawras S 1996 Mental translation into the first language during foreign-language reading. *The Language Teacher* 20(2): 6–12

Cohen A D and Hosenfeld C 1981 Some uses of mentalistic data in second-language research. *Language Learning* 31(2): 285–313

Cohen A D and Lebach S 1974 A language experiment in California: student, teacher, parent, and community reactions after three years. *Workpapers in teaching English as a second language* 8, University of California at Los Angeles, pp 33–46

Cohen A D and Olshtain E 1981 Developing a measure of sociocultural competence: The case of apology. *Language Learning* 31(1): 113–34

Cohen A D and Olshtain E 1985 Comparing apologies across languages. In Jankowsky J R (ed.) *Scientific and humanistic dimensions of language.* John Benjamins, Amsterdam, pp 175–84

Cohen A D and Olshtain E 1993 The production of speech acts by EFL learners. *TESOL Quarterly* 27(1): 33–56

Cohen A D and Olshtain E 1994 Researching the production of speech acts. In Tarone E *et al.* (eds.) *Research methodology in second language acquisition.* Lawrence Erlbaum, Hillsdale NJ, pp 143–56

Cohen A D, Olshtain E and Rosenstein D S 1986 Advanced EFL apologies: what remains to be learned. *International Journal of the Sociology of Language* 62(6): 51–74

Cohen A D and Scott K 1996 A synthesis of approaches to assessing language learning strategies. In Oxford R L (ed.) *Language learning strategies around the world: crosscultural perspectives* (Technical Report 13). Second Language Teaching & Curriculum Center, University of Hawaii, Honolulu HI, pp 89–106

Cohen A D and Swain M 1979 *Bilingual education: the 'immersion' model in the North American context.* In Pride J B (ed.) *Sociolinguistic aspects of language learning and teaching.* Oxford University Press, Oxford, pp 144–51

Cohen A D, Weaver S J and Li T-Y 1995 *The impact of strategies-based instruction on speaking a foreign language.* Research Report. Center for Advanced Research on Language Acquisition (CARLA), University of Minnesota, Minneapolis MN

Connor U M and Carrell P L 1993 The interpretation of tasks by writers and readers in holistically rated direct assessment of writing. In Carson J G and Leki I (eds.) *Reading in the composition classroom: second language perspectives.* Heinle & Heinle, Boston pp 141–160

Cook V J 1993 *Linguistics and second language acquisition.* St Martin's Press, NY

Cook V J 1994 *Internal and external uses of a second language.* Department of Language and Linguistics, University of Essex, England

Craik F I M 1977 Depth of processing in recall and recognition. In Dornic S (ed.) *Attention and performance* Vol. 6. Lawrence Erlbaum, Hillsdale NJ, pp 679–97

Craik F I M and Lockhart R S 1972 Levels of processing: a framework for memory research. *Journal of Verbal Learning and Verbal Behavior* 11: 671–84

Crookes G 1989 Planning and interlanguage variation. *Studies in Second Language Acquisition* 11(4): 367–83

Crutcher R J 1990 *The role of mediation in knowledge acquisition and retention: learning foreign vocabulary using the keyword method.* Technical Report No. 90–10. Institute of Cognitive Science, University of Colorado, Boulder

Cummins D D, Kintsch W, Reusser K and Weimer R 1988 The role of understanding in solving word problems. *Cognitive Psychology* 20: 405–38

Cummins J 1991 Conversational and academic language proficiency in bilingual contexts. *AILA Review* 8: 75–89

Cyr Paul 1996 *Le point sur les stratégies d'apprentissage d'une langue seconde.* Les Éditions CEC, Anjou (Québec), Canada

Dadour S and Robbins J 1996 University-level studies using strategy instruction to improve speaking ability in Egypt and Japan. In Oxford R L (ed.) *Language learning strategies around the world: cross-cultural perspectives* (Technical Report 13). Second Language Teaching & Curriculum Center, University of Hawai'i, Honolulu, pp 157–66

Dansereau D F 1985 Learning strategy research. In Segal J W *et al.* (eds.) *Thinking and learning skills: relating learning to basic research.* Lawrence Erlbaum, Hillsdale NJ, pp 209–40

Dechert H W and Raupach M 1989 *Transfer in language production*. Ablex, Norwood NJ

Derry S J and Murphy D A 1986 Designing systems that train learning ability: from theory to practice. *Review of Educational Research* 56: 1–39

Dickenson L 1992 *Learner autonomy 2: learner training for language learning*. Authentik Language Learning Resources Ltd, Dublin, Ireland

Dobrin D N 1986 Protocols once more. *College English* 48: 713–25

Dörnyei Z 1995 On the teachability of communication strategies. *TESOL Quarterly* 29(1): 55–85

Dörnyei Z and Scott M L 1997 Communication strategies in a second language: definitions and taxonomies *Language Learning* 47(1): 173–210

Dreyer C and Oxford R L 1996 Learning strategies and other predictors of ESL proficiency among Afrikaans speakers in South Africa. In Oxford R L (ed.) *Language learning strategies around the world: cross-cultural perspectives* (Technical Report 13). Second Language Teaching & Curriculum Center, University of Hawai'i, Honolulu, pp 61–74

Duffy G G, Book C and Roehler L R 1983 A study of direct teacher explanation during reading instruction. In Niles J A and Harris L A (eds.) *Searches in meaning in reading/language processing and instruction*. National Reading Conference, Rochester NY, pp 295–303

Ehrman M E 1996 *Understanding second language learning difficulties*. Sage, Thousand Oaks CA

Ehrman M E and Leaver B 1997 Sorting out global and analytic functions in second language learning. School of Language Studies, Foreign Service Institute, Arlington VA. Paper presented at the American Association for Applied Linguistics Annual Conference, March 8–11, 1997

Ehrman M and Oxford R L 1990 Adult language learning styles and strategies in an intensive training setting. *Modern Language Journal* 74(3): 311–27

Ellis G and Sinclair B 1989 *Learning to learn English: a course in learner training* (Teacher's Book, Learner's Book, Cassette). Cambridge University Press, Cambridge

Ellis R 1985 *Understanding second language acquisition*. Oxford University Press, Oxford

Ellis R 1994 *The study of second language acquisition*. Oxford University Press, Oxford

Ely C 1989 Tolerance of ambiguity and use of second language learning strategies. *Foreign Language Annals* 22(5): 437–45

Ericsson K A 1988 Concurrent verbal reports on text comprehension: a review. *Text* 8: 295–325

Ericsson K A and Simon H A 1980 Verbal reports as data. *Psychological Review* 87: 215–51

Ericsson K A and Simon H A 1993 *Protocol analysis: verbal reports as data*. Revised edn. MIT Press, Cambridge MA

Faerch C and Kasper G 1983a Plans and strategies in foreign language communication. In Faerch C and Kasper G (eds.) *Strategies in interlanguage communication*. Longman, London, pp 20–60

Faerch C and Kasper G 1983b Procedural knowledge as a component of foreign language learners' communicative competence. In Boete H and Herrlitz W (eds.) *Kommunication im (Sprach-) Unterricht.* Rijksuniversiteik, Utrecht, pp 169–99

Faerch C and Kasper G 1986 One learner – two languages: investigating types of interlanguage knowledge. In House J and Blum-Kulka S (eds.) *Interlingual and intercultural communication.* Gunter Narr, Tübingen, pp 211–27

Faerch C and Kasper G 1987 From product to process – introspective methods in second language research. In Faerch C and Kasper G (eds.) *Introspection in second language research.* Multilingual Matters, Clevedon, England, pp 5–23

Fanselow J F 1979 *First, I'd like to ask you a couple of questions!* Teachers College, Columbia University, NY

Farr R, Pritchard R and Smitten B 1990 A description of what happens when an examinee takes a multiple-choice reading comprehension test. *Journal of Educational Measurement* 27(3): 209–26

Felder R M and Henriques E R 1995 Learning and teaching styles in foreign and second language education. *Foreign Language Annals* 28(1): 21–31

Feldman U and Stemmer B 1987 Thin___ aloud a___ retrospective da___ in C-te___ taking: diffe___ languages – diff___ learners – sa___ approaches? In Faerch C and Kasper G (eds.) *Introspection in second language research.* Multilingual Matters, Clevedon, England, pp 251–67

Ferguson C A 1959 Diglossia. *Word* 15: 325–40

Fillmore C and Kay P 1983 *Final report to NIE: text semantic analysis of reading comprehension tests.* Institute of Human Learning, University of California, Berkeley CA

Flower L and Hayes J R 1984 Images, plans, and prose: the representation of meaning in writing. *Written Communication* 1(1): 120–60

Fowler B and Kroll B M 1978 Verbal skills as factors in the passageless validation of reading comprehension tests. *Perceptual and Motor Skills* 47: 335–8

Fransson A 1984 Cramming or understanding? Effects of intrinsic and extrinsic motivation on approach to learning and test performance. In Alderson J C and Urquhart A H (eds.) *Reading in a foreign language.* Longman, London, pp 86–121

Frenck-Mestre C and Vaid J 1992 Language as a factor in the identification of ordinary words and number words. In Harris R J (ed.) *Cognitive processing in bilinguals.* North-Holland, Amsterdam, pp 265–81

Friedlander A 1990 Composing in English: effects of a first language on writing in English as a second language. In Kroll B (ed.) *Second language writing: research insights for the classroom.* Cambridge University Press, Cambridge, pp 109–25

Fujiwara B 1990 Learner training in listening strategies. *JALT Journal* 12(2): 203–17

Galloway V and Labarca A 1991 From student to learner: style, process, and strategy. In Birckbichler D W (ed.) *New perspective and new directions in foreign language education.* National Textbook Company, Lincolnwood IL, pp 111–58

Garner R 1982 Verbal-report data on reading strategies. *Journal of Reading Behavior* 14(2): 159–67

Garner R 1987 *Metacognition and reading comprehension.* Ablex, Norwood NJ

Garner R 1990 When children and adults do not use learning strategies: toward a theory of settings. *Review of Educational Research* 60(4): 517–29

Gass S M and Neu J (eds.) 1996 *Speech acts across cultures: challenges to communication*. Mouton de Gruyter, Berlin

Gass S M and Selinker L 1983 *Language transfer in language learning*. Newbury House, Rowley MA

Gattegno C 1976 *The common sense of teaching foreign languages*. Educational Solutions, NY

Genesee F 1987 *Learning through two languages*. Newbury House, Rowley MA

Gerloff P 1987 Identifying the unit of analysis in translation: some uses of think-aloud protocol data. In Faerch C and Kasper G (eds.) *Introspection in second language research*. Multilingual Matters, Clevedon, England, pp 135–58

Gordon C 1987 *The effect of testing method on achievement in reading comprehension tests in English as a foreign language*. Unpublished master's thesis, Tel-Aviv University, Ramat-Aviv, Israel

Green J M and Oxford R 1995 A closer look at learning strategies, L2 proficiency, and gender. *TESOL Quarterly* 29(2): 261–97

Greene S and Higgins L 1994 'Once upon a time': the use of retrospective accounts in building theory in composition. In P Smagorinsky (ed.), *Speaking about writing: reflections on research methodology*. Sage, Thousand Oaks, CA, pp 115–40

Gruba P (forthcoming) *Strategies of videotext comprehension*. Unpublished PhD dissertation, Department of Applied Linguistics and Language Studies, University of Melbourne.

Gu Y 1994 Vocabulary learning strategies of good and poor Chinese EFL learners. In Bird N *et al.* (eds.) *Language and learning*. Hong Kong Education Department, Hong Kong, pp 376–401 (ERIC Document Reproduction Service ED 370 411)

Gu P Y 1996 Robin Hood in SLA: what has the learner strategy research taught us? *Asian Journal of English Language Teaching* 6: 1–29

Gu P Y and Johnson R K 1996 Vocabulary learning strategies and language learning outcomes. *Language Learning* 46(4): 643–79

Gu Y, Wen Q and Wu D 1995 How often is often? Reference ambiguities of the Likert-scale in language learning strategy research. *Occasional Papers in English Language Teaching* 5: 19–35 (English Language Teaching Unit, the Chinese University of Hong Kong) (ERIC Document Reproduction Service ED 391 358)

Hajer M, Messtringa T, Park Y Y and Oxford R L 1996 How print materials provide strategy instruction. In Oxford R L (ed.) *Language learning strategies around the world: cross-cultural perspectives* (Technical Report 13). Second Language Teaching & Curriculum Center, University of Hawai'i, Honolulu, pp 119–40

Hamp-Lyons L 1989 Raters respond to rhetoric in writing. In Dechert H W and Raupach M (eds.), *Interlingual processes*. Gunter Narr, Tübingen, pp 229–44

Haney W and Scott L 1987 Talking with children about tests: an exploratory study of test item ambiguity. In Freedle R O and Duran R P (eds.) *Cognitive and linguistic analyses of test performance*. Ablex, Norwood NJ, pp 298–368

Harley B, Allen P, Cummins J and Swain M 1990 *The development of second language proficiency*. Cambridge University Press, Cambridge

Harrison M, Freed B and Tucker G R 1994 *Learning about language learning: its role in foreign language instruction.* Program in Modern Languages, Carnegie Mellon University, Pittsburgh PA

Hatch E 1992 *Discourse and language education.* Cambridge University Press, Cambridge

Hatch E and Lazaraton A 1991 *The research manual: design and statistics for applied linguistics.* Newbury House / HarperCollins, NY

Hawras S 1996 *Towards describing bilingual and multilingual behavior: implications for ESL instruction.* Double Plan B Paper, English as a Second Language Department, University of Minnesota, Minneapolis

Heitzman S 1994 *Language use in full immersion classrooms: public and private speech.* Summa Thesis, Department of Linguistics, University of Minnesota, Minneapolis

Hidi S and Anderson V 1986 Producing written summaries: task demands, cognitive operations, and implications for instruction. *Review of Educational Research* 56(4): 473–93

Hill K 1994 *The contribution of multi-informant feedback to the development and validation of an oral proficiency test in two formats.* Unpublished MA thesis, Department of Linguistics and Language Studies, University of Melbourne, Australia

Hillocks G Jr 1994 Interpreting and counting: objectivity in discourse analysis. In P Smagorinsky (ed.) *Speaking about writing: reflections on research methodology.* Sage, Thousand Oaks, CA, pp 185–204

Holec H 1988 *Autonomy and self-directed learning: present fields of application.* Project No. 12: Learning and Teaching Modern Languages for Communication. Council for Cultural Co-operation, Strasbourg, France

Homburg T J and Spaan M C 1981 ESL reading proficiency assessment: testing strategies. In Hines M and Rutherford W (eds.) *On TESOL '81.* TESOL, Washington, D.C., pp 25–33

Hosenfeld C 1976 Learning about learning: discovering our students' strategies. *Foreign Language Annals* 9(2): 117–29

Hosenfeld C 1977 *A learning-teaching view of second-language instruction: the learning strategies of second language learners with reading-grammar tasks.* Unpublished PhD dissertation, Ohio State University, Columbus

Hosenfeld C 1984 Case studies of ninth grade readers. In Alderson J C and Urquhart A H (eds.) *Reading in a foreign language.* Longman, London, pp 231–49

Huckin T and Bloch J 1993 Strategies for inferring word-meanings in context: a cognitive model. In Huckin T *et al.* (eds.), *Second language reading and vocabulary learning.* Ablex, Norwood NJ, pp 153–78

Hugher A 1989 *Testing for language teachers.* Cambridge University Press, Cambridge

Hulstijn J 1997 Mnemonic methods in foreign language vocabulary learning: theoretical considerations and pedagogical implications. In Coady J and Huckin T (eds.) *Second language vocabulary acquisition.* Cambridge University Press, Cambridge, pp 203–24

James C 1991 The 'monitor model' and the role of the first language. In Ivir V and Kalogjera D (eds.) *Languages in contact and contrast: essays in contact linguistics to honour Rudolf Filipović.* eds. V. Ivir and D. Kalogjera. Mouton de Gruyter, The Hague pp 249–60

Jones S and Tetroe J 1987 Composing in a second language. In Matsuhashi A (ed.) *Writing in real time.* Ablex, Norwood NJ, pp 34–57

Kasper G (ed.) 1992 *Pragmatics of Japanese as a native and target language* (Technical Report 3). Second Language Teaching & Curriculum Center, University of Hawai'i, Honolulu HI

Kasper G (ed.) 1995 *Pragmatics of Chinese as a native and target language* (Technical Report 5). Second Language Teaching & Curriculum Center, University of Hawai'i, Honolulu HI

Kasper G and Dahl M 1991 Research methods in interlanguage pragmatics. *Studies in Second Language Acquisition* 13(2): 215–47

Kasper G and Schmidt R 1996 Developmental issues in interlanguage pragmatics. *Studies in Second Language Acquisition* 18(2): 149–69

Kaylani M 1996 The influence of gender and motivation on EFL learning strategies in Jordan. In Oxford R L (ed.) *Language learning strategies around the world: cross-cultural perspectives* (Technical Report 13). Second Language Teaching & Curriculum Center, University of Hawai'i, Honolulu, pp 75–88

Keller C M and Keller J D 1996 Imaging in iron, or thought is not inner speech. In Gumperz J J and Levinson S C (eds.) *Rethinking Linguistic Relativity.* Cambridge University Press, Cambridge pp 115–29

Kellerman E 1991 Compensatory strategies in second language research: a critique, a revision, and some (non-)implications for the classroom. In Phillipson R *et al.* (eds.) *Foreign/second language pedagogy research.* Multilingual Matters, Clevedon UK, pp 142–61

Kern R G 1989 Second language reading strategy instruction: its effects on comprehension and word inference ability. *Modern Language Journal* 73(2): 135–49

Kern R G 1994 The role of mental translation in second language reading. *Studies in Second Language Acquisition* 16(4): 441–61

Kesar O 1990 *Identification and analysis of reading moves in completing a rational deletion cloze.* Unpublished MA thesis, School of Education, Hebrew University, Jerusalem (in Hebrew)

Kessler C and Quinn E 1982 Cognitive development in bilingual environments. In Hartford B *et al.* (eds.) *Issues in international bilingual education: the role of the vernacular.* Plenum Press, NY

Kleiman A B, Cavalcanti M C, Terzi S B and Ratto I 1986 *Percepçao do léxico e sua funçao discursiva: algums fatores condicionantes* (Perception of the lexicon and its discourse function: some conditioning factors). Universidade Estadual de Campinas, Campinas, Brazil

Klein-Braley C 1981 *Empirical investigation of cloze tests: an examination of the validity of cloze tests as tests of general language proficiency in English for German university students.* Unpublished PhD dissertation, University of Duisburg, Duisburg, West Germany

Kobayashi H and Rinnert C 1992 Effects of first language on second language writing: translation versus direct composition. *Language Learning* 42(2): 183–215

Krashen S D 1985 The din in the head, input, and the language acquisition device. In *Inquiries and insights*. Alemany Press, Hayward CA, pp 35–42

Krashen S D and Terrell T D 1983 *The natural approach*. Pergamon Press, Oxford

Krings H P 1987 The use of introspective data in translation. In Faerch C and Kasper G (eds.) *Introspection in second language research*. Multilingual Matters, Clevedon, England, pp 159–76

Lado R 1986 Analysis of native speaker performance on a cloze test. *Language Testing* 3(2): 130–46

Lambert W E and Tucker G R 1972 *Bilingual education of children: the St Lambert experiment*. Newbury House, Rowley MA

Lapkin S, Swain M and Shapson S 1990 French immersion research agenda for the 90's. *The Canadian Modern Language Review* 46(4): 636–74

Larsen-Freeman D and Long M 1991 *Introduction to second language acquisition research*. Longman, London

Lay, N D S 1988 The comforts of the first language in learning to write. *Kaleidoscope* 4(1): 15–18

Levine A, Reves T and Leaver B L 1996 Relationship between language learning strategies and Israeli vs Russian cultural-educational factors. In Oxford R L (ed.) *Language learning strategies around the world: cross-cultural perspectives* (Technical Report 13). Second Language Teaching & Curriculum Center, University of Hawai'i, Honolulu, pp 35–43

Levenston E A 1979 Second language lexical acquisition: issues and problems. *Interlanguage Studies Bulletin – Utrecht* 4: 147–60

Lieberman D A 1979 Behaviorism and the mind: a limited call for a return to introspection. *American Psychologist* 34: 319–33

Lightbown P and Spada N 1993 *How languages are learned*. Oxford University Press, NY

LoCastro V 1994 Learning strategies and learning environments. *TESOL Quarterly* 28(2): 409–14

Lybeck K 1996 *Confessions for a learning strategies (or was it a foreign language?) instructor*. Center for Advanced Research on Language Acquisition, University of Minnesota MN

Lyons W 1986 *The disappearance of introspection*. MIT Press, Cambridge MA

MacKay R 1974 Standardized tests: objectives/objectified measures of 'competence.' In Cicourel A V *et al.* (eds.) *Language use and school performance*. Academic Press, NY, pp 218–47

MacLean M and d'Anglejan A 1986 Rational cloze and retrospection: insights into first and second language reading comprehension. *The Canadian Modern Language Review* 42(4): 814–26

Malakoff M E 1992 Translation ability: a natural bilingual and metalinguistic skill. In Harris R J (ed.) *Cognitive processing in bilinguals*. North-Holland, Amsterdam, pp 515–29

Mann S J 1982 Verbal reports as data: a focus on retrospection. In Dingwall S and Mann S (eds.) *Methods and problems in doing applied linguistic research*. Dept of Linguistics and Modern English Language, University of Lancaster, Lancaster UK, pp 87–104

McDonough S H 1995 *Strategy and skill in learning a foreign language*. Edward Arnold, London

Mehan H 1974 Ethnomethodology and education. In O'Shea D (ed.) *The sociology of the school and schooling*. National Institute of Education, Washington DC, pp 141–98

Mendelsohn D J 1994 *Learning to listen: a strategy-based approach for the second-language learner*. Dominie Press, San Diego CA

Mestre J P 1988 The role of language comprehension in mathematics and problem solving. In Cocking R R and Mestre J P (eds.) *Linguistic and cultural influences on learning mathematics*. Lawrence Erlbaum, Hillsdale NJ, pp 201–20

Motti S T 1987 *Competencia comunicativa em lingua estrangeira: o uso de pedido de disculpas* (Communicative competence in a foreign language: the use of apology). Program in Applied Linguistics, Pontificia Universidade Católica de São Paulo, São Paulo, Brazil

Murphy J M 1987 The listening strategies of English as a second language college students. *Research and Teaching in Developmental Education* 4(1): 27–46

Naiman N, Fröhlich M, Stern H and Todesco A 1978 The good language learner. *Research in Education Series No. 7*. Ontario Institute for Studies in Education, Toronto

Naiman N, Fröhlich M and Todesco A 1975 The good language learner. *TESL Talk* 6: 58–75

Nation R and McLaughlin B 1986 Novices and experts: an information processing approach to the 'good language learner' problem. *Applied Psycholinguistics* 7: 41–5

Neubach A and Cohen A D 1988 Processing strategies and problems encountered in the use of dictionaries. *Dictionaries: Journal of the Dictionary Society of North America* 10: 1–19

Nevo N 1989 Test-taking strategies on a multiple-choice test of reading comprehension. *Language Testing* 6(2): 199–215

Nickerson R S 1989 New directions in educational assessment. *Educational Researcher* 18(9): 3–7

Norris S P 1989 Can we test validly for critical thinking? *Educational Researcher* 18(9): 21–6

Nunan D 1992 *Research methods in language learning*. Cambridge University Press, Cambridge

Nunan D 1995 *Atlas: learning-centered communication*. The Atlas Series of ESL/EFL Courses. Heinle & Heinle, Boston

Nunan D 1996 *The effect of strategy training on student motivation, strategy knowledge, perceived utility and deployment*. The English Center, University of Hong Kong, Hong Kong

Nyhus S E 1994 *Attitudes of non-native speakers of English toward the use of verbal report to elicit their reading comprehension strategies*. Plan B Masters Paper, Department of English as a Second Language, University of Minnesota, Minneapolis

Nyikos M 1996 The conceptual shift to learner-centered classrooms: increasing teacher and student strategic awareness. In Oxford R L (ed.) *Language learning strategies around the world: cross-cultural perspectives* (Technical Report 13). Second Language Teaching & Curriculum Center, University of Hawai'i, Honolulu, pp 109–17

O'Loughlin K 1995 Lexical density in candidate output on direct and semi-direct versions of an oral proficiency test. *Language Testing* 12(2): 217–37

Olshtain E and Blum-Kulka S 1983 Cross-linguistic speech act studies: theoretical and empirical issues. In Mac Mathuna L and Singleton D (eds.) *Languages across cultures.* Irish Association for Applied Linguistics, Dublin

Olshtain E and Blum-Kulka S 1985 Crosscultural pragmatics and the testing of communicative competence. *Language Testing* 2(1): 16–30

Olshtain E and Cohen A D 1983 Apology: a speech act set. In Wolfson N and Judd E (eds.) *Sociolinguistics and language acquisition.* Newbury House, Rowley MA, pp 18–35

Olshtain E and Cohen A D 1989 Speech act behavior across languages. In Dechert H W *et al.* (eds.) *Transfer in production.* Ablex, Norwood NJ, pp 53–67

Olshtain E and Cohen A D 1990 The learning of complex speech behavior. *The TESL Canada Journal* 7(2): 45–65

Olson G M, Duffy S A and Mack R L 1984 Thinking-out-loud as a method for studying real-time comprehension processes. In Kieras D E and Just M A (eds.), *New methods in reading comprehension research.* Lawrence Erlbaum, Hillsdale NJ, pp 253–86

O'Malley J M and Chamot A U 1990 *Learning strategies in second language acquisition.* Cambridge University Press, Cambridge

O'Malley J M, Chamot A U, Stewner-Manzanares G, Küpper L and Russo R 1985 Learning strategies used by beginning and intermediate ESL students. *Language Learning* 35(1): 21–46

O'Malley J M, Chamot A U, Stewner-Manzanares G, Russo R and Küpper L 1985 Learning strategy applications with students of English as a second language. *TESOL Quarterly* 19(3): 557–84

Oxford R L 1989 Use of language learning strategies: a synthesis of studies with implications for strategy training. *System* 17(2): 235–47.

Oxford, R L 1990 *Language learning strategies: what every teacher should know.* Newbury House / Harper Collins, NY

Oxford R L 1993a Research on second language learning strategies. *Annual Review of Applied Linguistics* 13: 175–87

Oxford, R L 1993b *Style Analysis Survey.* University of Alabama, Tuscaloosa AL. Later published in Reid J (ed.) 1995 *Language learning styles in the ESL/EFL classroom.* Heinle & Heinle, Boston, pp 208–15

Oxford R L 1996a Employing a questionnaire to assess the use of language learning strategies. *Applied Language Learning* 7(1–2): 25–45

Oxford R L (ed.) 1996b *Language learning strategies around the world: crosscultural perspectives* (Technical Report 13). Second Language Teaching & Curriculum Center, University of Hawai'i, Honolulu HI

Oxford R L and Cohen A D 1992 Language learning strategies: crucial issues of concepts and classification. *Applied Language Learning* 3(1–2): 1–35

Oxford R L, Crookall D, Cohen A, Lavine R, Nyikos M and Sutter W 1990 Strategy training for language learners: six situational case studies and a training model. *Foreign Language Annals* 22(3): 197–216

Oxford R L and Burry-Stock J A 1995 Assessing the use of language learning strategies worldwide with the ESL/EFL version of the *Strategy Inventory for Language Learning. System* 23(2): 1–23

Oxford R L and Lavine R Z 1992 Teacher-student style wars in the language classroom: research insights and suggestions. *ADFL Bulletin* 23(2): 38–45

Oxford R L, Lavine R Z, Felkins G, Hollaway M E and Saleh A 1996 Telling their stories: language students use diaries and recollection. In Oxford R L (ed.) *Language learning strategies around the world: cross-cultural perspectives* (Technical Report 13). Second Language Teaching & Curriculum Center, University of Hawai'i, Honolulu, pp 19–34

Oxford R L and Leaver B L 1996 A synthesis of strategy instruction for language learners. In Oxford R L (ed.) *Language learning strategies around the world: cross-cultural perspectives* (Technical Report 13). Second Language Teaching & Curriculum Center, University of Hawai'i, Honolulu, pp 227–46

Oxford R, Nyikos M and Crookall D 1987 *Learning strategies of university foreign language students: a large-scale study.* Center for Applied Linguistics, Washington DC

Paivio A and Lambert W 1981 Dual coding and bilingual memory. *Journal of Verbal Learning and Verbal Behavior* 20: 532–9

Paribakht T 1985 Strategic competence and language proficiency. *Applied Linguistics* 6(2): 132–46

Parker J, Heitzman J, Fjerstad A J, Babbs L M and Cohen A D 1994 Exploring the role of foreign language in immersion education: implications for SLA theory and L2 pedagogy. In Eckman F R *et al.* (eds.) *Second language acquisition theory and pedagogy.* Lawrence Erlbaum, Manwah NJ, pp 235–53

Pearson P D and Dole J A 1987 Explicit comprehension instruction: a review of research and a new conceptualization of learning. *Elementary School Journal* 88: 151–65

Peyton J K and Reed L 1990 *Dialog journal writing with nonnative English speakers.* Teachers of English to Speakers of Other Languages, Alexandria VA

Pressley M and Afflerbach P 1995 *Verbal protocols of reading: the nature of constructively responsive reading.* Lawrence Erlbaum, Hillsdale NJ

Pressley M and Levin J R (eds.)1983 *Cognitive strategy research: educational applications.* Springer Verlag, NY

Politzer R L 1983 An exploratory study of self-reported language learning behaviors and their relation to achievement. *Studies in Second Language Acquisition* 6(1): 54–65

Poulisse, N 1990 *The use of compensatory strategies by Dutch learners of English.* Mouton De Gruyter, Dordrecht: Foris/Berlin

Poulisse N, Bongaerts T and Kellerman E 1986 The use of retrospective verbal reports in the analysis of compensatory strategies. In Faerch C and Kasper G (eds.) *Introspection in second language research.* Multilingual Matters, Clevedon, England, pp 213–29

Radford J 1974 Reflections on introspection. *American Psychologist* 29: 245–50

Raimes A 1987 Language proficiency, writing ability, and composing strategies: a study of ESL college student writers. *Language Learning* 37(3): 439–67

Ramírez A G 1986 Language learning strategies used by adolescents studying French in New York schools. *Foreign Language Annals* 19(2): 131–41

Rees-Miller J 1993 A critical appraisal of learner training: theoretical bases and teaching implications. *TESOL Quarterly* 27(4): 679–9

Ringbom H 1987 The role of the first language in foreign language learning. Multilingual Matters, Clevedon, UK

Rivers W M 1979 Learning a sixth language: an adult learner's daily diary. *Canadian Modern Language Review* **36**(1): 67–82

Riverside Publishing Co 1964 *La prueba Riverside de realización en español*. RPC, Circle Pines MN

Robinson M 1991 Introspective methodology in interlanguage pragmatics research. In Kasper G (ed.) *Pragmatics of Japanese as native and target language* (Technical Report 3). Second Language Teaching & Curriculum Center, University of Hawai'i, Honolulu, pp 29–84

Rosebery A S, Warren B and Conant F R 1992 Appropriating scientific discourse: findings from language minority classrooms. *The Journal of the Learning Sciences* **2**(1): 61–94

Rubin J 1975 What the 'good language learner' can teach us. *TESOL Quarterly* **9**(1): 41–51

Rubin J 1981 Study of cognitive processes in second language learning. *Applied Linguistics* **2**(2): 117–31

Rubin J 1996 Using multimedia for learner strategy instruction. In Oxford R L (ed.) *Language learning strategies around the world: cross-cultural perspectives* (Technical Report 13). Second Language Teaching & Curriculum Center, University of Hawai'i, Honolulu, pp 151–6

Rubin J 1997 *Developing monitoring and evaluating*. Paper presented at the American Association for Applied Linguistics Annual Conference, Orlando FL, March 8–11

Rubin J and Henze R 1981 The foreign language requirement: a suggestion to enhance its educational role in teacher training. *TESOL Newsletter* **17**(2): 17, 19, 24

Rubin J and Thompson I 1994 *How to be a more successful language learner*. 2d edn. Heinle & Heinle, Boston

Ruth L and Murphy S 1984 Designing topics for writing assessment: problems of meaning. *College Composition and Communication* **35**(4): 410–22

Ryan E B 1981 Identifying and remediating failures in reading comprehension: toward an instructional approach for poor comprehenders. In Mackinnon GE and Waller T G (eds.) *Reading research: advances in theory and practice 3*, pp 223–61

Sarig G 1987 High-level reading in the first and in the foreign languages: some comparative process data. In Devine J *et al*. (eds.) *Research in reading in English as a second language*. Teachers of English to Speakers of Other Languages, Washington DC, pp 105–20

Saville-Troike M 1988 Private speech: evidence for second language learning strategies during the 'silent' period. *Journal of Child Language* **15**: 567–90

Scarcella R C and Oxford R L 1992 *The tapestry of language learning: the individual in the communicative classroom*. The Tapestry Series of Language Learning. Heinle & Heinle, Boston

Schmeck R 1988 Individual differences and learning strategies. In Weinstein C *et al*. (eds.), *Learning and study strategies*. Academic Press, NY, pp 171–91

Schmidt R 1994 Deconstructing consciousness in search of useful definitions for applied linguistics. *AILA Review* **11**: 11–16

Schmidt R W and Frota S N 1986 Developing basic conversational ability in a second language: a case study of an adult learner of Portuguese. In Day R R (ed.) *Talking to learn: conversation in second language acquisition.* Newbury House, Rowley MA, pp 237–326

Schumann F E and Schumann J H 1977 Diary of a language learner: an introspective study of second language learning. In Brown H D *et al.* (eds.) *On TESOL '77.* TESOL, Washington DC, pp 241–9

Science Research Associates 1985 *SRA Survey of Basic Skills.* SRA, Chicago

Segal K W 1986 *Does a standardized reading comprehension test predict textbook prose reading proficiency of a linguistically heterogeneous college population?* Unpublished PhD dissertation, University of Texas at Austin

Seliger H W 1980 Utterance planning and correction behavior: its function in the grammar construction process for second language learners. In Dechert H W and Raupach M (eds.) *Temporal variables of speech.* Mouton, The Hague, pp 87–99

Seliger H W 1983 The language learner as linguist: of metaphors and realities. *Applied Linguistics* 4(3): 179–91

Seliger H 1984 Processing universals in second language acquisition. In Eckman F *et al.* (eds.), *Universals of second language acquisition.* Newbury House, Rowley MA, pp 36–47

Selinker L and Douglas D 1985 Wrestling with 'context' in interlanguage theory. *Applied Linguistics* 6(2): 190–204

Shohamy E 1994 The validity of direct versus semi-direct oral tests. *Language Testing* 11(2): 99–123

Skibniewski L 1990 The writing processes of advanced foreign language learners: evidence from thinking aloud and behavior protocols. In Fisiak J (ed.) *Papers and studies in contrastive linguistics.* Adam Mikiewicz University, Poznan, pp 193–202

Slobin D I From 'thought and language' to 'thinking for speaking'. In Gumperz J J and Levinson S C (eds.) *Rethinking Linguistic Relativity.* Cambridge University Press, Cambridge pp 70–96

Smagorinsky P 1989 The reliability and validity of protocol analysis. *Written Communication* 6: 463–79

Smagorinsky P (ed.) 1994 *Speaking about writing: reflections on research methodology.* Sage, Thousand Oaks CA

Spanos G, Rhodes N C, Dale T C and Crandall J A 1988 Linguistic features of mathematical problem solving: insights and applications. In Cocking R R and Mestre J P (eds) *Linguistic and cultural influences on mathematics.* Lawrence Erlbaum, Hillsdale NJ pp 221–40

Stansfield C W, Kenyon D M, Paiva R, Doyle F, Ulsh I and Cowles M A 1990 The development and validation of the Portuguese speaking test. *Hispania* 73: 641–51

Steinberg E R 1986 Protocols, retrospective reports, and the stream of consciousness. *College English* 48: 697–712

Stemmer B 1991 *What's on a C-test taker's mind? Mental processes in C-test taking.* Universitätsverlag Dr N Brockmeyer, Bochum

Stern H H 1975 What can we learn from the good language learner? *Canadian Modern Language Review* 31(3): 304–17

Stern H H 1983 *Fundamental Concepts of Language Teaching.* Oxford University Press, Oxford

Stevick E W 1989 *Success with foreign languages: seven who achieved it and what worked for them.* Prentice-Hall International, Hemel Hempstead UK

Stratman J F and Hamp-Lyons L 1994 Reactivity in concurrent think-aloud protocols. In Smagorinsky P (ed.), *Speaking about writing: reflections on research methodology.* Sage, Thousand Oaks CA, pp 89–112

Swain M 1984 A review of immersion education in Canada: research and evaluation studies. In California State Department of Education, *Studies on immersion education.* Office of Bilingual Bicultural Education, California State Department of Education, Sacramento CA, pp 87–112

Swain M 1988 Manipulating and complementing content teaching to maximize second language learning. *TESL Canada Journal* 6: 68–83

Swain M 1992 *The output hypothesis: a search for empirical evidence in a classroom second language acquisition context.* Description of Research Program funded by the Canadian Government. Modern Language Centre, OISE, Toronto

Swain M and Carroll S 1987 The immersion observation study. In Harley B *et al.* (eds.) *The development of bilingual proficiency: final report* (Vol. 2). Modern Language Centre, OISE, Toronto, pp 190–263

Swanson-Owens D and Newell G E 1994 Using intervention protocols to study the effects of instructional scaffolding on writing and learning. In Smagorinsky P (ed.) *Speaking about writing: reflections on research methodology.* Sage, Thousand Oaks CA, pp 141–62

Tarone E 1977 Conscious communication strategies in interlanguage. In Brown H D *et al.* (eds.), *On TESOL '77: teaching and learning English as a second language: trends in research and practice.* TESOL, Washington DC, pp 194–203

Tarone E 1981 Some thoughts on the notion of communication strategy. *TESOL Quarterly* 15(3): 285–95

Tarone E 1983 On the variability of interlanguage systems. *Applied Linguistics* 4(2): 143–63

Tarone E, Cohen A D and Dumas G 1976 A closer look at some interlanguage terminology: a framework for communication strategies. *Working Papers on Bilingualism* 9: 76–90. (Reprinted in Faerch C and Kasper G (eds.) 1993 *Strategies in interlanguage communication.* Longman, London, pp 4–14.)

Tarone E and Yule G 1989 *Focus on the language learner.* Oxford University Press, Oxford

Thompson I and Rubin J 1996 Can strategy instruction improve listening comprehension? *Foreign Language Annals* 29(3): 331–42

Titchener E B 1912 The schema of introspection. *American Journal of Psychology* 23: 485–508

Towell R and Hawkins R 1994 *Approaches to second language acquisition.* Multilingual Matters, Clevedon, England

Tréville M C and Duquette L 1996 *Enseigner le vocabulaire en classe de langue.* Hachette, Paris

Tuinman, J J 1973–74 Determining the passage dependency of comprehension questions in five major tests. *Reading Research Quarterly* 9: 206–23

Tyacke M 1991 Strategies for success: bringing out the best in a learner. TESL Canada Journal 8(2): 45–56

Upton T A 1993 *The influence of first and second language use on the comprehension and recall of written English texts by Japanese readers.* Unpublished PhD dissertation, University of Minnesota, Minneapolis

Vandergrift L 1992 *The comprehension strategies of second language (French) learners.* Unpublished PhD dissertation, University of Alberta, Edmonton, Canada

VanPatten B, Lee J F, Ballman T L and Dvorak T 1996 *¿Sabías que... ?: beginning Spanish.* 2nd edn. McGraw-Hill, NY

Vaughan C 1991 Holistic assessment: what goes on in the raters' minds? In Hamp–Lyons L (ed.) *Assessing second language writing in academic contexts.* Ablex, Norwood NJ, pp 111–25

Vogely A 1995 Perceived strategy use during performance on three authentic listening comprehension tasks. *The Modern Language Journal* 79(1): 41–56

Vygotsky L S 1961 Thought and speech. In Saporta S (ed.) *Psycholinguistics.* Holt, Rinehart & Winston, NY, pp 509–37

Waern Y 1988 Thoughts on text in context: applying the think-aloud method in text processing. *Text* 8: 327–50

Warren J 1996 How students pick the right answer: a 'think aloud' study of the French CAT. In Burston J, Monville-Burston M and Warren J (eds) *Issues and innovations in the teaching of French.* Occasional Paper No 15, *Australian Review of Applied Linguistics* 79–94

Weaver S J and Cohen A D 1994 Making learning strategy instruction a reality in the foreign language curriculum. In Klee C (ed.) *Faces in a crowd: the individual learner in multisection courses.* Heinle & Heinle, Boston, pp 285–323

Weaver S J and Cohen A D 1997 *Strategies-based instruction: a teacher-training manual.* Center for Advanced Research on Language Acquisition, University of Minnesota MN

Weaver S J, Alcaya C, Lybeck K and Mougel P 1994 *Speaking strategies: a list compiled by teachers in the experimental sections of the strategies-based instruction experiment.* Unpublished document, National Language Resource Center, University of Minnesota, Minneapolis MN

Weinstein C E and Underwood V L 1985 Learning strategies: the how of learning. In Segal J W *et al.* (eds.) *Thinking and learning skills: relating learning to basic research.* Lawrence Erlbaum, Hillsdale NJ, pp 241–59

Wenden A L 1985 Learner strategies. *TESOL Newsletter* 19(5): 1–7

Wenden A 1987a. How to be a successful language learner: insights and prescriptions from L2 learners. In Wenden A and Rubin J (eds.) *Learner strategies in language learning.* Prentice-Hall International, Englewood Cliffs NY, pp 103–17

Wenden A 1987b Incorporating learner training in the classroom. In Wenden A and Rubin J (eds.) *Learner strategies in language learning.* Prentice-Hall International, Englewood Cliffs NY, pp 159–68

Wenden A 1991 *Learner strategies for learner autonomy.* Prentice-Hall International, Englewood Cliffs NJ

Wenden A and J Rubin (eds.) 1987 *Learner strategies in language learning.* Prentice-Hall International, Englewood Cliffs NY

Wheatley G H 1991 Constructivist perspectives on science and mathematics learning. *Science Education* 75(1): 9–21

Willing K 1989 *Teaching how to learn: a guide to developing ESL learning strategies. Teacher's guide and activity worksheets.* National Centre for English Language Teaching and Research, Macquarie University, Sydney, Australia

Wolfson N 1989 *Perspectives: sociolinguistics and TESOL.* Newbury House / Harper & Row, NY

Woods D 1993 *Processes in ESL teaching: a study of the role of planning and interpretive processes in the practice of teachers of English as a second language.* Carleton Papers in Applied Language Studies, Occasional Papers 3

Zamel V 1983 The composing processes of advanced ESL students: six case studies. *TESOL Quarterly* 17(2): 165–87

Zuengler J 1993 Encouraging learners' conversational participation: the effect of content knowledge. *Language Learning* 43(3): 403–32

Index